BURT FRANKLIN BIBLIOGRAPHY AND REFERENCE SERIES #160

BENJAMIN FRANKLIN

FRANKLIN BIBLIOGRAPHY

A LIST OF BOOKS

WRITTEN BY, OR RELATING TO

BENJAMIN FRANKLIN

BY

PAUL LEICESTER FORD

BURT FRANKLIN BIBLIOGRAPHY AND REFERENCE SERIES #160

BURT FRANKLIN
NEW YORK

Published By
BURT FRANKLIN
235 East 44th St.
New York, N.Y. 10017

ORIGINALLY PUBLISHED
BROOKLYN: 1886
Reprinted 1968

Printed in U.S.A.

TO

HON. JOHN BIGELOW

AS A RECOGNITION OF HIS CONTRIBUTIONS TO

FRANKLIN LITERATURE

THIS LIST IS

DEDICATED.

CONTENTS.

EXPLANATORY.

/	signifies:	The end of a line on the title page.
. . .	"	A line omitted in the title.
. . . . .	"	Two or more lines omitted in the title.
*	"	That what is omitted is line for line the same as the preceding or indicated title.
+	"	That what is omitted is already sufficiently given in title of previous or numbered edition.
[ ]	"	Words or figures not in the title or text. Where brackets really occur they are represented by parenthesis.
Sic	"	That the word or sentence contains the error as printed, but this has only been used where doubt might arise. It is omitted in all obvious cases, or in mistaken or old-fashioned accentuation and spelling.

The initials at the end of the description indicate certain public libraries in which the publication can be consulted.

A.	signifies:	Astor Library.
A. P. S.	"	American Philosophical Society Library.
A. A. S.	"	American Antiquarian Society Library.
B.	"	Boston Public Library.
B. A.	"	Boston Athenæum Library.
B. M.	"	British Museum Library.
C.	"	Library of Congress.
H.	"	Library of Harvard University.
L.	"	Lenox Library.
M.	"	Massachusetts Historical Society Library.
N.	"	New York Historical Society Library.
P. H. S.	"	Pennsylvania Historical Society Library.
P.	"	Library Company of Philadelphia.
P. L.	"	Private Library.
S.	"	New York State Library.
S. D.	"	Department of State Library.
Y. C.	"	Yale College Library.

ERRATA.

Correct title of No. 289:

The / Examination of Dr. Benjamin Franklin / before an / Honourable Assembly, / relative to the / Repeal / of the / American Stamp Act, / in MDCCLXVI. / MDCCLXVII. / (Price One Shilling.)

No. 356. For "Transactions of the Royal Society," read "Memoirs of the Literary and Philosophical Society of Manchester."

No. 397. See note to No. 907.

ON a March night in the year 1722 there stole along Queen street, in the goodly and godly town of Boston, a lad of some sixteen years of age. Pausing in front of a building which James Franklin was then advertising in *The New England Courant* as "his Printing House over against Mr. Sheafs School" "near the Prison," the lad slipped a paper underneath the door, and then walked away.—Such was the surreptitious entrance of Benjamin Franklin into the world of literature. The next day, as this same 'prentice stood at his case in this printing office, he could hear his brother consulting with certain of that famous or infamous ilk, the "hell fire club," as to who could be the author of these sheets with the humble signature of "Silence Dogood;" and we can easily imagine his pride on hearing the writings praised, when the piece appeared in all the glory of type on the first page of *The New England Courant*, and when his eye met the notice in the same issue that "as the favor of Mrs. Dogood's Correspondence is acknowledged by the Publisher of this Paper, lest any of her Letters should miscarry, he desires they may be deliver'd at his Printing-Office, or at the Blue Ball in Union Street, and no questions will be ask'd of the Bearer."

In the piece so printed Mrs. Dogood introduces herself to the reader in due form, and announces that she "intends once a Fortnight to present them, by the Help of this Paper, with a short Epistle, which I presume will add somewhat to their Entertainment;" and she is as good as her word, for to the number of fourteen letters the widow gossips on college learning, female training and vices, pride, poetry in New England, hypocrites, widows, matchmaking, the drinker's vocabulary, Boston at night, religions, etc.

But James Franklin being involved in trouble with the government, more serious work soon claimed Mrs. Dogood, and in less than a year from the publication of the first of these letters, Franklin was masquerading before the public as the printer, publisher, and editor of that "Wicked Libel called the New England Courant," and with all the courage of years seventeen, was breaking lances against both Church and State. Not for long, however, for harsh words and blows soon made him a run-away, and forced James Franklin to advertise for a "likely lad for an apprentice." A likely lad may have been forthcoming, but *the* likely lad was lost to Boston for all time.

The young printer drifted to Philadelphia, where for some months he plied his trade. Then, induced by false promises of a chance of starting for himself, he went to London, only to learn, as Poor Richard wrote, that "experience keeps a dear school." However, "he that hath a trade, hath an estate," and so he quickly found work in the printing office of "Samuel Palmer, in Bartholomew-Close," and here he was set to composing William Wollaston's *Religion of Nature.* It was an absolutely inoffensive book, and the six editions and ten thousand copies sold of it in the fourteen years from its first publication probably did as little harm as any book ever printed; but to the young "doubter," with his mind unsettled by the writings of Shaftesbury and Collins, and his quarrels and controversies with the Boston clergy, it was an irritation to have to set the *a priori* propositions, and circular reasonings deduced therefrom, on good and evil, truth and falsehood, pleasure and pain. And so in his spare hours, he wrote and put into type a little tractate, animadverting on some of the reverend author's positions and arguments, and practically denying future life or rewards, the existence of natural religion, and the theological distinctions between man and beast. This *Dissertation on Liberty and Necessity, Pleasure and Pain*, has since been known as his "wicked tract," and Franklin lived to term it an "erratum" and to destroy almost all of the hundred copies he had printed. For a piece of philosophical reasoning it is certainly well written; but though the author lived to become more tolerant of opinions and beliefs, at this time he clearly believed his own aphorism, that "orthodoxy is my doxy, and heterodoxy your doxy."

And then in 1726 he returned to Philadelphia and worked as a journeyman in the printing office of Samuel Keimer, but soon set up for himself, with Hugh Meredith, the "New Printing-Office near the Market." In after years Franklin took pride in styling himself "B. Franklin, Printer," but even in this first year of independence he proved himself something more. It was an experimental time in finance, and the colonies, occupying a peculiar position, were trying sundry schemes to benefit themselves; and among others that of creating wealth with a printing press. In the course of his twenty years active service at his press, Franklin succeeded in so doing, but in 1729 he thought he saw a quicker way, and so there came from his pen and office *A Modest Enquiry into the Nature and Necessity of a Paper Currency*, in which an immediate issue was advocated with so much success as to overcome the opposition thereto, and win sufficient converts to carry through the project. It was a theory of money which Franklin never quite outgrew, and so we may take his arguments as honest; yet one cannot but suspect that the printer's economic reasonings may have been influenced by the knowledge that he would be the printer of the "very profitable jobb." Whatever the causes which produced the pamphlet, or the fallacies it contained, it added its mite to the facts and theories, then so few and crude, which to-day are almost a science.

Then a project which had been brewing some time in

Franklin's mind began to take definite form. The printer aspired to be an editor, and preparations for the starting of a paper were in progress, when Franklin, who had yet to teach Poor Richard that "three can keep a secret, if two are dead," let a gossiping journeyman into his confidence, who told it to Samuel Keimer, his old master, and before Franklin's plans were matured he found the former had seized on the idea and that the field was already occupied. He had his revenge, however, for setting pen to paper he wrote a series of essays not unlike those of Mrs. Dogood, well entitled "The Busybody," and by sending them to the old established paper, drew attention from the new enterprise, which soon languished, and before a year passed by purchase into Franklin's hands. Under its new management, it quickly throve and in time became the greatest paper in the colonies, so far as regards circulation and advertising patronage. At that time the editor's task was considered one entirely of compilation, outsiders being trusted to supply the essays and squibs; which besides the advertisements, the shipping news, and what was clipped from the London papers, practically constituted the newspaper of the period; but Franklin was, nevertheless, a constant contributor to *The Pennsylvania Gazette*, while it remained in his hands, and in it appeared a number of his collected essays as well as many which are still inedited.

The great source of profit at that time to the printer was the almanac which came yearly from his press, and was the *vade mecum* in every household which could spare the necessary two or three pence annually; and so when Franklin set up his press he arranged with Thomas Godfrey, a local scientist of some note, to furnish him with the "copy" for an annual issue—an arrangement which continued three years, when Discordia, in the person of Mrs. Godfrey, produced the apple of discord. Franklin had rented the upper part of his office to the Godfreys, boarding with them, and Mrs. Godfrey naturally attempted a match between the young printer and her niece. All went as she desired, till the question of actual marriage was reached, when the practical lover, who advised one to "never take a wife till you have a house (and a fire) to put her in," intimated that he should expect as much money with the lady as would pay the debt on his printing office. It was in vain that the parents protested they had not the wherewithal. Franklin told them to mortgage their house, and he does not seem to have suffered much when the match fell to the ground. But if the broken heart was a matter of small importance, the broken friendship proved otherwise, for he not only lost his tenant, but the philomath carried his "copy" to a rival printer, and he was left in the lurch for his issue.

In this predicament he apparently wrote his own almanac, but knowing that his name would hardly give it currency among readers who still looked upon it as dealing in magic, witchcraft, and astrology, he adopted that of Richard Saunders, an English philomath of the seventeenth century of great popularity; but since quite eclipsed by his more popular western namesake. Under this name, therefore, the initial number was issued in the latter part of December, 1732, when, in spite of its late publication, three "impressions" were called for by the popular demand; and from that time it was not merely the most esteemed almanac in Pennsylvania, but had a sale as far north as Rhode Island, and as far south as the Carolinas. The secret of its success was its humor. The calculations were no more accurate, the poetry no better, nor the printing clearer, than were the half dozen competitors which then came from the Pennsylvania presses; but in the colorless life of the frontier settlements, the advent of this little pamphlet of a dozen leaves was one of the events of the year, and it is not strange that the sense and nonsense of Poor Richard, which afterwards gained such a place and name in' the literary centers of Europe, should surpass its competitors, and keep the presses busy printing the ten thousand copies annually called for. The humor was everywhere—in the advertisement that announced its publication, in the title page and preface, sprinkled in the calendar, the weather predictions, the eclipses and the prophecies. Where other philomaths lost their tempers, Franklin cracked a joke; where they made mysteries of the trade, he gave a humorous account of the way it is done. Much was coarse, as suited the times and people; but Franklin's indelicacy is tinctured with genuine wit; and not merely broad for broadness' sake. The poetry is wretched; but even if he wrote it, which there is good cause to doubt, we know from other rhymes that he was not a poet. Poor Richard is by no means all original, and he pilfered from many sources; but nearly everything had been filtered through Franklin's brain, and bore the stamp of his mind. It was all written for the common people, and never made the mistake of overshooting their heads, yet in spite of this, the writings in the twenty-five almanacs which Franklin sent forth are to-day almost the sole literary production of colonial America which is read save by antiquaries.

The great mass of American literature and printing of that time was of a religious character, and Franklin was next to swell this class. A church quarrel was on the tapis, and Franklin sided with the young and eloquent, though "unsound and dangerous" clergyman, who drew about him the "free-thinkers, deists and nothings;" and, finding him unable to defend himself, Franklin wrote for him "an artful dialogue" in the paper, and also three pamphlets. Poor Richard advised one never to "misinform your doctor nor your lawyer," but seems not to have practised as he preached, for the charges against his client were soon substantiated, and so Franklin had his trouble for nothing (unless the printer's profits paid him), and disgusted once more with religion, he went back to his private prayer book and home service, and advertised that he would shortly print, in addition to *Every man his own Lawyer* and *Every man his own Doctor*, which at that time he was selling, a work entitled *Every man his own Priest;* while the Reverend Samuel Hemphill and the three polemical tractates disappeared into an oblivion from which the most painstaking of his editors have never drawn them.

Franklin had already given the colonies the best newspaper and almanac published at that time, but this was not the whole service the printer rendered. From his press came the first novel, the first classic both translated and printed in this country, one of the first anti-slavery pamphlets, the first planned American magazine, the first periodical in a foreign tongue, the first bookseller's catalogue, and the first library catalogue printed south of Boston. And in his *Proposal for Promoting Useful Knowledge* and his *Account of the New Invented Pennsylvanian Fire-Places* we have two of the earliest American attempts in science and invention.

In 1746 he published a pamphlet entitled *Reflections on Courtship and Marriage*, which but for the certain proof one would hardly think could be written by him (though on a subject he was fond of writing on) so unlike is it to his usual simple and felicitous style. But the author confesses that it was not written for the public, having "such a careless Negligence of Dress," and it is unfair to judge such a piece by the literary tenets of this century, for the four editions of this pamphlet attest that at the time it was considered a work of merit; and it was the first of Franklin's writings reprinted in Europe.

In this same year Franklin first stepped into politics, and so, as a natural consequence we soon find him writing on that subject. The European powers were fighting as usual, and America must defend herself as best she could from England's enemies. In Pennsylvania this was an even more difficult task than in the other colonies, for the Friends, by their belief were opposed to all warfare, and exercised a controlling influence in the government. To overcome this Franklin wrote *Plain Truth*, which though it "bore somewhat hard on both parties" and was promptly replied to by a couple of writers, "wonderfully spirited us up to defend ourselves and the country," and proved the entering wedge by which Pennsylvania was by degrees changed from the submissive tenets inculcated by William Penn.

From this time until his sailing for England in 1757, his pen was constantly at work in politics, drafting "associations," "advertisements," "memorials," "proclamations," "messages," "resolutions," "reports," "acts," and other political pieces. And in his "Plan of Union," submitted to, and accepted by the Albany Congress of 1754, we have the first real plan for the permanent arrangement of the English sway on this continent as well as for the changing of thirteen colonies into a united country; and the only one proposed, till the old loyalty and love of the "mother" country had been so changed as to make true union no longer possible. As in the case of his articles of confederation, moved in the Continental Congress, the times were not ripe for it, and both the home and colonial governments gave it the cold shoulder.

The cause of better education had received attention from him as early as 1743, but meeting with disappointments, it was laid aside till the conclusion of peace, when in 1749 he distributed with the copies of his newspaper his *Proposals relating to the Education of Youth in Pennsylvania*, containing the plan for the formation of an academy, and an outline of what should be taught; which was followed in two years by his *Idea of an English School*, in which is contained one of the first protests, in this country at least, against the total subservience of all institutions of learning to the classics and mathematics. Nor were his services limited to these publications, for he personally aided in obtaining money and teachers for the school which was started, and he was a trustee and constant worker for the enterprise, till politics got possession of it, and it became a hot-bed of writers opposed to him and his party. Then he turned his attention to the Pennsylvania Hospital, which he had been instrumental in founding, and of which in 1754 he had published a short *Account*, as an advertisement of its good work; and these two institutions thus became to a certain extent political factors for the two local parties.

For a number of years Franklin and some of his friends had been studying and experimenting in the then fashionable science of electricity, and in 1747 he first began the communication of the results to Peter Collinson of London —results which in time made both Franklin and America famous in the world of science, but which at first were not even deemed worthy of a place in the *Transactions of the Royal Society*, were sneered and laughed at by many of the scientists, and Franklin's existence even questioned. Yet once in print, the letters ran through nine editions, gained him admission to the Royal Society and the award of the Copley medal; and for twenty-five years made electricity and Franklin almost synonymous words.

And then, in 1757, Franklin composed his most popular piece. It was in effect a skimming of the cream from the twenty-four issues of *Poor Richard's Almanac*, being a selection of the aphorisms and humorous sayings run into one continuous speech which purported to be delivered by an old man named "Father Abraham" to the people collected about an auction sale. Originally printed in Poor Richard for 1758, it was quickly reprinted in separate form, and under the titles of "Father Abraham's Speech, "The Way to Wealth," and "La Science du Bonhomme Richard" it has proved itself one of the most popular American writings. Seventy editions of it have been printed in

English, fifty-six in French, eleven in German, and nine in Italian. It has been translated into Spanish, Danish, Swedish, Welsh, Polish, Gaelic, Russian, Bohemian, Dutch, Catalan, Chinese, Modern Greek and Phonetic writing. It has been printed at least four hundred times, and is to-day as popular as ever.

Sent to England in 1757 on the colonial affairs of Pennsylvania, Franklin not only contributed to the newspapers of that country, with a view to influencing public opinion on the matter in dispute, but he also composed his *Historical Review*, which is the largest of his publications, and must be ranked among the ablest of his partisan writings. The necessity of the case required an anonymous printing, and Franklin even went so far as positively to deny the authorship, but a contemporary letter of his son fixes it on him, and his grandson gives Franklin's reasons for concealing himself.

But his writings in his six years' agency in England were by no means limited to this question of local politics, and in the *London Chronicle* and *Grand Magazine* he was, under various pseudonyms, defending the colonies from the sneers of the mother country, philosophically discussing population and love, and even before the conquest of Canada was complete, was pleading that it should not be returned to France at the signing of peace.

The *bête noire* of the colonies at that time was the French possession of that country. The great enemy of England, France could and did, whether at peace or war in Europe, instigate and aid the Indians in their constant harrying of the back settlements, and so check the growth of this western England. Its conquest was therefore hailed with universal joy in the colonies, which was only tempered by the fear that it would be traded back to France at the peace. And the fear was not without cause. It was not only held by a large party in England that the little sugar island of Guadaloupe was of more value to

Great Britain than the Canadian conquests, but that the presence of the French on the American continent was necessary in order that the American Colonies should be kept from growing too strong and made to look to the mother country for protection. These arguments were discussed and criticised in a pamphlet written jointly by the Earl of Bath and James Douglas, entitled *A Letter addressed to Two Great Men*, which "was a good deal talked on" and drew forth many answers, among them *Remarks* by William Burke, who favors the opposite view. This pamphlet drew from Franklin his *Interest of Great Britain*, which his biographers have claimed exercised great influence in ministerial circles; but unless the piece itself can be cited as such, the evidence is lacking. It however had "a great run in the Coffee Houses," and William Burke in replying to him, styled him "the ablest, the most ingenious and the most dexterous writer" on that side of the question.

It was in this period also, that Franklin wrote his "Parable against Persecution." The idea was taken, beyond doubt, from Jeremy Taylor's *Liberty of Prophesying*, who took it from George Gentius, who took it from Saadi, who only quoted it. Under Franklin's pen it was shaped into biblical language, printed on a sheet of paper and laid into his Bible, from which it was read aloud to theologians and friends, whose comments afforded infinite amusement to him. Against his wishes, copies were begged by friends and in time stole into the *London Chronicle, Gentleman's Magazine*, and finally into Lord Kames' *Sketches of the History of Man*, and there met with comparison with the version as printed by Taylor; and charges of plagiarism, which have been published and republished endlessly, were thereon founded. It need only be said that although Franklin had so changed it as to make it practically a new composition, he never claimed it as original; but if this was plagiarism, we can only regret that Franklin did not do more of it. This piece is also interesting, being, so far as I can learn, the only one of Franklin's writings which underwent revision and corrections for a new edition, unless we except the enlargements of his newspaper squibs on "Human Vanity" and "Drinking Dictionary," both of which were practically entirely rewritten, so as to leave little of the original, beyond the idea.

Returning from his mission to England in 1763, he was at once involved in one of the bitterest and fiercest political struggles this country has ever seen, and one which produced such an extraordinary number of publications that one printer sarcastically changed his imprint to "Quilsylvania." Franklin's pen was among the most fertile, and within a year wrote the *Narrative of the late Massacres; Cool Thoughts; Petition to the King; Remarks on the late Protest;* and the preface to the *Speech of Joseph Galloway*, and in these pieces we have almost the only angry utterances or attempts at a personal vindication that Franklin ever put in print.

In 1764 Franklin was once more sent to England, again as Pennsylvania's colonial agent, but really to act, in his ten years' stay, as the agent of the whole thirteen colonies. In their behalf he was examined before Parliament relative to the hated Stamp Act, and as most of the questions and answers had been concerted beforehand between him and the opposers of the act, his *Examination* was practically America's answer and argument. And when, possibly in altered form, it stole surreptitiously into print, it became the most popular pamphlet that had ever been written by an American or had dealt with an American subject.

From this time till his return to America in 1775, his pen was constantly engaged in fighting for or on the American side of the dispute. He caused the ablest of the American pamphlets to be reprinted in England, sometimes adding a preface by himself; he furnished other writers with the materials for writing pamphlets, and he was continually writing in the *London Chronicle, Gentleman's Magazine, Political Register, London Packet, Public Advertiser,* and *Public Ledger,* and in this form appeared two of his cleverest political satires, the *Rules for Reducing a Great Empire,* which England so successfully practiced, and the "Prussian Edict," purporting to be Frederick II's assumption of sovereignty over Great Britain, because of the original colonization from Germany; which was so well done that it was by some for a time actually believed. In addition to his writings on the Anglo-American troubles, he also contributed extensively on the more abstract political affairs, and both in periodicals, and in notes to a friend's pamphlet, has left us his views on trade, money, manufactures, smuggling, pauperism, emigration and colonizing.

A private venture also produced two pamphlets from him on the latter question. A number of gentlemen had formed a company and petitioned for a grant of land on the Ohio. Lord Hillsborough, after having encouraged the company, brought in an adverse report, to which Franklin wrote a reply, and published the two pieces in a pamphlet. The Lords Commissioners of the Treasury having granted the petition, the cry was at once raised by those opposed to the scheme, or interested in rival ones, that this was "a job," to which Franklin again replied in another pamphlet, but for some reason suppressed it almost at once.

In 1772 he also undertook, at the request of Sir Francis Dashwood, Lord Le Despencer, a curious task. The latter, a notorious roué and deist, having first reformed himself, next conceived the idea of reforming the Book of Common Prayer. In this he asked Franklin's assistance; who wrote the preface and abridged the Catechism and Psalms, and in 1773 their work was printed in the finest style at the expense of Lord Le Despencer. The English Church, however, did not take warmly to an improvement from such a source, and it was hardly noticed in that country; but in America, where it was known as "Franklin's Prayer Book," it attracted more attention, and when after the separation, "The Church" in this country set to work to compose its system and rituals, we find that the gentlemen who prepared the "proposed" Prayer Book studied this with care, and adopted certain ideas from it.

In these years he was also writing more or less on scientific subjects, and in his visit at Tuyford in 1771, he began his autobiography, the history of which is deferred to another part of this sketch.

And then in 1775 he was, like the stranger in his parable against persecution, driven forth "with blows into the wilderness." Deprived of his offices and pay, insulted in and by the Privy Council, and attacked in press and Parliament, he still sought and worked for peace and union, till threatened arrest made him take ship for America. Here he was at once elected to the Continental Congress and the Pennsylvania Convention. In the former, though placed on many committees, none of the famous "addresses" or "declarations" of that body can claim more than a revision from him, and but for his proposed "articles of confederation," which necessitating and antedating independence, as it did by nearly a year, was premature and passed by in silence, he was a worker rather than an orator and writer, in his two years' attendance. In the Convention, however, he was largely responsible for the wretched state constitution it adopted, as well as for the articles of association it drew up.

Sent in 1776 by the Congress to France, his pen was soon at work, not merely on the routine addresses, memorials and letters intended to persuade the French government or inform that at home, but in satires on the English methods of conducting the war, use of the Indians, Hessians, etc., in exposing the financial straits and impending ruin of that country, and in urging the advantages of loans to America; while there is good authority for ascribing to him the partial editing of a periodical which was intended to influence the French people in favor of the American cause, and prepare them for the treaties of amity and alliance to which Franklin eventually set his name.

It was during his nine years' service in France that he also wrote most of what have since been known as the "bagatelles." Little essays on many subjects, composed for the amusement of "la société choisie de Franklin," they were written in his happiest vein, and fifteen or twenty copies printed on his private press at his home in Passy for the little circle for whom they were intended. And in this shape also first appeared two pieces of more serious import, being his *Advice to Emigrants*, which can be almost as well applied to-day as at the time it was written, and his *Remarks on the Savages*, wherein he points out the superiority of them, in some particulars, to those who claimed for themselves a much higher plane.

In these years he also added a short fragment to the autobiography, and wrote in science on rainfall, meteorology, and mesmerism, to which during his voyage to America he added his *Maritime Observations* and his *Causes and Cures of Smoky Chimneys*. And in his letter on criminal law and privateering, and the treaty he made with Prussia, we have projects so enlightened and merciful that even his own country failed to carry them into effect.

Once more in his native country, he was laid hold of by the public, and placed in positions that left him little time for writing; yet he contributed on scientific matters to the *Transactions of the American Philosophical Society*, and wrote anonymously on politics, education, newspapers, slavery, and other subjects, in the newspapers; prepared his speeches in the Federal Convention, and added another section to his autobiography.

Begun as already stated, in 1771, in a temporary lull of the American dispute, the life was laid aside after having been brought down only to 1731. Left with his other papers when he sailed for France, it suffered their fate, but by good chance was rescued by his old friend, Abel James, who was so charmed by the reading of it that he sent Franklin a copy and begged him to complete it. Franklin sent this to Benjamin Vaughan; and upon receiving his approval of it, in 1784, though without his notes and materials, and not even having a copy of what he had written, he added a few pages. But without his papers he could not go far, and once more it was laid aside. Urged to it by his friends, he in 1788 continued the narrative to 1757; but his time was mortgaged to the public, and when at last it became his own, he found that the gout and stone were faster workers than the man, and they wrote "finis" to the real life, when that on paper had but passed over a little more than half its story.

To judge Franklin from the literary standpoint is neither easy nor quite fair. The printer of newspapers and pamphlets was almost from the beginning the writer of them, yet he never was a literary man in the true and common meaning of the term. Omitting his scientific writings and autobiography, there is hardly a published line from his pen which was not anonymously written to exert a transient influence, fill an empty column, or please a friend. The larger part of his writing was not only done in haste, but never even read in proof, and printers and editors often took strange liberties in the way of omission and alteration. To apply the ordinary canons of literary criticism to these productions is absurd. Another difficulty in attempting an estimate of his writings is their variety and range of subject. Theoretical and polemical theology, sociology, morality, philanthropy, music, education, medicine, philosophy, poetry, politics, political and natural science, all received attention from his mind and pen. He had distinct literary ease—Poor Richard was never at a loss for an aphorism, simile or story to illustrate or strengthen an argument, could take another's idea and improve it, could imitate other and by-gone styles of writing, could refute a whole argument by a dozen words scribbled in the margin, and write letters for a single eye of as much interest and excellence as the piece meant to be read by thousands. Of course much of this matter is printed and reprinted only because Franklin wrote it, but so it is largely of writers who have made literature their profession. Some of it is poorly, some coarsely written. Much of it, save to the historian or antiquarian, may be classed with Carlyle's "gone-nothingness," but to this self-educated boy and busy, practical man, we owe the most popular autobiography ever written; the piece which of all American literature has been the oftenest printed and translated; an imitation of a chapter of the Bible which would be an addition even to that "Book of books;" a collection of social and political satires which may stand comparison with those of almost any of the great satirists; a series of letters on electricity which rank high in that science; a private correspondence as readable as Walpole's or Chesterfield's; and a selection from all these has gone through more editions and probably been more read in the last hundred years than the "works" of any author here or abroad. He seems to have hit that point described by Poor Richard in the stanza:

"Some books we read, tho' few there are that hit
The happy *point* where wisdom joins with wit."

* *

Poor Richard told his readers that "If you would not be forgotten, as soon as you are dead and rotten, either write things worth reading, or do things worth the writing," and Franklin was so busy doing both these, that once written and sent to the press, his contributions to literature rarely received further attention from him. But in addition to this neglect, fate seems to have conspired against his writings. In 1776, when he left this country, he put his papers in the care of his friend, Joseph Galloway, who within a year became a fugitive loyalist. In the confusions of the two evacuations of Philadelphia, the trunk containing them was.broken open, and its contents scattered in the streets. Nor did his books fare much better, for English officers were quartered in his house, and Major André played the biblioklept before he played the spy.

On his return from France, Franklin brought with him his later MSS. and books, which added to the fragments of his former collection, probably constituted the finest one at the time in this country. By his will, with unimportant exceptions, Franklin left these to his grandson, William Temple Franklin. The latter carried Franklin's own writings and part of his library to England, where after putting them to the use mentioned elsewhere, the MSS. were deposited at his banker's, and the books were hypothecated, and eventually brought back to America, only to be scattered. On Temple Franklin's death, his widow left the MSS. on a shelf in a tailor's shop, from which they passed into the possession of a gentleman who sold them to Henry Stevens, from whom they eventually came to their proper resting place in the Department of State. The remainder of the MSS. and library were left in Philadelphia in the care of a friend, from whom the former passed to the American Philosophical Society, and the fragments of the latter, after division and theft, came into the possession of the Historical Society of Pennsylvania.

Except for the printer's profits on some of his earlier writings, none of Franklin's compositions brought him any remuneration, though many others, and especially those of his own trade, have coined money from his brain. From 1759, nearly every pamphlet of his was published without his knowledge, or at once pirated as soon as printed, and except for the slight assistance given to the editors of the three editions subsequently mentioned, no collected edition received the slightest authorization from him. We thus owe the discovery and preservation of almost his entire works to those who were actuated either by friendship or hope of profit.

In 1751, when Peter Collinson sent Franklin's letters on electricity to the press, the collecting of his writings began. These passed through three editions, and with the supplementary experiments made in time a volume of some size, which in 1769, was further increased by the addition of his philosophical writings and of those he had printed in the *Gentleman's Magazine* under his own name. This edition, which probably passed under the author's eye, was reprinted in 1774.

In 1772, Barbeu Dubourg, a French friend of Franklin's, who had already edited some of his tracts, prepared a translation into French of this edition, with additions, in which Franklin gave him some assistance, so far as the supplying of new matter, and to this is probably due the appearance of his "Observations on the Increase of Mankind," "Poor Richard," and the familiar letters.

In 1779, Benjamin Vaughan collected all he could discover of the political, philosophical and miscellaneous writings of Franklin which had not been printed in the edition of 1769, and printed them as a companion volume to that edition. In this were "The Interest of Great Britain," "The Albany Papers," "Causes of the American Discontents," "Prussian Edict," "Rules for Reducing a Great Empire," and a number of other pieces first printed here as his, and everything printed in Dubourg's edition which had not been already printed in the English edition of 1769. That Franklin made suggestions for this collection is beyond doubt, and he also prepared the "Addenda and Corrigenda" for it, which is the nearest approach he made to editing his own writings.

In 1787, Dr. Edward Bancroft published a collection of Franklin's philosophical and miscellaneous writings, wholly limited to what he had written since the publication of the edition of 1779. This was the last collection published in his life time.

William Temple Franklin, his literary legatee, began the preparation of an edition in 1790, but other editors proved themselves faster workers. The first part of the autobiography was, in spite of his request, printed in the French language, from a translation made of one of the several MS. copies which were in existence at this time, and re-translations of this were quickly made and printed in England and America, and have been oftener printed than the true version.

One of these translations was made by Benjamin Vaughan, to which he added a collection of essays and extracts from letters which had not been printed in the three previous English collections; and this edition of 1793, with minor corrections and additions, has had an almost boundless popularity, considerably more than one hundred editions of it having been printed.

In 1806, a Mr. Marshall, assisted by Benjamin Vaughan, collected into a three-volume edition the matter contained in the four English collections of 1769, 1779, 1787 and 1793, to which was added whatever had come to light since they were printed. This was the first edition, therefore, which gave the purchaser more than a section of Franklin's works.

The long delay in the appearance of the authorized edition of Franklin's writings, as well as the sneers of the *Edinburgh Review* at the lack of an American edition led William Duane to begin the editing and publication in Philadelphia of a six-volume edition in 1808, which was not completed till 1818. Much matter was included in this for the first time, and here was printed the largest of Franklin's works, the "Historical Review;" but the slip-shod editing, numerous errors and poor typographical execution seriously marred the value of the edition.

At last, in 1818, Franklin's literary legatee issued three volumes of his writings, which though not purporting to be his complete works, added much to what had theretofore been printed (except in the Duane edition), and included the true English text of one of Franklin's copies of the autobiography, and his familiar and private letters.

From this time, though many minor collections of his writings were printed, nothing new was added till 1833, when Jared Sparks edited a small volume of new letters, some of his political pamphlets and annotations, and the "Craven Street Gazette."

A year later, William Duane re-edited, with corrections and additions, his edition of 1808–18, and published it in a compact two-volume edition, making it the best and most serviceable then published.

From 1836 to 1840, Jared Sparks edited his ten-volume collection of Franklin's works, which till recently was *the* edition of his writings, and which even now is not entirely superseded. The editor availed himself of all previous editions, and from other sources added much new matter; and was the first of the many editors, unless we except Benjamin Vaughan, who seemed to have the slightest idea of what an editor's duties were. In his other literary work he laid himself open to severe and merited criticism; but this cannot apply to his edition of Franklin.

In 1868, John Bigelow repaired one of Temple Franklin's most serious blunders by recovering and editing the original autobiography as Franklin wrote it.

The recent edition of Franklin's works edited by this gentleman fittingly closes this resumé of Franklin literature. As great an advance on Sparks' edition, as Sparks' was on the previous ones; with much added matter and information, and the correction of some errors, it is open to but two criticisms—the limited edition and the use of the word "complete" on the title page.

The writings of Franklin will never be complete. If his known or recognizable pamphlets and contributions to periodicals not in the two great collections of his writings (and these together would add nearly a half more to what has been collected) were brought together and printed with those already edited, the writings would still only be a portion, though a large one, of what he wrote. That these will in time be gathered is hardly to be questioned, and in this future collection it is to be hoped will be included his hitherto suppressed or expurgated writings, so that we may have all sides of the man, and judge him accordingly. But it is time to print and read the letters of "Silence Dogood" and the sayings of "Poor Richard."

**

Franklin's long and prominent career has also produced a class of literature which must be noticed—that written to oppose or deal with his acts, opinions or personality.

These Frankliniana began in 1734, in the prefaces of the almanacs of Titan Leeds and John Jerman, rival philomaths of Poor Richard, who disliking what the latter had humorously said of them, replied in language more strong than choice. During his editorship of *The Pennsylvania Gazette*, he occasionally crossed swords with the rival newspaper, *The American Weekly Mercury*, generally getting from that sheet as good as he sent, and in this paper appeared John Webbe's side of the controversy over the *American Magazine*, and Franklin's behavior as postmaster. His *Plain Truth*, in opposition to one of the Friends' tenets, with the subsequent action it caused, produced a pamphlet warfare, half political, half religious in its nature.

His electrical experiments and theories produced an almost endless mass of literature, from the writings of his ardent exponents and defenders, Dalibard, Canton, Watson, Henley, Priestley, Ingen-Housz, Beccaria, and Winthrop, to those of Nollet and Wilson, who sneer at or endeavor to refute his theories, and who prove themselves little better scientists than Rev. Thomas Prince, who not only declared these discoveries unchristian, but in his pamphlet on the earthquake of 1755, charged that Franklin's lightning-rods, by drawing the electricity from the air into the earth, had caused that great natural phenomenon.

The political course and pamphlets of Franklin during the controversy over the proprietary government in Pennsylvania gave rise to a series of most bitter and partisan writings, in which Franklin was savagely attacked by Rev. William Smith and Hugh Williamson, and defended by his son William Franklin, by John Hughes and Isaac Hunt, while the whole subject was treated by a host of anonymous scribblers in press and pamphlet with a personality and indecency never equalled by any other American political controversy.

Charged with having suggested, planned and promoted the passage of the Stamp Act, he was vigorously assailed in this country, chiefly by those who were already ranked among his enemies, and these charges were later served up to his disadvantage in England by Josiah Tucker and others.

His political opinions and actions on the Anglo-American disputes were praised in the speeches or writings of Chatham, Burke, Willoughby and Price, and criticised with bitterness and ridicule by Wedderburn, Mauduit, Chalmers and Tickell, all placemen under the George III-North government.

Franklin's proposed "Articles of Confederation," though little noticed in the Congress, provoked some discussion and criticism in the press. The Pennsylvania Constitution, accredited in France to his pen, was much noticed as such there, and drew forth encomiums from Turgot, Mably and Price, which were criticised by John Adams.

Franklin's Commissionership and Ministry to France produced much criticism and controversy, a part of which was from Lord Stormont, and "Grub Street," which Franklin called "Stormonts," but the larger part was written by his own countrymen, Arthur Lee, John Adams and Ralph Izard, all of whom were, we fear, partially influenced by disappointment in diplomatic advancement. But for a suppression by the endeavors of Washington, he would also have been severely handled after his death on these same grounds; and the matter has been largely gone over in recent histories and biographies.

The publication of a surreptitious and inaccurate version of one of his speeches in the Federal Convention, in which he gave only a partial approval of the Constitution, led to more or less criticism in the papers by Anti-Federalists, who charged him with supporting a government which he did not like; but such was the popularity of the man in these last years, that the author of one of the worst of these writings found it policy to suppress the most indecent part of it, in its republication.

On his death, Franklin was eulogised by William Smith, Rochefoucauld, Mirabeau, Condorcet, and in numerous resolutions passed by public bodies or societies. In early life Franklin had written a satirical "receipt" for a funeral elegy, and when Benjamin Rush attempted a few sentences in praise of Franklin in his "Discourse" before the American Philosophical Society in 1786, Franklin had taken especial pains to have them suppressed in the printed copy; but I think he would have enjoyed listening to the glowing periods and indiscriminate panegyrics of William Smith, and then have read over the lampoons and pasquinades with which the reverend gentleman had for over ten years bedaubed and bespattered him.

The entire life and character of Franklin have also met with more or less unfavorable comment. A writer who did not care to give his name to the public (thereby showing his wisdom) published in 1777 a letter on him which is not worthy of notice, even as an attack, for his chief charges are that Franklin was self-educated and a printer. In 1790, a Mr. Wilmer, a fugitive loyalist from Maryland, wrote and had "printed for the author" what purported to be a "Memoir" of Franklin, wherein we are told of his having to fly from Boston for some crime there committed, of his theft and utilization of others' discoveries in electricity, of his planning of the Stamp Act and other political trickery, and of the many women whom he had brought to shame. Another Maryland fugitive, Jonathan Boucher, who in 1774 had preached a sermon holding Franklin up to scorn, in 1797 printed it, with an appendix of matter relating to Franklin, made up chiefly from Wedderburn's speech and Wilmer's "Memoir," with the additional charges that he was a plagiarist and a deist, which charges the author discusses in the order here given. William Cobbett, while in America, had a very acrimonious newspaper warfare with Benjamin Franklin Bache, Franklin's grandson, and in the course of it, as one method of attack, tells the grandson and his readers of the immorality, hypocrisy, craft and meanness of "Old Franklin," the "old Zanga" and "malicious old hypocrite." Another inimical characterization of him is contained in Horace Smith's *Life of Rev. William Smith.* Franklin had been instrumental in obtaining for Smith the provostship of the Philadelphia Academy, and according to his own statement had made him an "enemy by doing him too much kindness." At all events, Smith soon became one of the bitterest and most active workers and writers of the political party opposed to Franklin; who naturally broke with him, and in private letters at least expressed his mind of him freely. In order to justify his ancestor, the author of this biography raked together all he could find discreditable to Franklin, and after suppression and revision by a wiser and cooler pen, inserted it in the first volume, and then in the second volume reprints his great-grandfather's funeral "rhapsody" on Franklin, in which he is painted with every greatness and virtue.

In spite of Franklin's having written so charming a sketch of part of his own life, he has been a favorite subject to biographers. Over fifty lives of him, varying in importance from the long and full ones of Mr. Bigelow and Mr. Parton, to the little juveniles which even the author deemed too insignificant to give his or her name have been written; while in both his contemporary and more recent magazines, or collections of essays are contained many biographical sketches of some importance. The names most noticeable in these biographies are those of John Bigelow, Edward Everett, Nathaniel Hawthorne, Theodore Parker, James Parton, Robert Walsh, and Robert C. Winthrop.

But this by no means ends the Franklin literature. We have essays and tracts dealing with particular incidents or matter relating to him, references of more or less importance in many books, birth-day orations, and publications relating to statues, pictures, medals, memorial windows, and other monuments to commemorate his services to his country and mankind.

This great mass of literature, by, pro, and con, has in turn produced a large number of critiques and reviews, for the most part anonymous, and buried in the periodical literature of many countries. Among those whose authorship is known we find the names of Lord Jeffrey, Lord Brougham, Josiah Quincy, Henry T. Tuckerman, William Cullen Bryant and Thomas Hughes.

Two other classes of books are connected with Franklin—those addressed to, or dedicated to, and works bearing his imprint, or upon which he is known to have worked as a journeyman printer.

***

With the production of these Frankliniana have come special collections of this matter in public and private libraries, outside of the general works which could be obtained with ease.

First among these is the Boston Public Library. Mr. Justin Winsor, in 1869, began the systematic collection of a Franklin alcove, on the ground "that Franklin is to Boston" as Shakespeare is to England. In 1881, Dr. Samuel A. Green presented the library with one hundred and fifty volumes, and by purchase, gift, and exchange, the collection now numbers over six hundred volumes, written by, printed by, or relating to "Boston's boy."

The Historical Society of Pennsylvania has the fragments, being some hundred and fifty volumes of bound pamphlets, of Franklin's library, purchased from the Athenæum, which had bought them of William Duane. It contains few of Franklin's own pieces, but many that are of interest as dedicated to, presented to, or otherwise connected with him. The Society also has the finest collection of his Philadelphia imprints, a scrap-book of MSS., clippings, and relics relating to, and a collection of some two hundred volumes of his writings and other miscellaneous books, mostly the duplicates and additions collected by Henry Stevens in connection with his "Stevens-Franklin Collection."

In the Library of Congress are the two hundred volumes collected by Henry Stevens and sold to the U. S. Government in the "Stevens-Franklin Collection," and the library already had nearly one hundred volumes relating to him.

The Lenox Library has a number of Franklin imprints, including the finest set of Poor Richard's Almanacs I have seen, and a number of pamphlets with autograph annotations by Franklin, which were stolen from the Philadelphia Athenæum, and bought by this library at the auction sale of Mr. George Brinley's books.

The library of the British Museum has nearly two hundred volumes of Frankliniana, but little of rarity.

Of private collections of books, I have only made use or know of those of Mr. George Brinley, sold at auction in 1880, which contained some hundred and fifty volumes, for the most part of rare and interesting books; and that of Mr. Gordon L. Ford, of Brooklyn, which numbers some two hundred volumes, the rarities of which are sufficiently noticed in the body of this list.

In the Department of State at Washington are the MSS. of the Stevens-Franklin Collection, together with the Franklin MSS. in the papers of the Continental Congress. In the American Philosophical Society are the bulk of the letters to Franklin by his friends and correspondents, filling over fifty volumes. The Yale College, Harvard College, and New York Historical Society libraries also possess MSS. written by and relating to him.

Mr. Clarence S. Bement and Mr. Charles R. Hildeburn, both of Philadelphia, have fine collections of the engraved portraits of Franklin, the former containing in the neighborhood of four hundred, and the latter over three hundred.

Mr. W. H. Huntington, an ardent Franklinist and antiquary, formed a very fine collection of Franklin matter, which on his death he left to the Metropolitan Museum of New York; but for reasons given elsewhere, the compiler is unable to state the nature of the collection. Many other collections have been examined, but these seem all requiring mention.

* *

The attempt to first catalogue any proportion of this matter was made by Joseph Sabin, who in his *Dictionary of Books relating to America,* under the head of Franklin, described with more or less fulness not quite two hundred works, and here a number of errors have led his successors into mistakes which I have endeavored to correct in this work. This list was reprinted with additions in the third volume of Mr. Bigelow's *Life of Franklin.*

In Mr. Stevens' *Bibliographic Essay* on Franklin, he describes with accuracy, and often with interesting notes, the two hundred works contained in his Stevens-Franklin Collection.

The most exhaustive list, however, is that written by Mr. Lindsay Swift, and printed by the Boston Public Library. This contains titles not only of the five hundred and fifty volumes then in that library, but also of all others that were given by Sabin, Hildeburn, Stevens, or other bibliographers. It contains not only the works by or relating to him, but also a list of the productions of his press.

The *Catalogue* of the Library of the British Museum describes with satisfactory fulness the works relating to him in that library.

In Mr. Charles R. Hildeburn's *Issues of the Pennsylvania Press* are catalogued with great fulness and accuracy the issues of Franklin's Philadelphia printing office.

In the various issues of Poole's and Fletcher's Indices of Periodical Literature are given a proportion of the magazine literature relating to Franklin.

**
*

From all these lists the compiler has derived much aid, which he has endeavored to acknowledge in the proper places. He has also examined the collections of books already described, with the exception of that in the Metropolitan Museum, to which access was forbidden, with gross rudeness, by Prof. Isaac H. Hall. With this solitary exception the compiler has received the utmost courtesy and aid from the librarians and curators of both these larger collections and many of lesser importance.

From these two sources the following list has been chiefly compiled, though much has been collected from many books and individuals. The compiler owes thanks to Mr. Lindsay Swift and Dr. Samuel A. Green, of Boston; Mr. Gordon L. Ford and Mr. Worthington C. Ford, of Brooklyn; Mr. John Bigelow, Mr. George H. Moore, Mr. W. Eames, and Mr. William Kelby, of New York; Mr. Charles R. Hildeburn, Mr. F. D. Stone, Mr. Bumford Samuels and Mr. Henry Phillips, of Philadelphia; and Mr. A. R. Spofford and Mr. Theodore F. Dwight, of Washington, for their assistance and courtesy; and especial thanks and gratitude to Mr. Lindsay Swift, Mr. W. W. Pasko, and Mr. W. Eames, for their comparisons and corrections of the proof sheets of this list.

PAUL LEICESTER FORD.

97 Clark St., Brooklyn, N. Y.

PART I.

BOOKS AND PAMPHLETS

WHOLLY OR PARTLY WRITTEN BY

FRANKLIN.

.*. The titles in this part are arranged chronologically under the
year in which they were written, and editions of each grouped chronologically under the first edition. Collected works are arranged under
the date of printing, except reprints, which are grouped under the first
edition. All editions of Father Abraham, however, even if containing
other pieces, are classed under that heading, and all editions of the
Autobiography are gathered in one series.

1719. Ballad.

[The Lighthouse Tragedy.   Boston: Printed by James Franklin.]

Broadside.

1

1719. Ballad.

[The Taking of Teach, the Pirate.   Boston: Printed by James Franklin.]

Broadside.

2

∗∗∗ Hypothetical titles of two pieces, not now extant, though the inventive Mr. Weems, in his *Life of Benjamin Franklin*, gives a stanza from the second (which fortunately for Franklin, we know to be by another hand), and *The Memorial History of Boston* (II., 174), suggests another, on no better authority.

∗∗∗ "I now took a fancy to poetry, and made some little pieces; my brother, thinking it might turn to account, encouraged me, and put me on composing occasional ballads.   One was called *The Lighthouse Tragedy*, and contained an account of the drowning of Captain Worthilake, with his two daughters; the other was a sailor's song, on the taking of *Teach* (or Blackbeard) the pirate.   They were wretched stuff, in the Grub-street-ballad style; and when they were printed he sent me about the town to sell them.   The first sold wonderfully, the event being recent, having made a great noise.   This flattered my vanity; but my father discouraged me by ridiculing my performances, and telling me verse-makers were generally beggars." *Autobiography*, 93.

1721. The New England Courant.

The [No. 1 / New England Courant / from Monday, August 17, to Monday, August 24, 1721. / [colophon] Boston: Printed by James Franklin, in Queen Street, where / Advertisements are taken in. [?]

Folio.

3

∗∗∗ This, the fifth paper published in what is now the United States, was printed by the brother of Benjamin Franklin, who as his apprentice aided in its manufacture from its commencement; was the real publisher during his brother's imprisonment, and the ostensible publisher after the Massachusetts House of Representatives had forbidden James Franklin to continue its publication; and under his name it was pub-

[1]

lished till long after he had run away from his brother, if not till the discontinuance of the paper.

⁎⁎⁎ But in addition to this connection with Franklin, this paper is still more interesting as containing the first of Franklin's writings now extant. Under the pseudonym of "Silence Dogood" Franklin commenced in No. 35 (March 26, 1722) a series of essays, "in the manner of the Spectator" on a variety of subjects, which are among the most charming and readable of his writings, but as yet not printed in any edition of his works, though Buckingham in 1850 (*Specimens of Newspaper Literature*, 1, 62), in reprinting portions of two, accredited them to Franklin's pen; and Franklin in his outline of the autobiography virtually claims them for himself. It is probable that Franklin wrote other pieces for the Courant, but which they are is largely guess-work.

⁎⁎⁎ In 1856, the first number of the paper published in Benjamin Franklin's name was reprinted as follows:

The [No. 80 / New England Courant. / From Monday, February 4 to Monday, February 11, 1723. [colophon] Boston: Printed and sold by Benjamin Franklin in Queen Street, where / Advertisements are taken in. / Fac-Simile of the first Paper ever issued by Franklin, and / now printed (Sept. 17, 1856) on a press once used by him.

Folio.   1 l.   B.   4

⁎⁎⁎ An imperfect file is in the Massachusetts Historical Society.

1725. Dissertation on Liberty and Necessity. London. 1725.

A / Dissertation / on / Liberty and Necessity, / Pleasure and Pain. / . . . . . / London: / Printed in the year MDCCXXV.

8vo.   pp. 32.   P.L., C.   5

⁎⁎⁎ "At Palmer's I was employed in composing for the second edition of Wollaston's 'Religion of Nature.' Some of his reasonings not appearing to me well founded, I wrote a little metaphysical piece in which I made remarks on them. It was entitled 'A Dissertation on Liberty and Necessity, Pleasure and Pain.' I enscribed it to my friend Ralph; I printed a small number. It occasion'd my being more consider'd by Mr. Palmer as a young man of some ingenuity, tho' he seriously expostulated with me upon the principles of my pamphlet, which to him appear'd abominable. My printing this pamphlet was another erratum." *Autobiography*, 141.

⁎⁎⁎ "There were only a hundred copies printed, of which I gave a few to friends; and afterwards disliking the piece, as conceiving it might have an ill tendency, I burnt the rest, except one copy." *Franklin to Vaughan.*

⁎⁎⁎ Mr. Sparks searched in vain for this so-called "wicked tract" of Franklin's, and it is therefore omitted in his edition of the *Writings;*

as also in Mr. Bigelow's; though Mr. Parton had printed it entire in the appendix to his *Life of Franklin*, from a MS. copy of the original tract, two of which have been discovered by Henry Stevens. Of these Mr. Stevens wrote: "Then there was Franklin's 'Liberty and Necessity,' London, 1725, bought for 2s.6d., offered to the British Museum with its story for one guinea and declined on account of price, then offered to Mr. Brown and Mr. Lenox at five guineas and declined by both; subsequently thrown into auction at Messrs. Puttick & Simpson's with nearly a half page note, where it fetched 19 guineas, and was bought by Mr. Hotten against the British Museum; on Mr. Hotten's death in 1872 it was sold again by Puttick & Simpson for £22 10s. [to Henry Huth] again against the British Museum. Neither the Museum nor Mr. Brown nor Mr. Lenox ever secured this rare little book. My own copy (for I had a duplicate) is now slumbering in the 'Stevens Franklin Collection' in the Department of State at Washington . . . in which I had valued it at £100. It is rather remarkable that both of the only two copies now known, out of the 100 that Franklin printed himself at Palmer's at the age of 18, should have thus passed through my hands."

∗∗∗ Franklin is evidently mistaken in saying that it was the second edition of Wollaston; for that was published before the author's death, October 29, 1724, while Franklin did not reach London till December 24, 1724. Hence he must have worked on the third edition, printed in 1725, with the following title: The / Religion / of / Nature / Delineated / . . . . . / London: / Printed by Samuel Palmer, in Bartholomew-Close, / and sold by B. Lintot, W. and J. Innys, J. Osborn and / T. Longman, and J. Batley. 1725. 4to. pp. 219, (12).   C., B.   6

1725. Dissertation on Liberty and Necessity. Dublin: 1733.

A / Dissertation / on / Liberty and Necessity, / Pleasure and Pain. / In a Letter to a Friend / . . . . . / Dublin: / Printed in the year MDCCXXXIII.

8vo. pp. 16.   c.   7

∗∗∗ Franklin did not know of this edition, and Mr. Stevens claims that the copy contained in his "Franklin Collection" is "believed to be unique," rendering it probable that it is the same copy which Mr. James Crossley describes in *Notes and Queries*, first series, v. 6.

1725. Dissertation on Liberty and Necessity. London. 1854.

A / Dissertation / on / Liberty and Necessity, / Pleasure and Pain. / . . . . . . / London: / Printed in the Year MDCCXXV. [colophon] . . . a facsimile reprint by

Charles Whittingham . . . from the / original edition in the possession of Henry Stevens . . . / London.

8vo. pp. 32.   P. H. S.   8

* Only 25 copies printed.

* In the catalogue of the Stevens' Franklin Collection, there is given a title of an edition of this pamphlet, printed with two prefaces, in London in 1881, but it was never completed.

1728. Rules for a Club.

Benjamin Franklin's / Rules for a Club established in Philadelphia, / übertragen und ausgelegt / als / Statut für eine Gesell-schaft von Freunden / der Humanität / von / Johann Gottfried Herder. / 1792. / Aus dem Nachlaß veröffentlicht / und / Eduard Simson / zum 22. Mai 1883 / zugeeignet / von / Bernhard Suphan, / Berlin, / Weid-mannsche Buchhandlung.

Sm. 4to. pp. 30.   B., P. H. S.   9

* The constitution of the "Junto."

1729. Enquiry into Paper Money.

A Modest / Enquiry / into the / Nature and Necessity / of a / Paper-Currency. / . . . / . . . / . . . / Philadelphia: / Printed and Sold at the New Printing- / Office, near the Market, 1729.

8vo. pp. 36.   P., P. H. S., C.   10

* "About this time there was a cry among the people for more paper money, only fifteen thousand pounds being extant in the province, and that soon to be sunk. The wealthy inhabitants oppos'd any addition, being against all paper currency, from an apprehension it would depreciate, as it had done in New England, to the prejudice of all creditors. We had discuss'd this point in our Junto, where I was on the side of an addition, being persuaded that the first small sum struck in 1723 had done much good . . . Our debates possess'd me so fully of the subject, that I wrote and printed an anonymous pamphlet on it. . . . It was well receiv'd by the common people in general; but the rich men dislik'd it, for it increas'd and strengthen'd the clamor for more money, and they happening to have no writers among them that were able to answer it, their opposition slacken'd, and the point was carried by a majority in the House." *Autobiography,* 185.

1729. Pennsylvania Gazette.

Numb. XL. / The Pennsylvania Gazette. / Containing the freshest Advices Foreign and Domestic. / From Thurs-

day, September 25. to Thursday, October 2. 1729. / . . .
[colophon] Philadelphia: Printed by B. Franklin and
H. Meredith, at the New Printing-Office near the Market,
where Advertisements / are taken in, and all Persons may
be supplied with this Paper, at Ten Shillings a year.

Folio and 4to.   P., P. H. S.   11

*** Continued, with many changes of title, imprint, and size till 1821.

*** The publication of a newspaper was one of Franklin's pet
schemes, but having mentioned the idea to others, it was seized upon
by Keimer (a rival printer), who forestalled him by starting *"The Universal Instructor in all Arts and Sciences, or The Pennsylvania Gazette,"*
which he printed till its fortieth number, when having disposed of his
printing office, he parted with it to Franklin at a nominal sum, having
at that time ninety subscribers. With Number 40 the title was cur-
tailed to *"The Pennsylvania Gazette,"* and it became the leading
newspaper of the day, with a large circulation and advertising patronage. For nearly twenty years (1729–1748), Franklin was virtually the
sole editor and proprietor, and for eighteen more (1748–1766) jointly so
with David Hall. A few of the articles which it was supposed he
wrote for the paper were printed in Duane's edition of his writings,
from which they were taken by W. T. Franklin, Sparks, and Bigelow
for their editions, though the former two expressed doubts as to some
of them. In both Parton's and McMaster's biographies, other pieces
are ascribed to his pen, not hitherto printed as his. That Franklin
contributed many pieces is hardly to be questioned, but it is equally
certain that few of them can be awarded to him with sufficient evidence
to entitle them to a place in his writings.

*** In spite of its large circulation, no complete series is at present
known to exist, those in the Historical Society of Pennsylvania and
the Library Company of Philadelphia being the most perfect. In
Hildeburn's *"Issues of the Press in Pennsylvania"* is a most minute
and careful collation of as perfect a file as could be found. Brief histories of the paper are printed in Thomas' *"History of Printing in
America;" "Potter's American Monthly,"* IV. 7; and *"The Magazine
of American History,"* XV. 452.

1732. Poor Richard's Almanac for 1733.

Poor Richard, 1733. / An / Almanack / For the Year of
Christ / 1733, / Being the First after Leap Year; / And
makes since the Creation Years / By the Account of the
Eastern Greeks 7241 / By the Latin Church, when ☉ ent ♈
6932 / By the Computation of W. W. 5742 / By the Roman

Chronology 5682 / By the Jewish Rabbies 5494 / Wherin is contained / The Lunations, Eclipses, Judgment of / the Weather, Spring Tides, Planets Motions & / mutual Aspects, Sun and Moon's Rising and Set- / ting, Length of Days, Time of High Water, / Fairs, Courts, and observable Days. / Fitted to the Latitude of Forty Degrees, / and a Meridian of Five Hours West from London, / but may without sensible Error, serve all the ad- / jacent Places, even from Newfoundland to South- / Carolina. / By Richard Saunders, Philom. / Philadelphia: / Printed and sold by B. Franklin, at the New / Printing-Office near the Market [1732.]

Sm. 8vo. pp. (24).　　　　　　　12

*** "In 1732 I first publish'd my Almanack, under the name of *Richard Saunders;* it was continu'd by me about twenty-five years, commonly call'd *Poor Richard's Almanac.* I endeavor'd to make it both entertaining and useful, and it accordingly came to be in such demand, that I reap'd considerable profit from it, vending annually near ten thousand. And observing that it was generally read, scarce any neighborhood in the province being without it, I consider'd it as a proper vehicle for conveying instruction among the common people, who bought scarcely any other books; I therefore filled all the little spaces that occur'd between the remarkable days in the calendar with proverbial sentences, chiefly such as inculcated industry and frugality, as the means of procuring wealth, and thereby securing virtue." *Autobiography*, 235.

*** Poor Richard is beyond question the most famous of almanacs, and is, with but one exception, the most charming and readable of Franklin's writings. Yet the series has never been reprinted, and (except the few extracts given in the later editions of his writings, and the uncompleted attempt of Mr. Doggett mentioned below), can only be consulted in the original issues, which are of the greatest rarity, and, as shown by the following list, widely scattered:

1733. P. H. S., A. P. S.	1742. C., P.	1751. L., P. H. S., P.
1734.	1743. C., P.	1752. L., P. H. S., C., P.
1735.	1744. P. H. S., P.	1753. L., P. H. S., C., P.
1736. L., P. H. S.	1745. L., P.	1754. L., P. H. S., C., P.
1737. L., P. H. S.	1746. L., P.	1755. L., P. H. S., C., P.
1738. L., P.	1747. L., P.	1756. L., P. H. S., C., P.
1739. P.	1748. L., P. H. S., C., P	1757. L., P. H. S., C., P.
1740. L., C., P.	1749. L., P. H. S., P.	1758. L., P. H. S., C., P.
1741. P. H. S., C., P.	1750. P. H. S., C., P.	

_**_* The fame of the almanac has made it a popular title for other series, which as they contain nothing of Franklin's, I have merely included in the Reference List. John Doggett, however, began to reprint the whole series, so far as "the editorial matter of Franklin" in the following:

"Poor Richard." / Poor Richard's Almanac / for / 1850, / as written by / Benjamin Franklin, / for the years / 1733–1734–1735. / The Astronomical calculations / by Prof. Benj. Peirce, of Harvard University, / . . . . . / To which is added, / the Commencement of the Life / of / the Great Philosopher, / Written by Himself / Annual Illustrated Edition. / New-York: / John Doggett, Jr., 64 Liberty-Street, / . . . / 1849. / 12mo., pp. 60, plates, covers.   B., P. H. S.   13

"Poor Richard." / Poor Richard's Almanac / for / 1851, / as written by / Benjamin Franklin, / for the years / 1736–1737–1738. / . . . / New-York: / John Doggett, Jr., 59 Liberty-Street. / 1850.   12mo., pp. 60, plates, covers.   B., P. H. S.   14

Poor Richard's Almanac / for / 1852, / as written by / Benjamin Franklin, / for the years / 1739–1740–1741. / . . . . . / New-York: / John Doggett, Jr., 59 Liberty-Street. / 1851.   12mo., pp. 48, plates, covers.   B., P. H. S.   15

_**_* All ever printed.

1732. *Poor Richard's Almanac for 1733.*

Poor Richard, 1733. / [_*12_*] / Philadelphia: / Printed and sold by B. Franklin, at the New / Printing-Office near the Market. / The Third Impression.

Sm. 8vo. pp. 24.   P. H. S.   16

1732. *Poor Richard's Almanac for 1733.*

Poor Richard, 1733. / [_*12_*] / Philadelphia: / Printed and sold by B. Franklin, at the New / Printing-Office near the Market / [Reprinted in fac-simile, Philadelphia: G. S. Appleton, 1847.]

12mo. pp. 2, 36.   L., B.   17

_**_* With a preface by Charles Marshall. It was an advertising dodge.

1733. *Poor Richard's Almanac for 1734.*

Poor Richard, 1734. An Almanack for the Year of Christ, 1734, ... By Richard Saunders, Philom. Philadelphia: Printed and sold by B. Franklin, at the New Printing-Office near the Market. [1733.]

Sm. 8vo. pp. (24).   18

1734. Poor Richard's Almanack for 1735.

Poor Richard, 1735. An Almanack for the Year of Christ, 1735, ... By Richard Saunders, Philom. Philadelphia: Printed and sold by B. Franklin, at the New Printing-Office near the Market. [1734.]

Sm. 8vo. pp. (24).

19

1735. Introduction to Moral Distiches.

Cato's / Moral / Distiches / Englished in Couplets. [By James Logan] / Philadelphia: / Printed and Sold by B. Franklin, 1735.

4to. pp. vi, 23.

P. 20

_**_* Includes an introduction from "The Printer to the Reader." The work is reprinted, and fully described in Phile's *Philobiblion*, II. 25.

1735. Defense of Hemphill.

A / Defense / Of the Rev. Mr. Hemphill's / Observations: / or, An / Answer / to the / Vindication of the Reve- / rend Commission. / . . . . . . / Philadelphia: / Printed and Sold by B. Franklin at the New Printing- / Office near the Market.   1735.

8vo., pp. 47, (1).

B. 21

_**_* "About the year 1734 there arrived among us from Ireland a young Presbyterian preacher, named Hemphill, who delivered with a good voice, and apparently extempore, most excellent discourses, which drew together considerable numbers of different persuasions, who join'd in admiring them. Among the rest, I became one of his constant hearers, his sermons pleasing me, as they had little of the dogmatical kind, but inculcated strongly the practise of virtue . . . Those, however, of our congregation, who considered themselves as orthodox Presbyterians, disapprov'd his doctrine, and were join'd by most of the old clergy, who arraign'd him of heterodoxy before the synod, in order to have him silenc'd. I became his zealous partisan, and contributed all I could to raise a party in his favor. . . . There was much scribbling pro and con upon the occasion; and finding that, tho' an elegant preacher, he was but a poor writer, I lent him my pen, and wrote for him two or three pamphlets, and one piece in the Gazette of April, 1735. Those pamphlets, as is generally the case with controversial writings, tho' eagerly read at the time, were soon out of vogue, and I question whether a single copy of them now exists." *Autobiography*, 239.

⁎ Neither this, nor numbers 22 and 25 are contained in any edition of Franklin's writings.

1735. Letter to a Friend.

A Letter to a Friend in the Country, / Containing the Substance of a / Sermon / Preach'd at Philadelphia, in the Congregation of / The Rev. Mr. Hemphill, / Concerning the Terms of Christian and / Ministeriaˡ Communion. / . . . . . / Philadelphia: / Printed and Sold by B. Franklin at the New Printing- / Office near the Market. 1735.

8vo.   pp. 40.   B.   22

⁎ Answered in:

Remarks / Upon a Pamphlet Entitled, / A Letter to a Friend in the / Country containing the Sub- / stance of a Sermon / preached at / Philadelphia, / in the Congregation of the / Rev. Mr. Hemphill. / . . . . . / Philadelphia: Printed and Sold by Andrew / Bradford at the Bible in Second Street. 1735. 8vo. pp. 32.   M.   23

1735. Poor Richard's Almanac for 1736.

Poor Richard, 1736. / An Almanack / For the Year of Christ / 1736, / . . . . . / By Richard Saunders, Philom. / Philadelphia: / Printed and Sold by B. Franklin, at the New / Printing-Office near the Market. [1735.]

8vo.   pp. (24).   L., P. H. S.   24

1735. Observations on the Proceedings.

Some / Observations / on the / Proceedings / against / The Rev. Mr. Hemphill; / with a / Vindication of his Ser- mons. / Philadelphia: / Printed and Sold by B. Franklin. 1735.

8vo.   pp. 32.   P. H. S.   25

⁎ Answered in:

A / Vindication / of the / Reverend Commission / of the / Synod: / In Answer to / Some Observations / On their Proceedings against the Reverend / Mr. Hemphill. / . . . . . / Philadelphia: / Printed and Sold by Andrew Bradford at the / Bible, in Second-Street. MDCCXXXV. 8vo. pp. (2), 63.   Y. C.   26

1735. Observations on the Proceedings, 2d Edition.

Some / [⁎25⁎] / Sermons. / The Second Edition. / Phila- delphia: / Printed and Sold by B. Franklin. 1735.

8vo.   pp. 32.   27

1736. Way to make Money Plenty.
The Art of Making Money Plenty / In every Man's Pocket; by / Doctor Franklin. / [n. p. 183–.]

Sm. 4to., Broadside.   P. L.   28

1736. Way to make Money Plenty.
The Art of making Money Plenty / in every Man's Pocket / By / Doctor Franklin / . . . [New York:] M. J. Stockwell [1866.]

4to.   Broadside.   P. L.   29

_**_* An advertisement, in the form of a rebus. There are other issues, from the same plate, with the advertisement of John C. Stockwell and Hopkins & Son.

1736. Hints for getting riches.
Necessary Hints / to / those who would be Rich. / An Essay / By Dr. Benjamin Franklin. / [London: W. Turner. 1805.]

Min. pp. 2.   P. H. S.   30

_**_* First printed in Poor Richard's Almanac for 1737.

1736. Poor Richard's Almanac for 1737.
Poor Richard, 1737. / An / Almanack / For the Year of Christ / 1737. / . . . . . / By Richard Saunders, Philom. / Philadelphia: / Printed and sold by B. Franklin, at the New / Printing-Office near the Market. [1736.]

Sm. 8vo. pp. (24).   L., P. H. S.   31

1737. Poor Richard's Almanac. 1738.
Poor Richard, 1738. / An / Almanack / For the Year of Christ / 1738. / . . . . . By Richard Saunders, Philom. / Philadelphia: / Printed and sold by B. Franklin, at the New / Printing-Office near the Market. [1737.]

Sm. 8vo. pp. (24).   L., P.   32

1738. Poor Richard's Almanac for 1739.
Poor Richard, 1739. / An Almanack / For the Year of Christ / 1739. / . . . . . / By Richard Saunders, Philom. / Philadelphia: / Printed and sold by B. Franklin, at the New / Printing-Office near the Market. [1738.]

Sm. 8vo. pp. (24).   P.   33

1739. Poor Richard's Almanac for 1740.

Poor Richard, 1740. / An / Almanack / for the Year of Christ / 1740. / . . . . . / By Richard Saunders, Philom. / Philadelphia: / Printed and sold by B. Franklin, at the New / Printing-Office near the Market. [1739.]

12mo. pp. (24).   P. 34

1740. Poor Richard's Almanac for 1741.

Poor Richard, 1741 / An / Almanack / For the Year of Christ / 1741. / . . . . . / By Richard Saunders, Philom. / Philadelphia: / Printed and sold by B. Franklin, at the New / Printing-Office near the Market. [1740.]

Sm. 8vo. pp. (24).   P. H. S., C., P. 35

1741. General Magazine.

The / General Magazine, / And / Historical Chronicle, / For all the British Plantations in America. / (To be Continued Monthly.) / January, 1741 / Vol. I. / Philadelphia: / Printed and Sold by B. Franklin.

8 Nos. 8vo.   C., P. H. S. 36

⁎⁎⁎ The first magazine planned, and the second issued, in this country. Franklin was the editor, but I do not think wrote anything for it. See McMaster's *Benjamin Franklin*, 129, and *Hildeburn*, I, 159.

1741. Poor Richard's Almanac for 1742.

Poor Richard, 1742. / An / Almanack / For the Year of Christ / 1742. / . . . . . / By Richard Saunders, Philom. / Philadelphia: / Printed and sold by B. Franklin, at the New / Printing-Office near the Market. [1741.]

12mo. pp. (24).   P., C. 37

1742. Poor Richard's Almanac for 1743.

Poor Richard, 1743. / An / Almanack / For the Year of Christ / 1743. / . . . . . / By Richard Saunders, Philom. / Philadelphia: / Printed and sold by B. Franklin, at the New / Printing-Office near the Market. [1742.]

Sm. 8vo. pp. (24).   C., P. 38

1743. Poor Richard's Almanac for 1744.

Poor Richard, 1744. / An / Almanack / For the 'Year of Christ / 1744. / . . . . . / By Richard Saunders, Philom.

/ Philadelphia: / Printed and sold by B. Franklin, . . . / also by Jonas Greene. . . . [1743.]

Sm. 8vo. pp. (24).   P., P. H. S. 39

1743. Prospectus of Philosophical Society.

A Proposal for Promoting / Useful Knowledge among the / British Plantations in America. [Philadelphia, Printed by B. Franklin, 14 May, 1743.]

Folio, 1 l.   c. 40

ᕠ The original prospectus of the American Philosophical Society, to which Franklin alludes in his *Autobiography*, p. 260.

ᕠ "Benjamin Franklin, the writer of this Proposal, offers himself to serve the Society as their Secretary, till they shall be provided with one more capable." *Proposal.*

1744. Account of Pennsylvania Fire Place.

An / Account / Of the New Invented / Pennsylvanian / Fire-Places: / Wherein / Their Construction and Manner of / Operation is particularly explained; / Their Advantages above every other / Method of Warming Rooms de- / monstrated; / And all Objections that have been raised against / the Use of Them, answered and obviated. / With Directions for putting them up, and for Using / them to the best Advantage. With a Copper-Plate, / in which several Parts of the Machine / are exactly laid down, from a Scale of equal Parts. / Philadelphia: / Printed and Sold by B. Franklin. 1744.

8vo. pp. (2), 37, (1), folding plate.   P. H. S., P. 41

ᕠ Mr. Sparks states that there are several other editions of this pamphlet; but I have only been able to find the one below.

ᕠ For an account of this stove, see Sparks' *Works of Franklin*, VI, 34; and *Autobiography*, 273.

1744. Account of Pennsylvania Fire Place. Venice. 1778.

Descrizione / della / Stufia di Pennsilvania / inventati / dal / Franklin Americano. / In Venizia, MDCCLXXVIII. / Delle Stampe di Antonio Graziosi / . . .

Sm. 4to. pp. 47, plate.   P. H. S. 42

1744. Catalogue of Books.

A / Catalogue / of / Choice and Valuable / Books / con-

sisting of / Near 600 Volumes in most Faculties / and
Sciences, viz: / Divinity, History, Law, Ma- / thematics,
Philosophy, Phy- / sic, Poetry, &c., / which will begin /
To be sold for ready money only, by Benj. / Franklin at
the Post office in Philadelphia, / on Wednesday the 11th
of April 1744 at nine / o clock in the morning: And for
Despatch, the / lowest Price is mark'd in each Book. /
The sale to continue Three Weeks, and no longer: And
what then remains will be sold at an advance Price. /
Those Persons that live remote by sending their / Orders
and money to said B. Franklin, may / depend on the
same justice as if present.

16mo. pp. 60. P. L. 43

⁎ Title through the courtesy of Mr. Thomas J. McKee of New
York.

1744. *Preface to Cato Major.*

M. T. Cicero's / Cato Major, / or his / Discourse / of / Old-
Age: / With Explanatory Notes. / Philadelphia: / Printed
and Sold by B. Franklin, / MDCCXLIV.

8vo. pp. viii, 159. P. H. S., B., C. 44

⁎ I have included this not only because it contains Franklin's
"The Printer to the Reader," but also because in later editions the
authorship had been improperly ascribed to him, although in his preface he distinctly states the translation and notes to be the work of
James Logan. It is the finest piece of printing from Franklin's press,
and is eagerly sought for by collectors, an uncut copy having sold as
high as $260.

⁎ "I formerly sent you from Philadelphia part of an edition of
Tully on Old Age, to be sold in London; and you put the Book, if I
remember right, into the Hands of Mr. Becket for that Purpose.
Probably he may have some of them still in his Warehouse, as I never
had an Account of their being sold. I shall be much obliged by your
procuring and sending me one of them." *Franklin to Strahan*, Dec.
4th, 1781.

⁎ Reprinted as follows:

Cato Major; / or, a / Treatise / on / Old Age, / by / M. Tullius Cicero.
/ With / Explanatory Notes from the Roman / History. / By the Hon-
ourable / Mr. Logan. / Philadelphia, Printed. / Glasgow, Re-printed by
R. Urie. / M.DCC.LI. 12mo. pp. 168, (3). P. H. S. 45

Cato Major; or, a Treatise on Old Age, by M. Tullius Cicero. With

Explanatory Notes from the Roman History. Philadelphia: Printed by William Dunlap, 1758. 16mo. pp. 168.   46

Cato Major; / or, a / Treatise / on / Old Age, / by / M. Tullius Cicero. / with / Explanatory Notes from the / Roman History. / By the Honour-able / James Logan, Esq; / President of the Council, and Chief Jus-/tice of the Province of Philadelphia. [sic] / The Fourth Edition. / Phila-delphia, Printed. / Glasgow, Reprinted by R. Urie. / M.DCC.LVIII. 12mo. pp. 168, (3).   P. H. S.   47

M. T. Cicero's / Cato Major, / or Discourse on / Old Age. / Addressed to / Titus Pomponius Atticus. / With Explanatory Notes. / By Benj. Franklin, LL.D. / Philadelphia: / Printed by B. Franklin. / London: / Re-Printed for Fielding and Walker, / Pater-Noster Row / MDCC-LXXVIII. / 8vo. pp. (4), 163, portrait.   P. H. S.   48

⁎ In this edition Franklin's preface is so altered, as to make it ap-pear that he was the translator. It was a publisher's trick to sell the book, but led Mr. Duane, when publishing Franklin's writings in 1808, to include it among them (IV, 250), and also to issue a separate edition as below.

Marcus Tullius Cicero's / Cato Major; / or a / Discourse on Old Age. / Addressed to / Titus Pomponius Atticus. / With Explanatory Notes, / by Benjamin Franklin, L.L.D. / Philadelphia: W. Duane. [1809.] 8vo. pp. (4), 251–357.   C.   49

1744. Poor Richard's Almanac for 1745.

Poor Richard, 1745. / An / Almanack / for the Year of Christ / 1745. / . . . . . / By Richard Saunders, Philom. / Philadelphia: / Printed and sold by B. Franklin. / [1744.] 12mo. pp. (24).   L.   50

1745. Poor Richard's Almanac for 1746.

Poor Richard, 1746. / An / Almanack / for the Year of Christ, / 1746. / . . . . . / By Richard Saunders, Philom. / Philadelphia: / Printed and Sold by B. Franklin. [1745.] 12mo. pp. (24).   L., P.   51

1745. Suppressed Letter.   Washington: 1885.

June 25, 1745. / To —— / [Washington: 1885.] 4to. 2ll.   P. L.   52

⁎ Only a few copies printed in lithographic text from the original in the Department of State. The letter was written to William Frank-lin, and has never been embodied in any edition of Franklin's writings.

⁎ In the catalogue of the Stevens Franklin Collection, there is noted, "Dr. Franklin's Two New Bagatelles [on Perfumes and on Marriage] Edited and now first printed from the original autograph

manuscripts in the possession of Henry Stevens of Vermont.   London : Privately printed. 1881. 64mo.''—According to Mr. Henry N. Stevens, this was never printed.

1745. Suppressed Letter.   New York: 1887.

Benjamin Franklin [1745. / Copy of a Letter in the possession of the State Department / at Washington, D. C. / June 25, 1745. / My Dear Friend:— / . . .

8vo. pp. 3.   P. L. 53

    ₌ Printed in the same form and type (though on different paper) as Mr. Bigelow's edition of Franklin.

1745. Suppressed Letter.   1887.

A / Philosopher / in / Undress. / ''So you may make a secret of it too, if you please, and oblige / all your friends with it.''   Franklin to his wife. / 25 Copies printed.—1887.

Sm. 4to. pp. (4).   P. L. 54

    ₌ Printed on one side of paper only.

1745. Suppressed Letter.   New York: 1888.

Ben Franklin on Marriage, etc. / An authentic letter of Benjamin Franklin in / the Collection of Franklin's Cor- respondence, / purchased by the United States at a cost of / $30,000, now in the possession of the Depart- / ment of State at Washington, D. C.: / [New York: 1888.]

8vo. pp. (2).   P. L. 55

1746. Poor Richard's Almanac for 1747.

Poor Richard, 1747. / An / Almanack / For the Year of Christ / 1747, / . . . . . / By Richard Saunders, Philom. / Philadelphia: / Printed and Sold by B. Franklin. [1746.]

12mo. pp. 24.   P. 56

1746. Reflections on Marriage.   Philadelphia: 1746.

Reflections / on / Courtship and Marriage: / In / Two Letters / to a / Friend. / Wherein a Practicable Plan is laid down for / Obtaining and Securing / Conjugal Felicity. / Philadelphia: / Printed and Sold by B. Franklin, / M,DCC,XLVI.

Sm. 4to. pp. vii. 68.   P. H. S. 57

    ₌ Dr. Benjamin Rush states that this is by Franklin, but it has not been included in any edition of his writings. Sabin mentions an edi- tion with the same imprint and collation, ''Philadelphia. 1749.''

_**_* "Mr. Hildeburn states that the third edition (1758) refers to Franklin as the author." *Swift.*

1746. Reflections on Marriage. Edinburgh: 1750.

Reflections / on / Courtship / and / Marriage: / In two Letters to a Friend. / Wherein a practical Plan is laid down for / Obtaining and Securing / Conjugal Felicity. / To which is annexed, / A Letter to a very young Lady on her / Marriage. By Dr. Swift. / Philadelphia, Printed. / Edinburgh, Reprinted, / For William Gray, junior. / MDCCL / (Price Eight Pence.)

8vo. pp. iv. 52.   P. L, 58

1746. Reflections on Marriage. Philadelphia: 1758.

Reflections on Courtship and Marriage; In Two Letters to a Friend.   Wherein a Practicable Plan is laid down for Obtaining and Securing Conjugal Felicity.   To which is added, A Letter from the late Dean Swift, to a very young Lady on her Marriage, containing salutory Advice relating to her conduct thro' Life.   The Third Edition.   Philadelphia : Printed and Sold by William Dunlap, at the Newest-Printing-Office, on the South Side of the Jersey Market.   1758.

o. pp.   59

_**_* Title from *Hildeburn.*

1746. Reflections on Marriage. 1759.

Reflections on Courtship and Marriage, with a plan of Conjugal Felicity, etc., with an appendix on Jealousy. 1759.

12mo. pp. portrait.   60

_**_* Title from stock catalogue of John Salkeld.

1747. Association for Defense.

[An Association for the general Defense of the City and Province.   Philadelphia: B. Franklin.   1747.]

Broadside.   61

_**_* A hypothetical title of a piece unnoticed by all editors of Franklin, and bibliographers.

_**_* "Having settled the draft of it ['instrument of Association'] with a few friends, I appointed a meeting of the citizens in the large building before mentioned. The house was pretty full; I had prepared

a number of printed copies, and provided pens and ink dispers'd all over the room. I harangued them a little on the subject, read the paper, and explained it, and then distributed the copies, which were eagerly signed." *Autobiography*, 263.

₊*₊ See Hildeburn's *Issues of the Pennsylvania Press*, 1747-8, for many pamphlets attacking and defending the principles of defensive warfare, which this association was formed to encourage.

1747. Proclamation for a Fast.

G. [Royal Arms] R. By the Honourable the President and Council of the Province of Pennsylvania. A Proclamation for a general Fast. . . . [Philadelphia: B. Frank-' lin: 1747.]

Folio. Broadside.   62

₊*₊ The Council appointed Abraham Taylor and Thomas Hopkinson to draft this Proclamation. *Pa. Archives*, v, 169.

₊*₊ "My activity . . . was agreeable to the governor and council; they took me into confidence, and I was consulted by them in every measure wherein their concurrence was thought useful to the association. Calling in the aid of religion, I propos'd the proclaiming of a fast, to promote . . . our undertaking. They embrac'd the motion; but, as it was the first fast ever thought of in the province, the secretary had no precedent from which to draw the proclamation. My education in New England, where a fast is proclaimed every year, was here of some advantage: I drew it in the accustomed style; it was translated into German, printed in both languages, and divulg'd thro' the province." *Autobiography*, 265.

1747. Proclamation for a Fast.

[Same, in German. Philadelphia: Printed by B. Franklin. 1747.]

Folio. Broadside.   63

₊*₊ The allusion to this German edition in Franklin's autobiography is the only trace I have been able to find of it.

1747. Plain Truth.

Plain Truth: / Or, / Serious Considerations / On the Present State of the / City of Philadelphia, / and / Province of Pennsylvania. / By a Tradesman of Philadelphia. / . . . [16 lines] . . . / [Philadelphia:] Printed [by B. Franklin] / in the Year MDCCXLVII.

8vo. pp. 22, (2).   P. H. S. 64

₊*₊ The Boston Public Library list, quoting Westcott, mentions a second edition, with a cut of "Hercules and the Waggoner" added, but though a second edition was printed, there is no difference between the two; and Westcott was probably misled by Sparks, who believed that the first edition was published earlier than 1747.

∗ "I determined to try what might be done by a voluntary association of the people. To promote this, I first wrote and published a pamphlet, entitled PLAIN TRUTH, in which I stated our defenseless situation in strong lights, with the necessity of union and discipline for our defense, and promis'd to propose in a few days an association to be generally signed for that purpose. The pamphlet had a sudden and surprising effect." *Autobiography*, 263.

∗ "Though *Plain Truth* bore somewhat hard on both parties here, it has had the happiness not to give much offence to either. It has wonderfully spirited us up to defend ourselves and the country, to which end great numbers are entering into an association, of which I send you a copy enclosed."

∗ This pamphlet may be considered the first wedge by which the inhabitants of Pennsylvania were changed from the Quaker doctrine of submission, to that of defensive warfare. The controversy gave rise to many publications, and among them to two direct answers to Plain Truth, as follows:

Necessary / Truth: / Or / Seasonable / Considerations / for the / Inhabitants of the / City of Philadelphia, / and / Province of Pennsylvania. / In Relation to the Pamphlet call'd / Plain Truth: / And Two other Writers in the / Newspapers. / . . . . . / Philadelphia: / Printed [by W. Bradford] in the Year MDCCXLVIII. 8vo. pp. 16. P.,P.H.S.   65

∗ Mr. Sabin refers the authorship to Franklin, which is of course absurd. Mr. Hildeburn proves it to be by Samuel Smith, the historian of New Jersey. See *Issues of the Pennsylvania Press*, 1099.

A / Treatise / Shewing / The Need we have to rely upon / God as sole Protector of this Province; / . . . . . / Together with / Something in Answer to a late Performance, intituled, Plain Truth; discovering the falsity therein con- / tained, with Remarks on the Author's Irreligion. / . . . . . / By one that wisheth well to all Mankind. / Philadelphia: / Printed by Godhard Armbrister, / in Arch-Street. 1748.

8vo. pp. (26).   P.   66

1747. *Plain Truth.*

Die / Lautere Wahrheit, / Oder / Ernstliche Betrachtung / des gegenwärtigen Zustandes / Der / Stadt Philadelphia, / und der / Provintz Pensylvanien. / Von einem Handwercksmann in Philadelphia. / Aus dem Englischen übersetzt durch J. Crell. / Gedruckt, und zu finden bey Gotthard Armbruester. [1747.]

8vo. pp. 20.   P. H. S.   67

1747. Poor Richard's Almanac for 1748.

Note, This Almanack us'd to contain but 24 Pages, and | now has 36; yet the Price is very little advanc'd. | Poor Richard improved: | Being an | Almanack | and | Ephemeris | of the | Motions of the Sun and Moon; | the true | Places and Aspects of the Planets; | the | Rising and Setting of the Sun; | and the | Rising, Setting and Southing of the Moon, | for the | Bissextile Year, 1748. | Containing also, | The Lunations, Conjunctions, Eclipses, Judg- | ment of the Weather, Rising and Setting of the | Planets, Length of Days and Nights, Fairs, Courts, | Roads, &c. Together with useful Tables, chro- | nological Observations, and entertaining Remarks. | Fitted to the Latitude of Forty, Degrees, and a Meridian of near | five Hours West from London; but may, without sensible Error, | serve all the Northern Colonies. | By Richard Saunders, Philom. | Philadelphia: | Printed and Sold by B. Franklin. [1747.]

8vo. pp. (36).   L., C., P. H. S. 68

1748. Advice to Young Tradesmen. Philadelphia: [1800?]

Advice to a Young Tradesman. Philadelphia. Printed by D. Humphreys. [n. d.]

Folio. Broadside.   B. M. 69

_ Title from British Museum Catalogue.

1748. Advice to Young Tradesmen. London: 1805.

Advice | to a | Young Tradesman: | An Essay | By Dr. Benjamin Franklin | [London: W. Turner, 1805.]

Min. pp. 4.   P. H. S. 70

1748. Advice to Young Tradesmen. Dublin: [1820?]

Advice to young persons intended for Trade. By Benjamin Franklin. To which is added, Golden Rules for Young Shopkeepers [By Sir R. Phillips. Dublin.]

16mo.   B. M. 71

_ Title from British Museum Catalogue.

1748. Advice to Young Tradesmen. London: 1824.

Practical Wisdom: or the manual of life. The counsels of eminent men to their children. Comprising those of

Sir Walter Raleigh, Lord Burleigh . . . . . and Benjamin Franklin, with the lives of the Authors. London, 1824.

12mo.   B. M.   72

₊*₊ Title from British Museum Catalogue.

1748. Poor Richard's Almanac for 1749.

. . . . . Poor Richard improved: / Being an / Almanack / . . . . . / For the / Year of our Lord 1749. / . . . . . / By Richard Saunders, Philom. / Philadelphia: / Printed and Sold by B. Franklin, and D. Hall. [1748.]

Sm. 8vo. pp. (36).   L., P. H. S.   73

1749. Poor Richard's Almanac for 1750.

Poor Richard improved: / Being an / Almanack / . . . . . / For the / Year of our Lord 1750. / . . . . . By Richard Saunders, Philom. / . . . . . / Philadelphia: / Printed and Sold by B. Franklin, and D. Hall.   1749.]

Sm. 8vo. pp. (36).   C., P. H. S.   74

1749. Education of Youth.

Proposals / Relating to the / Education / of / Youth / in / Pensilvania. / Philadelphia: / Printed in the Year, M.DCC.XLIX.

8vo. pp. 32.   B. A., P. H. S.   75

₊*₊ See *Autobiography*, 275; *Sparks' edition*, I, 569; II, 133.

1750. Poor Richard's Almanac for 1751.

Poor Richard improved: / Being an / Almanack / . . . . . / For the / Year of our Lord 1751. / . . . . . / By Richard Saunders, Philom. / . . . . . / Philadelphia: / Printed and Sold by B. Franklin, and D. Hall. [1750.]

Sm. 8vo. pp. (36).   L., C., P. H. S.   76

1751. Electrical Experiments. London: 1751.

Experiments / and / Observations / on / Electricity, / made at / Philadelphia in America, / By / Mr. Benjamin Franklin, / and / Communicated in several Letters to P. Collinson, / of London, F. R. S. / London: / Printed and sold by E. Cave, at St. John's Gate. 1751. / (Price 2s. 6d.)

4to. pp. (4), 86, (2), plate.   B., P. H. S., C.   77

_**_* "I . . . wrote him [Collinson] several letters containing accounts of our experiments. He got them read in the Royal Society, where they were not at first thought worth so much notice as to be printed in their Transactions. . . . The papers, however, being shown to Dr. Fothergill, he thought them of too much value to be stifled, and advis'd the printing of them. Mr. Collinson then gave them to *Cavé* for publication in his Gentleman's Magazine; but he chose to print them separately in a pamphlet, and Dr. Fothergill wrote the preface. Cave, it seems, judged rightly for his profit, for by additions that arrived afterward, they swell'd to a quarto volume, which has had five editions." *Autobiography*, 331.

*_** These experiments and discoveries, which have given Franklin such fame, were the work of four men: Benjamin Franklin, Philip Syng, Thomas Hopkinson and Ebenezer Kinnersley; but owing to Franklin writing of them to England, they were published in his name, and have redounded to his credit solely. In Franklin's own copy of the work he has, however, noted the initials of the discoverer against each experiment, as follows:

Page 12,	line	1.	"T. Hopkinson."
" 13,	"	14.	"Philip Syng."
" 16,	"	7.	"P. S."
" 17,	"	24.	"P. S."
" 19,	"	1.	"E. Kinnersly."
" 19,	"	6.	"Do."
" 19,	"	9.	"Do."
" 27,	"	6.	"E. Kinnersly."
" 33,	"	15.	"E. Kinnersly."
" 33,	"	17.	"Do."
" 33,	"	20.	"Do."
" 49,	"	6.	"E. K. and B. F."

*_** In Duane's editions (from which Sparks reprints) are other notes as to the experimenters.

*_** For the supplementary experiments, see 1753 and 1754.

1751. Electrical Experiments. London: 1754.

New Experiments / and / Observations / on / Electricity. / Made at / Philadelphia in America, / By / Benjamin Franklin, Esq; / and / Communicated in Several Letters / To Peter Collinson, Esq; of London, F. R. S. / Part I. / The Second Edition / London: / Printed and Sold by D. Henry and R. Cave, at / St. John's Gate. 1754.

4to. pp. (2), 86, plate.   P. H. S., C.   78

1751. Electrical Experiments. London: 1760.

New Experiments / [*78*] / Part I. / The Third Edition. / London: / [*78*] / St. John's Gate. 1760. / (Price 2s. 6d.)

4to. pp. (2), ii, (2), 86, plate.   P. H. S., C. 79

1751. Electrical Experiments. Paris: 1752.

Expériences / et / Observations / sur / l'Électricité / faites / A Philadelphie en Amérique; / Par / M. Benjamin Franklin; / & communiquées dans plusieurs Lettres / à M. P. Collinson . . . / . . . . . / Traduites de l'Anglois. / A Paris, Chez Durand, ruë St. Jacques, au Griffon / M.D.CC.LII. . . .

16mo. pp. 24, lxx, (9), 222, (29), plate.   B. 80

1751. Electrical Experiments. Paris: 1756.

Experiences / et / Observations / sur / l'Électricité / faites / A Philadelphie en Amérique / Par / M. Benjamin Franklin; / & communiquées dans plusieurs Lettres à M. P. / Collinson, . . . / Traduites de l'Anglois. / Seconde Édition. / Revûë, corrigée & augmentée d'un supplement considé- / rable du même Auteur, avec des Notes & des / Expériences nouvelles. / Par M. D'Alibard. / Tome Seconde. / A Paris, / Chez Durand, ruë du Foin, au Griffon. / M.DCC.- LVI. / . . .

2 vols. 12mo. pp. (2), 349, (1), plate.   Y. C. 81

*** I have been able to find only volume II of this edition. This edition contains the "Supplementary Experiments."

*** "A very incorrect French translation fell into the hands of the celebrated Buffon. . . . He prevailed on his friend, M. Dalibard, to give his countrymen a more correct translation." *Stuber.*

1751. Electrical Experiments. Leipsic: 1758.

Des / Herrn Benjamin Franklin / Esq. / Briefe / von der / Elektricitot. / Aus dem Englandischen ubersetzet, / nebst Anmerkungen / von / J. C. Wilcke. / Leipzig, 1758. / verlegts Gottfried Kiesewetter, / Buchh. in Stockholm.

12mo. pp. (26), 354, plate.   C. 82

1751. Plan of School.

Idea of the English School, / Sketch'd out for the Consideration of the Tru- / stees of the Philadelphia Academy. / [Philadelphia: B. Franklin, and D. Hall.   1751.]

8vo. pp. 8.   B., P. H. S. 83

₊ Usually appended to:

A / Sermon / on / Education. / Wherein / Some Account is given of the / Academy, / Established in the / City of Philadelphia. / Preach'd at the Opening thereof, on the Seventh / Day of January, 1750–1. / By the Reverend Mr. Richard Peters. / Philadelphia: / Printed and Sold by B. Franklin, and D. Hall, / at the Post-Office. MDCCLI. 8vo. pp. vii, (1), 48, 8.   B., P. H. S. 84

1751. Letter on the Indians.   New York: 1751.

The / Importance / of / Gaining and Preserving / the / Friendship / of the / Indians / to the / British Interest, / Considered. / New York: / Printed and Sold by James Parker, at the New / Printing-Office, in Beaver-Street, 1751.

8vo. pp. 31.   P. 85

₊ The appendix of four pages is a letter, which Mr. Bigelow prints as Franklin's.   The pamphlet is by Archibald Kennedy.

1751. Letter on the Indians.   London: 1751.

The Importance. [+85+] London: E. Cave. M.DCC.-LII.

8vo. pp. 31.   86

1751. Increase of Mankind.   Boston: 1755.

Observations / on the late and present / Conduct of the French, / With / Regard to their Encroachments / upon the British Colonies / in North America. / Together / With remarks on the Importance / of these Colonies to Great-Britain. / To which is added, wrote by another Hand: / Observations concerning the Increase / of Mankind, Peopling of Countries, &c. / Boston: / Printed and Sold by S. Kneeland in Queen- / Street.   1755.

4to. pp. (8), iv, 47, 15.   M. 87

₊ The "Observations concerning the Increase of Mankind" was written by Franklin in 1751, and is sometimes found separate from the rest of the work, as it is separately paged and has a half title, but I do not think it was so issued.   The main work is by William Clarke.

1751. Increase of Mankind.   London: 1755.

Observations / [+87+] / By William Clarke, M. D. / of

Boston in New-England. / To which is added, wrote by another Hand, / Observations concerning the Increase of Man- / kind, peopling of Countries, &c. / Boston printed: / London: Reprinted for John Clarke, / under the Royal Exchange, Cornhill.   1755.

8vo.   pp. viii, 54.   s. 88

1751. Poor Richard's Almanac for 1752.

Poor Richard improved: / Being an / Almanack / . . . . . / For the / Year of our Lord 1752: / . . . . . / By Richard Saunders, Philom. / Philadelphia: / Printed and Sold by B. Franklin, and D. Hall. [1751.]

Sm. 8vo.   pp. (36).   L., C., P. H. S.   89

1752. Poor Richard's Almanac for 1753.

Poor Richard improved, / Being an / Almanack / . . . . . / For the / Year of our Lord 1753: / . . . . . / By Richard Saunders, Philom. / Philadelphia: / Printed and Sold by B. Franklin, and D. Hall. [1752.]

Sm. 8vo.   pp. (36).   L., C., P. H. S.   90

1753. Letter to Whitefield.

A Letter from Benjamin Franklin to a Gentleman in New Jersey, dated Philadelphia, June 6th, 1753. Nottingham. [n. d.]

Broadside.   91

⁎⁎⁎ Title from the John Allan auction catalogue, lot 1151. See *Sparks*, VII, 74.

1753. Poor Richard's Almanac for 1754.

Poor Richard improved: / Being an / Almanack / . . . . . / For the / Year of our Lord 1754: / . . . . . / By Richard Saunders, Philom. / Philadelphia: / Printed and Sold by B. Franklin, and D. Hall. [1753.]

Sm. 8vo.   pp. (36).   L., C., P. H. S. 92

1753. Supplementary Experiments.   London: 1753.

Supplemental / Experiments and Observations / on / Electricity, / Part II. / made at / Philadelphia in America, / By / Benjamin Franklin, Esq, / and / Communicated in several letters to Peter Collinson, Esq, / of London, F. R. S.

/ London: / Printed and sold by E. Cave, at St. John's Gate. 1753. / (Price 6d.)

4to. pp. (2), 89–107, (1).   B., P. H. S. 93

*** See Nos. 77 and 96.

1753. Supplementary Experiments. London: 1754.

New Experiments / and / Observations / on Electricity. / Made at / Philadelphia in America, / By / Benjamin Franklin, Esq; / and / Communicated in several Letters to Peter Collinson, Esq; / of London, F. R. S. / Part II. / The Second Edition. / London: / Printed and Sold by D. Henry, and R. Cave, at St. / John's-Gate. 1754. / (Price 6d.)

4to. pp. (2), 89–109, (1).   B., C. 94

1753. Supplementary Experiments. London: 1762.

New Experiments / [*94*] / Part II. / The Third Edition / London: / Printed by R. Cave, at St. John's-Gate. MDCCLXII. / (Price 6d.)

4to. pp. (2), 89–109, (1).   C. 95

1754. New Experiments. London: 1754.

New Experiments / and / Observations / on / Electricity. / made at / Philadelphia in America. / By Benjamin Franklin, Esq; / Communicated to P. Collinson, Esq; of London, F. R. S. / And read at the Royal Society June 27, and July 4, 1754. / To which are added / A Paper on the same Subject by J. Canton, M. A. F. R. S. and read at / the Royal Society Dec. 6, 1753; and another in defense of Mr. Franklin / against the Abbe Nollet, by Mr. D. Colden, of New York. / Part III. / London: / Printed and sold by D. Henry and R. Cave, at St. / John's-Gate. 1754. (Price 1s.)

4to. pp. (4), 111–154.   C. 96

1754. New Experiments. London: 1765.

New Experiments / [*96*] / Part III / The Fourth Edition / London: / Printed and sold by R. Cave, at St. John's-Gate. / 1765. (Price 1s.)

4to. pp. (2), 111–154.   97

1754. Poor Richard's Almanac for 1755.

Poor Richard improved: / Being an / Almanack / . . . . .
/ For the / Year of our Lord 1755: / .. . . . . / By Richard Saunders, Philom. / Philadelphia: / Printed and Sold
by B. Franklin, and D. Hall. [1754.]

Sm. 8vo.   pp. (36).   L., C., P. H. S.   98

1754. Pennsylvania Hospital.   Philadelphia: 1754.

Some / Account / of the / Pennsylvania Hospital; / From
its first Rise, to the Beginning / of the Fifth Month, called
May, 1754. / Philadelphia: / Printed by B. Franklin, and
D. Hall.   MDCCLIV.

8vo.   pp. 40.   P. H. S.   99

_**_* Not printed in any edition of Franklin, though undoubtedly by
him.   See Wood's *Address on the Centennial of the Pennsylvania
Hospital. Philadelphia: 1851*, 19.   In Sabin's *Dictionary of Books
relating to America*, a "Continuation" to the above, published in 1761,
is also referred to Franklin, but it must be erroneously, for he was at
that time in Europe.

1754. Pennsylvania Hospital.   Philadelphia: 1817.

Some / Account / of the / Pennsylvania Hospital; / from
its first Rise / to the / Beginning / of the / Fifth Month,
called May, 1754 / Philadelphia: / Printed at the Office of
the / United States' Gazette. / 1817.

8vo.   pp. 145.   C., P. H. S.   100

_**_* Pages 1–69 are a reprint of the above pamphlet, the remainder
being the "Continuation."

1755. Advertisement.

Advertisement. / Lancaster, April 26, 1755. / . . . . .
/ B. Franklin. / [Lancaster: Printed by W. Dunlap.
1755.]

Broadside.   101

_**_* An advertisement for 150 wagons to accompany Braddock's
Army, issued by Franklin at the General's request.   See *Autobiography*, 303, and *Pennsylvania Archives*, II, 295, 309 and 310.

1755. Poor Richard's Almanac for 1756.

Poor Richard improved: / Being an / Almanack / . . . . .
/ For the / Year of our Lord 1756: / . . . . . / By Richard

Saunders, Philom. | Philadelphia: | Printed and sold by B. Franklin, and D. Hall. [1755.]

Sm. 8vo. pp. (36).   L., C., P. H. S.   102

1755 or 56. Proposal to clean streets.

103

~*~*~ An unknown piece. "I then wrote and printed a paper setting forth the advantages to the neighborhood." *Autobiography*, 286.

1756. Poor Richard's Almanac for 1757.

Poor Richard improved: | Being an | Almanack | . . . . . | For the | Year of our Lord 1757: | . . . . . | By Richard Saunders, Philom. | Philadelphia: | Printed and sold by B. Franklin, and D. Hall. [1756.]

Sm. 8vo. pp. (36).   P. H. S.   104

1757. Preface to Hopkin's Memoirs.

An | Abridgement | of | Mr. Hopkin's | Historical Memoirs, | Relating to the | Housatunnuk, or Stockbridge Indians: | . . . . . | Philadelphia: | Printed and Sold By B. Franklin, and D. Hall. | M,DCC,LVII.

8vo. pp. 40.   P. H. S.   105

~*~*~ Contains an Introduction by Franklin.

1757. Poor Richard's Almanac for 1758.

Poor Richard Improved: | Being an | Almanack | . . . . . | For the | Year of our Lord 1758: | . . . . . | By Richard Saunders, Philom. | Philadelphia: | Printed and Sold by B. Franklin, and D. Hall. [1757.]

Sm. 8vo. pp. (36).   L., C., P. H. S.   106

~*~*~ The last of the series edited by Franklin. It contains the many proverbs of the former issues collected into one piece, which has become famous under the titles of "The Speech of Father Abraham;" "The Way to Wealth;" "La science du bonhomme Richard;" etc. See the following list of editions and the *Autobiography*, 236.

1757. Way to Wealth. Boston: [1760.]

Father | Abraham's | Speech | To a great Number of People, | at a Vendue of Merchant- | Goods; | Introduced to The Publick | By Poor Richard, | (A famous Pennsylvanian Conjuror and | Almanack-Maker) | In Answer to the following Questions. | Pray, Father Abraham, what | think you of the Times? Won't | these heavy Taxes quite ruin the |

Country? How shall we be ever / able to pay them? What would / you advise us to? / Printed and Sold by Benjamin Mecom, at the New / Printing-Office, near the Town-House, in Boston. /

12mo. pp. 16, plate.   L., B. 107

*** The first separate edition of this wonderfully popular piece, which has been oftener printed and translated, I believe, than any other work from an American pen. Enjoying such a great popularity, it has been simply impossible to find and note all the editions, and the present titles are only offered as a basis for some future list. Many of them are without date, place, or printer, so as to render their classification and finding of great difficulty. This is, I hope, so far as the latter, overcome by the special index at the end of this list of editions. No attention has been paid to works containing it, unless the title or Franklin's name was on the title.

1757. Way to Wealth.   New Haven: [1767?]

Father Abraham's / Speech / to a / great number of People, / at a Vendue of Merchant / Goods; / Introduced to The Publick / By Poor Richard, / (a famous Conjuror and Almanack-Maker) / In Answer to the following Questions, / Pray, Father Abraham, what / think you of the Times? / Won't these heavy Taxes quite / ruin the Country? How shall we be / ever able to pay them? What would you advise us to do? / Printed and sold by T. & S. Green, in New Haven. [1767?]

8vo. pp. 16.   B. 108

1757. Way to Wealth.   London: 1774.

The / Way to Wealth, / as clearly shewn in the / Preface / of / An Old Pennsylvania Almanack, / Intituled, / Poor Richard Improved. / London: / Printed and Sold by M. Lewis, No. 1.   Paternoster- / row 1774. / (Price 1d. or 10d. per doz.)

12mo. pp. 12.   P. L. 109

1757. Way to Wealth.   [London: 1774.]

The / Way to Wealth; / as clearly shewn in the / Preface / of an old / Pennsylvania Almanack, / intitled / Poor Richard Improved.

8vo. pp. 16.   P. L. 110

 ₓ*ₓ Either this or the succeeding edition was priced by Ashton Nield (*Bibliotheca Americana*, No. 118) at 5 guineas. Of it he said: "I trace no other copy of this edition. It was not in the Franklyn [sic] collection sold for £5,000 to the American Government. A former owner has written upon the title 1774 as the date."

1757. Way to Wealth. [*London: 1774?*]
 The / Way to Wealth, / as clearly shewn in the / Preface / of / An old Pennsylvania Almanack, / intitled, / Poor Richard Improved.
8vo. pp. 16.   P. L. III

1757. Way to Wealth. [*London: 1775?*]
 The Way to Wealth, / As clearly shewn in the / Preface of an Old Pennsylvania Almanack, / intitled, Poor Richard Improved.
8vo. pp. 8.   C. 112

 ₓ*ₓ The place and date are given according to the Stevens' list.

1757. Way to Wealth. [*Paris:*] *1777.*
 La Science / du Bonhomme Richard, / ou / Moyen Facile / de payer les Impôts. / Traduit de l'Anglois, / [Vignette] / A Philadelphie. / Et se trouve / A Paris, chez Ruault, Libraire / rue de la Harpe. / 1777.
12mo. pp. 151, (1), 4, covers. C., P. H. S. 113

 ₓ*ₓ Contains also the Examination relative to the Stamp Act, and the Constitution of Pennsylvania. Translated by Francis A. Quétant.

1757. Way to Wealth. 2d Edition. Paris: 1778.
 La Science / du bonhomme Richard, / ou / Moyen facile / de payer les Impôts, / traduit de l'Anglois. / Seconde édition, / exactement semblable à la premiere. / A Philadelphie. / Et se trouve / A Paris, chez Ruault, Libraire, / rue de la Harpe, 1778.
12mo. pp. 151, (5).   P. H. S. 114

1757. Way to Wealth. 3d Edition. Paris: 1778.
 La science / du bonhomme Richard, / moyen facile / de payer les impôts. / Traduite de l'Anglois. / Troisieme édition, / exactement semblable à la premiere. / A Philadelphie. / Se vend à Paris, / chez Ruault, Libraire, rue de la Harpe. / M.DCC.LXXVIII.
12mo. pp. 151, (5).   P. H. S. 115

1757. Way to Wealth. 4th Edition. [Paris:] 1778.

La science / du bonhomme Richard, / moyen facile / de payer les impôts. / Traduite de l'Anglois. / Quarantieme edition. / A Philadelphie. / Se vend à Paris, / chez Jean François Bastien, / Libraire, rue du Petit-Lion. F. S.-G. / M.DCC.LXXVIII.

12mo. pp. 151.   P. H. S.   116

1757. Way to Wealth. Paris: 1778.

La science / du bonhomme Richard, / Par M. Franklin: / Suivie / des Commandemens / de l'Honnête-Homme, / Par M. Feutry / Prix quatre sous. / Se vend à Paris, / chez Ruault, Libraire, rue de la Harpe / 1778.

Min. pp. 48, covers.   B.   117

1757. Way to Wealth. Paris: 1779.

La Science / du Bonhomme Richard, / ou / le moyen facile / de payer les Impots dans les possession / de l'Amérique Angloise; / contenant en outre, un Discours de S. E. Mr. Jean / Hancock, président du Congrès de Philadelphie. / L'Interrogatoire que Mr. Francklin subit au mois / de Février de 1766 devant le Parlement d'An- / gleterre. La Constitution de la Republique de / Pensylvania, / telle qu'elle a été établie par la / Commission général de Philadelphie au mois de / Juillet 1776; & l'Interrogatoire de Mr. Penn, / à la Barre du Parlement au mois de Novembre de la / même année. / Ouvrages traduits de l'anglais qui / mettant dans tout leur jour les / principes & la suite / des Contestations qui divisent les Insurgents avec / la mere patrie. / A Philadelphie, / et se trouve à Lausanne, / chez François Grasset & Comp. / M.D.C.C.LXXIX.

Min. pp. 166, covers.   P. H. S.   118

1757. Way to Wealth. London: [1779].

The Way to Wealth: / As clearly shewn in the Preface of an old Pennsylvanian Almanack, intitled, Poor Richard, Improved, / Written by Dr. Benjamin Franklin.—Extracted from the Doctor's Political Works. [London: Printed for J. Johnson, 1779.]

Folio. Broadside, (11 x 14½).   P. L.   119

₊*₊ "This piece has been printed on a single sheet of paper, of a small size fit for framing, and may be had of the publisher of this work, price two-pence." Note to Franklin's Works, 1779.

1757. Way to Wealth. London: [1780?]

The Way to Wealth, as clearly shewn in the Preface of an old Pennsylvanian Almanack, intitled, Poor Richard Improved. London [1780?]

Folio. Broadside.

₊*₊ Title from British Museum Catalogue.   119*

1757. Way to Wealth. Dublin: 1782.

The / Way to Wealth / as clearly shewn in the / Preface / of an Old / Pennsylvania Almanack, / intitled, / Poor Richard Improved. / Dublin: / Printed by Wogan, Bean, and Pike / No. 23 Old Bridge / MDCCLXXXII.

Min. pp. 16.   P. H. S.   120

1757. Way to Wealth. Paisley: 1784.

The Way to Wealth as shown in the Preface of an Old Pennsylvanian Almanack. Paisley, 1784.

12mo. pp. 16.   121

₊*₊ Title from Puttick & Simpson's Catalogue of Americana (Stevens) sold May 21, 1863, lot 304.

1757. Way to Wealth. Paris: 1785.

Calandrier de Philadelphie, ou le moraliste Américain, pour tous les jours de l'année. Édition augmentée de l'auis de ceux qui veulent passer en Amérique. A Philadelphie, pour la présente année. [Paris, 1785.]

12mo. pp. 15, xli, 118.   122

₊*₊ Ce Calendrier est la traduction du Pauvre Richard, . . . et augmenté de l'avis pour ceux vondraient émigres. Title and note from Leclerc's *Bibliotheca Americana*. 1878.

1757. Way to Wealth. Canterbury: 1785.

The Way to Wealth, as clearly shewn in the Preface of an old Pennsylvania Almanack intitled Poor Richard improved. Canterbury, printed by Simmons and Kirkby,

Broadside.   123

_**_* Title from Puttick & Simpson's sale catalogue, Dec. 13, 1870.

1757. Way to Wealth. Edinburgh: 1785.

A / Collection / of / Gaelic Proverbs / and / Familiar Phrases; / Accompanied with / An English Translation, / Intended to facilitate the Study of the Language; Illustrated with Notes. / To which is added, / The Way to Wealth, / By Dr. Franklin, / Translated into Gaelic, / by Donald Macintosh. / . . . . . / Edinburgh: / Printed for the Author, and sold by Messrs. Donaldson, Creech, Elliot, and Sibbald, ... / M.DCCLXXXV.

12mo. pp. x, 83.   c. 124

*_** "The translation of Franklin's Way to Wealth was done by R[obert] Macfarland, by desire of the Earl of Buchan." Preface to *A Collection of Gaelic Proverbs. Edited by A. Nicholson.*

_**_* See No. 166.

1757. Way to Wealth. Paris: 1786.

La / Science / du / Bonhomme / Richard, / Moyen facile de payer les Impôts; Avec l'Interrogatoire de M. Franklin & / plusiere Pièces interessantes qui n'étoient / point dans les éditions précédentes. / Ouvrages traduit de l'Anglois. / A Philadelphie, / Et se trouve à Paris, / Chez Royez, Libraire, quai des Augustins / 1786.

Min. pp. 15.   P. L. 125

_**_* Includes the Remarks on the Savages.

1757. Way to Wealth. London: 1788.

Lord Chesterfield's / Advice to his Son / . . . . . . / to which are added, / . . . . . / Dr. Franklin's Way to Wealth. / London: / Printed for W. Richardson, at the Royal / Exchange / MDCCLXXXVIII.

12mo. pp. vii, (4), 201, (3).   P. H. S. 126

1757. Way to Wealth. Lansingburgh: 1789.

The Way to Wealth, / as clearly shown in the preface of / An old Pennsylvania Almanack, / entitled, / Poor Richard Improved. / Written by / Dr. Benjamin Franklin. / London printed. / Lansingburgh; Reprinted by / Babcock & Hickok. / M,DCC,LXXXIX.

12mo. pp. 15.   B. 127

_**_* Apparently reprinted from a London edition of 1784.

1757. Way to Wealth. Newburyport: [*179–.*]

The / Way to Wealth, / clearly shown in a variety of / Useful and Interesting / Maxims; / or / Poor Richard Improved, / By Dr. Benjamin Franklin. / Extracted from the / Doctor's Political Works. / Newburyport: Printed and sold by / William Barrett, / Merrimac-Street.

12mo. pp. 12.   A. A. S.   128

1757. Way to Wealth. Worcester: 1790.

The / Way to Wealth; / as clearly shewn in the preface of an old / publication entitled, / "Poor Richard Improved." / By Benjamin Franklin, L. L. D. / Printed at Worcester, Massachusetts / By Isaiah Thomas, / Sold at his Bookstore in Worcester, and by him / and Company in Boston. / MDCCXC.

12mo. pp.   A. A. S.   129

1757. Way to Wealth. Birmingham: 1791.

The / Way to Wealth, / as clearly shewn in the / Preface / of an old / Pennsylvanian Almanack, / intitled, / Poor Richard Improved. / Written by / Dr. Benjamin Franklin. / Birmingham, / Printed by J. Thompson. / MDCCXCI.

12mo. pp. 23.   L. I. H. S.   130

1757. Way to Wealth. London: 1793.

Lord Chesterfield's / [_*126_*] / London: / Printed for W. Richardson, at the Royal-Exchange. / 1793.

12mo. pp. vii, (4), 203, (1).   P. H. S.   131

1757. Way to Wealth. Leeds: 1793.

Bad as the Times are, / They that will be Counselled / may / Yet be helped! / Leeds / Printed by Thomas Gill, (1793).

8vo. pp. 15.   P. H. S.   132

_**_* "Poor Richard" and the "Art of Making Money."

1757. Way to Wealth. Paris: 1794.

La Science / du / Bonhomme Richard / de / Benjamin Franklin, / Précédée d'un abrégé de la Vie de / Franklin, et suivie de son Inter- / rogatoire devant la Chambre des /

Communes. / . . . / . . . / A Paris, / A l'Imprimerie des Sciences et Arts, / rue Thérèse, près la rue Helvétius. / L'an II de la Republique françoise.

12mo.   pp. (2), lxiv, 119, cover.   133

⁎ The life, according to *Quérard*, is by J. B. Say.

1757. Way to Wealth. Lausanne: 1795.

Manuel / de / Philosophie Pratique, / Pour servir de suite à la Science / du Bon-homme Richard, /|Par Francklin, [sic] / Suivi de l'art de voir / Fragmens traduits de l'Anglais, . . . / . . . . . / A Lausanne, / Chez Hignou et Compe. / . . . / 1795.

Min.   pp. 130.   134

1757. Way to Wealth. Paris: 1795.

The /. Way to Wealth / or / Poor Richard Improved / By Benj. Franklin. / Paris, / Printed for Ant. Aug. Renouard, / Apolline's street, No. 25. / M.DCC.XCV.

12mo.   pp. (2), 181, (4), portrait.   P. H. S., B.   135

⁎ The prettiest edition yet printed, of which six copies were printed on large paper and eight on vellum.

⁎ The second title, at page 34, is :

La Science / du / Bonhomme Richard, / ou Moyen facile / de payer les impôts. / Par Benj. Franklin. / Paris, / Chez Ant. Aug. Renouard, / rue Appoline, No. 25. / M.DCC.XCV.

⁎ A supplementary 28 pages is contained in some copies, being :

Observations / sur / les Sauvages du Nord / de l'Amerique, / par Franklin.

1757. Way to Wealth. Danbury: 1795.

The / Way to Wealth, / as clearly shown in the Preface of / an old Pennsylvania Almanack, / Entitled / " Poor Richard Improved." / Written by / Dr. Franklin. / Danbury: / Printed and sold by N. Douglas / MDCCXCV.

12mo.   pp. 11.   136

1757. Way to Wealth. Philadelphia: 1796.

The / Immortal Mentor: / or, / Man's Unerring Guide / to a / Healthy, Wealthy, and / Happy Life. / In three Parts. / By / Lewis Cornaro, Dr. Franklin, and / Dr. Scott. / . . . / . . . / . . . / . . . / . . . / Philadelphia: /

Printed for the Rev. Mason L. Weems, / by Francis and
Robert Bailey, / No. 116, High-Street. / 1796.

12mo. pp. vi, 321.   P. L.   137

1757. Way to Wealth. [*Manchester: 1796?*]

Bowle's Moral Pictures, or Poor Richard Illustrated,
being Lessons for Young and Old on Industry, Temperance, Frugality, &c. [Manchester: 1796.]

Folio. Broadside.   137*

₊*₊ Title from A. Neild's *Bibliotheca Geographica*, No. 138.

1757. Way to Wealth. London: 1797.

The Way to Wealth, to which is added Select Thoughts.
London: 1797.

12mo. pp.   138

₊*₊ Title from British Museum Catalogue.

1757. Way to Wealth. Manchester: 1798.

Moral Philosophy, Conduct, &c. / Way to Wealth, by
Dr. Franklin / [etc.] . . . . . / Manchester, / Printed at
the Office of G. Nicholson, No. 9 Spring-Gardens /
. . . . . / Anno 1798.

Min. pp. 28.   F. H. S.   139

1757. Way to Wealth. Riom: 1799.

La Science / du / bonhommé Richard, / Par. Franklin. /
A Riom, / de l'Imprimerie de J. C. Salles, / An 7. /

Min. pp. 44, portrait.   C.   140

1757. Way to Wealth. Salem: [*1800?*]

The / Way to Wealth, / as clearly shewn in the / Preface
of an Old Pennsylvania Almanack, / intitled / Poor Richard Improved, / By Dr. Benjamin Franklin. / Extracted
from the Doctor's Political Works. / Salem, / Printed by
T. C. Cushing. [1800?]

12mo. pp. 16.   C.   141

1757. Way to Wealth. Nottingham: [*1800?*]

The / Way to Wealth, / Written by the late / Dr. Frank-
lin. / Extracted from his Political Works. / . . . . . /
Nottingham: / Printed by C. Sutton, Bridlesmith-Gate /
(Price One Penny.)

12mo. pp. 11.   P. H. S.   142

1757. Way to Wealth. Copenhagen: 1801.

Nytaansgave for Unge og Gamle, eller den Kunst at blive riig og lykkelig.   Oversat af Carl Fr. Primon. Kjobenhavn: 1801.

o.   pp.   142*

₊*₊ Title from *Swift*. He states that it was also printed with the title: Den gamle Richards Kunst at blive riig og lykkelig. En Lommebog for hvert Aarh. Oversat af Carl Fr. Primon. Kjobenhavn. 1801.

1757. Way to Wealth. New York: 1802.

Way to Wealth. By Benjamin Franklin. New York: 1802.

Folio.   Broadside.   143

₊*₊ Title from C. W. Frederickson's Auction Catalogue, lot 2833.

1757. Way to Wealth. Edinburgh: 1801.

The True Root of Scarcity; or, Sure Road to Competence in times of Dearth. Edinburgh: C. Stewart & Co. M,DCCC,I.

12mo.   pp. 23.   143*

1757. Way to Wealth. Philadelphia: 1802.

The / Immortal Mentor: [₊137₊] Philadelphia: / Printed for the Rev. Mason L. Weems. / 1802.

12mo.   pp. (4), 321.   P. L.   144

1757. Way to Wealth. Birmingham: 1805.

Poor Richard's / Maxims; / or, / The Way to Wealth, / By the Celebrated / Doctor Franklin. / Birmingham: / Printed and sold by Surnney and Ferrall, / No. 75, High Street. / 1805. / . . .

12mo.   pp. 18.   c.   145

1757. Way to Wealth. Nottingham: [1805?]

The Way to Wealth. Nottingham. [1805?]

12mo.   146

₊*₊ Title from British Museum Catalogue. Perhaps the same as No. 142.

1757. Way to Wealth. Dedham: 1807.

Father / Abraham's / Speech / To a great Number of People, at a Vendue / of Merchant-Goods; / Introduced to

the Public by / Poor Richard, / a famous Pennsylvania
Conjurer, and / Almanac-Maker, / In Answer to the following Questions: / Pray, Father Abraham, what think
you of / the Times? Won't these heavy Taxes quite / ruin
the Country? How shall we ever / be able to pay Them?
What do you advise us to? / To which are added, / Several
curious Pieces of Writing. / Dedham: / Printed by H.
Mann, / for Wm. Tileston Clapp. Boston / . . . . . /
January 1807.

12mo. pp. 24.   C.   147

1757. Way to Wealth. Philadelphia: 1808.

The Way to Wealth; or, "Poor Richard improved."
Philadelphia: J. Johnson. 1808.

Min. pp.   148

 ⁎ Title from Swift's list.

1757. Way to Wealth. Coventry: 1808.

The / Prompter; / or / Common Sayings, and Subjects, /
which are full of Common Sense, / the best Sense in the
World. / By Noah Webster, / . . . / To which is added, /
The Way to Wealth. / By B. Franklin, LL.D. / Coventry:
/ Printed by and for Pratt, Smith, & Lesson. / Also sold
by Longman, Hurst, Rees, & Orme; / Craddock & Joy,
and R. Scholey, London. / 1808.

12mo. pp. (8), 88, plate.   P. L.   149

1757. Way to Wealth. Philadelphia: 1809.

Franklin's / Way / to Wealth. / Franklin's Weg, / reich zu
werden. / Philadelphia: / Published by Johnson and Warner,
No. 147, / Market-Street. / 1809. / Adams, Printer.

Min. pp. 41, (3), 4 plates.   B.   150

1757. Way to Wealth. Besançon: 1809.

Principes élémentaires de morales, ou traité abrégé des
devoirs de l'Homme. Par Étienne Gabriel Peignot.
Suivie de la Science du Bonhomme Richard et du Sifflet,
oppuscules de B. Franklin. Besançon, imprimerie de Tau-
lin. 1809.

12mo. pp. xii, 104.

 ⁎ Title from *Swift.*

1757. Way to Wealth. Mill-Hill: 1810.

The / Immortal Mentor. / [+137+] / Published by Daniel Fenton / Mill-Hill, near Trenton. / Printed by Brown and Merritt, Philadelphia / 1810.

12mo. pp. (4), 323, (3).   P. L. 152

1757. Way to Wealth. Newcastle: [1810?]

The Way to Wealth.   The Whistle, a story and a new method for ordering expenses . . . To which is added a discourse on frugality by R. Robinson. Newcastle: [1810?]

12mo. pp.   153

⁎⁎ Title from British Museum Catalogue. See No. 163.

1757. Way to Wealth. Wien: 1812.

Sicherer Weg zu einer festen moral. Gesundheit zu gelangen und sich darin lebenslang zu erhalten. Wien: Wimmer. 1812.

4to.   153⁎

⁎⁎ Title from *Swift*.

1757. Way to Wealth. Berlin: 1812.

Sprüchwörter des alten Heinrich und Engels Lebens-weirsheit des alten Witt. Berlin: Mittler. 1812.

8vo. pp.   154

⁎⁎ Title from *Swift*.

1757. Way to Wealth. Blackburn: 1812.

Way to Wealth.   Blackburn: 1812.

12mo. pp.   155

⁎⁎ Title from the British Museum Catalogue.

1757. Way to Wealth. London: [1814?]

Franklin's / Way to Wealth; / or, / "Poor Richard Improved, &c." / A New Edition: / Corrected and enlarged by Bob Short, / And adorned with copper-plates. / London, / Printed by W. Darton, Jun. / 58 Holburn Hill.

16mo. pp. 36.   c. 156

⁎⁎ The Plates are dated 1814.

1757. Way to Wealth. London: 181–?

Franklin's / Way to Wealth; / or, / "Poor Richard Improved, Etc." / A New Edition: / Corrected and enlarged by Bob Short; / and adorned with Engravings. / London: / Darton and Clarke, / Holborn Hill.

Min.   pp. 36, covers.   P. H. S.   157

₊*₊ The title on cover is:

Franklin's / Way to Wealth; / or, / Poor Richard Improved: / To which is added, / Alphabetical Maxims, / worthy / the remembrance and regard / of all. / Selected by Bob Short / London: / Darton and Clark. / . . . / Price Sixpence.

1757. Way to Wealth. London: 1816.

Poor Richard's Almanack / The Way to Wealth, / As clearly shewn in the Preface to an old / Pennsylvanian Almanack / entitled / Poor Richard Improved; / and / The Whistle, a True Story. / By Benjamin Franklin. / London. / Privately Printed. / 1816.

12mo.   pp. 23, (1).   S. D.   158

1757. Way to Wealth. Newipswich: 1816.

The / Way / to / Wealth. / By Dr. Franklin. / To / which are added his / Advice to Young Tradesmen, / and / Sketches of his Life and Char- / acter. / . . . . . / Newipswich: / Published by Simeon Ide. / 1816.

Min.   pp. 72.   B.   159

1757. Way to Wealth. London: 1816–7.

Lord / Chesterfield's Advice / to his Son, / . . . . . To which are added; / Franklin's / Way to Wealth: / . . . . . / London: / Printed for G. Walker. / . . . . . / 1817.

Min.   pp. (8), 114, plate.   P. H. S.   160

₊*₊ The title on cover is:

Lord / Chesterfield's Advice / to His Son / Franklin's Way to Wealth. / London, / Printed for G. Walker & Co. / 1816.

1757. Way to Wealth. Hartford: 1817.

Allen's / New-England / Almanack, / for the year of our Lord / 1817: / . . . . . / Containing, . . . / . . . . . / Poor Richard; / or, / The Way to Wealth—By Dr. Franklin. / By A. Allen, Philo. / Hartford: / Printed and sold, / . . . by / Peter B. Gleason & Co. / . . .

12mo.   pp. (24).   P. L.   161

₊*₊ The leaves are unpaged, so that "The Way to Wealth / By Dr. Franklin" is sometimes found separate. They may be told by the three paragraphs at the end of the piece.

1757. Way to Wealth. Milan: 1817.

La Maniera di farsi ricco, di Beniamino Franklin. Edi-
gione centesimaprima. Milano: Giovanni Silvestri, 1817.

o. pp.   162

_**_* Title from *Swift.*

1757. Way to Wealth. Newcastle: [1817?]

The / Way to Wealth; / or the admonitions of / Poor
Richard. / The / Art of making Money Plenty / in every
man's Pocket. / The Whistle, / A Story. / And a new
Method for Ordering Expenses / very suitable to the times
/ By Dr. Franklin / To which is added / A Discourse on /
Frugality, / by Robert Robinson. / Printed by J. Marshall /
old Flesh Market, New Castle / . . . / . . .

Min. pp. 24.   c. 163

_**_* This edition also is found bound in a volume of chap books en-
titled "A Right Pleasant and Famous Book of Histories Collected by
William Garret. Newcastle MDCCCXVIII." See No. 153.

1757. Way to Wealth. Stockport: 1818.

The Way to Wealth. Stockport: 1818.

Min. pp.   164

_**_* Title from *British Museum Catalogue.*

1757. Way to Wealth. London: 1818.

The Prompter; or, Essays on common things and common subjects . . . . . To which is added, The Way to
Wealth. By Dr. Franklin. London, 1818.

12mo. pp.   165

_**_* Title from *British Museum Catalogue.*

1757. Way to Wealth. Edinburgh: 1819.

Mackintoshes / Collection / of / Gaelic Proverbs, / and
Familiar Phrases; / Englished anew / To which is added,
/ 'The Way to Wealth,' / by / Benjamin Franklin, LL.D.
/ Edinburgh: / Printed by Charles Stewart, / for William
Stewart, No. 61, South-Bridge Street. / 1819.

12mo. pp. (4), 11, (1), 239.   c. 166

_**_* See No. 124.

1757. Way to Wealth. Bermondsey: 1819.

The Way to Wealth. Bermondsey: 1819.

8vo. pp.   167

_**_* Title from *British Museum Catalogue.*

1757. Way to Wealth.   Wien: 1819.

Tugendübungen, guter Rath an Handwerker, Mittel, reich zu Werden.   Wien: Mayer.   1819.

8vo. pp.   168

1757. Way to Wealth.   Paris: [182–?]

La Science / du / Bonhomme Richard, / Par Benjamin Franklin; / l'Histoire du Sifflet, / et / le Testament / de Fortuné Ricard. / Paris, / Adolphe Riom et Compagnie, /

· · · · ·

12mo. pp. 35.   P. L.   169

1757. Way to Wealth.   London: [182–?]

The / Way to Wealth. / By Dr. Franklin. / . . . . . / London / Printed and sold by J. Bailey, / No. 55, East Smithfield / Price Three Pence.

12mo. pp. 12.   P. H. S.   170

The title on cover is: *The | Way to grow Rich | (By Dr. Franklin)* / · · ·

1757. Way to Wealth.   Copenhagen: 1820.

Den gamle Richards Kunst at blive rig og lykkelig; tilligemed tre nyttige Huustavler og en sandfærdig Historie.   Em Lommebog for alle Stænder.   Af Benj. Franklin.   Andet, forbedr. og med Tillæg ferogede, danske Oplag.   Kjobenhavn: 1820.

o. pp.   170*

₊*₊ Title from *Swift.*

1757. Way to Wealth.   New York: 1820.

Franklin's / Way to Wealth; / or, / Poor Richard Improved. / Industry leads to Wealth. / New York: / Published by S. Wood & Sons, / . . . / and Samuel S. Wood & Co. . . / Baltimore, / 1820.

Min, pp. 44.   P. H. S.   171

1757. Way to Wealth.   New York: [182–?]

Franklin's / Way to Wealth / New York: / Published by Samuel Wood & Sons; / And Samuel S. Wood & Co. / Baltimore.

Min. pp. 4–?   S. D.   171*

1757. Way to Wealth. Preston: [*1820?*]

The Servant's Companion, / . . . . . / Also, / Poor Richard's Maxims / By Dr. Franklin. / The whole arranged by / By [sic] S. M. T. Millington / Preston: / Printed and sold by George Bateman / . . . . . [1820?]

12mo. pp. 60.   P. H. S.   172

1757. Way to Wealth. Montroulez: [*1820?*]

Guizieguez ar Pautr-cos Richard. Troet eus al levr gallec B. Franklin. [Morlaix:]. Montroulez, eus a imprimerie Lédan.

Min. pp. 15.   B. M.   173

    ⁎ See 198*.

1757. Way to Wealth. Paris: 1821.

Proverbs et Sentences du Bonhomme Richard. Paris: 1821.

Min. pp. 8.   174

1757. Way to Wealth. Paris: 1822.

La science du bonhomme Richard suivie du Testament de Fortuné Ricard, Par Mathon de la Cour. Paris. Kleffer. 1822.

Min. pp.   175

    ⁎ Title from *Quérard.*

1757. Way to Wealth. Paris: 1822.

La Science du bonhomme Richard, suivie d'extraits de ses œuvres. Précédé de l'éloge funèbre de Franklin par Mirabeau. Paris, A. Bailleul. 1822.

Min. pp.   176

    ⁎ Title from *Quérard.* See No. 201.

1757. Way to Wealth. London: 1823.

The Way to Wealth. London. 1823.

12mo. pp.   177

    ⁎ Title from *Swift.*

1757. Way to Wealth. Geneva: 1823.

La Science / du / Bonhomme Richard / Par Franklin / suivi / du Testament de Fortuné Ricard, / Maître d'Arithmétique / Par Mathon de la Cour / A Genève, / Chez Manget et Cherbuliez, / Imprimeur-Libraires. / 1823.

Min. pp. xij, 95, covers.   178

1757. Way to Wealth.   Paris: 1823.
Η ΕΠΙΣΤΗΜΗ / ΤΟΥ / ΚΑΛΟΥ ΡΙ ΧΑΡΔΟΥ / ΣΥΝΤΕ ΘΕΙΣΑ / ΥΠΟ ΤΟΥ
Β. ΦΡΑΓΚΛΙΝΟΥ / . . . / . . . / . . . / ΕΝ ΠΑΡΙΣΙΟΙΣ, / ΕΚ ΤΗΣ
ΤΥΠΟΓΡΑΦΙΑΣ ΦΙΡΜ / ΝΟΥ ΔΙΔΟΤΟΥ / 1823.

Min. pp. 81, portrait.   H. 179

1757. Way to Wealth.   Paris: 1823.
La Science du Bonhomme Richard.   Paris: Didot. 1823.

12mo. pp.   180

.*.* Title from *Quérard.*

1757. Way to Wealth.   London: [1824.]
The / Way to Wealth; / or, Poor Richard Improved. /
By Benjamin Franklin / Published by / The Christian
Tract Society / No. 17. / London: / Sold by Sherwood,
Neebly and Jones, 20 Paternoster-Row, / . . . . / Price One
Penny / . . . . . / Stower & Smallfield, Printers, Hack-
ney.

12mo. pp. 11.   P. H. S. 181

1757. Way to Wealth.   Paris: 1824.
La Science du Bonhomme Richard.   Paris: Sanson.
1824.

Min. pp.   182

.*.* Title from *Swift.*

1757. Way to Wealth.   Paris: 1824.
La science du bonhomme Richard, suivie de la Véritable
poule noire.   Paris, Sanson.   1825.

Min. pp.   183

.*.* Title from *Quérard.*

1757. Way to Wealth.   Paris: 1825.
La science du bonhomme Richard.   Paris.   A. A.
Renouard.

Min. pp.   184

.*.* Nous [A. A. Renouard] publions *La Science du Bonhomme
Richard* à part précédé d'un calendrier pour l'Année, 1825; le prix est
de 25 cent. et de 20 fr. les cent exemplaires." Preface, *Melanges,* 1824.

1757. Way to Wealth.   Paris: 1825.
Conseils pour faire fortune, ou La Science du bonhomme
Richard.   Paris.   A. A. Renouard.   1825.

Min. pp. 36.   185

.*.* Title from *Quérard.*

1757. Way to Wealth. London: 1825.
The Way to Wealth. London: 1825.

Min. pp.   186

₊*₊ Title from Ms. list of Henry Stevens & Son.

1757. Way to Wealth. Paris: 1826.
La Science du Bonhomme Richard. Paris: A. A. Renouard. 1826.

Min. pp.   187

₊*₊ Title from *Swift.*

1757. Way to Wealth. Windsor: 1826.
The / Way / to / Wealth. / By Dr. Franklin, / to which is added / his / Advice to Young Tradesmen / and / Sketches of his Life and Character. / Windsor, Vt. / Published by Simeon Ide. / 1826.

Min. pp. 80.   c. 188

1757. Way to Weatth. Paris: 1827.
La Science / du Bonhomme / Richard / Par / Benjamin Franklin / . . . / . . . / Paris / Imprimé par C. L. F. Panckoucke / Chevalier de la Légion d'Honneur / M DCCC XXVII.

Large folio. pp. (4), xvj, 16, covers.   c. 189

₊*₊ A white elephant.

1757. Way to Wealth. Dijon: 1827.
La Science du Bonhomme Richard, et Conseils pour faire fortune, avec une notice sur Franklin, et l'ordonnance de Louis XVIII, sur la caisse d'épargnes et de prévoyance. Dijon: Lagier. 1827.

Min. pp.   190

₊*₊ Title from *Swift.*

1757. Way to Wealth. The Hague: 1828.
De / Weg tot Geluk / naar / Benjamin Franklin. / (Prij's vii § Cents.) / 's Gravenhage / Ter Drukkerij van im de Lyon / lange Porrten. No. 438. / 1828.

12mo. pp. 16, covers.   B. 191

1757. Way to Wealth. Paris: 1828.
La sciencia da bon homen Riccardo, on meios de fazer fortuna. Paris: A. A. Renouard. 1828.

Min. pp. 32.   192

₊*₊ Title from *Quérard.*

1757. Way to Wealth.   Paris: 1828.
La Science du bonhomme Richard, suivie de la Véritable poule Noire.   Paris.   Sanson.   1828.

Min. pp.   193

_**_* Title from *Swift*.

1757. Way to Wealth.   Nantes: 1829.
Moyens d'avoir toujours de l'Argent dans sa poche. Nantes: imprimerie de Mellinet-Malassis.   1829.

12mo. pp. 194.   194

1757. Way to Wealth.   London: [183–?]
The Way to Wealth / As plainly shewn in the Preface to an Old Pensylvania Almanack, entitled "Poor Richard Improved" written by Dr. Benjamin Franklin.—Extracted from the Doctor's Political Works. / G. Cooke, . . . Dunstan's Hill, Tower Street, London; . . .

Folio. Broadside.   P. L.   195

1757. Way to Wealth.   Paris: [183–?]
La Science / du Bonhomme / Richard / et Autres Œuvres Morales de / Benjamin Franklin, / Suivie du Testament / de Fortuné Ricard / 4e Édition / A Paris / Chez Phillippart, Libraire / 2 Boulevart Montmartre / . . . . .

Min. pp. 63, covers.   P. H. S. 196

_**_* The title on cover is:
Bibliothèque / Pour Tout le monde / Directeur: Ad. Rion / Franklin / Œuvres Choisis. / Bonhomme Richard, etc. / Paris, / Phillippart Libraire.

1757. Way to Wealth.   [Paris: 183–?]
Petit Cours de Morale. / . . . . / La Science / du Bonhomme Richard. / Par Franklin. / . . . . . . / Chez Montizon, imprimeur-lithographe, place Dauphine, ...

Min. pp. [33–] 48.   B.   197

_**_* Printed in lithographic script.

1757. Way to Wealth.   Limoges: [183–?]
Benjamin Franklin / La Science / du Bonhomme Richard / et Conseils pour Faire Fortune / avec / Une Notice

sur l'Auteur et Introduction et Notes / a cette éditeur. /
Limoges / Eugène Ardant et Cie, Éditeurs.

12mo. pp. 71.   B. 198

₊*₊ Contains, besides what is mentioned on the title page, Franklin's "Conseils" and "le Testament de Fortuné Ricard." The Introduction is by Paul Jonhanneaud.

1757. Way to Wealth. Nottingham: 1830.
The Way to Wealth.   Nottingham: 1830.

Min. pp.   199

₊*₊ Title from *British Museum Catalogue*.

1757. Way to Wealth. Paris: 1830.
La science du bonhomme Richard.   Paris: A. Hiard.
1830.

12mo. pp. 30.   200

₊*₊ Title from *Swift*.

1757. Way to Wealth. Paris: 1831.
La Science / du / Bonhomme Richard / Par Franklin,
Imprimeur, / suivie de / l'Histoire du Sifflet, / et du Testament / de Fortuné Ricard / Nouvelle Édition, / . . . /
. . . / Paris, / Klefer, Imprimeur-Libraire, / rue de Touraine-s-Germain, No. 5; Garnier, Libraire, au Palais-Royal. / 1831.

Min. pp. 122, (2), portrait.   B. 201

₊*₊ See No. 175. Some copies were printed on red, white and blue paper.

1757. Way to Wealth. Morlaix: 1832.
Guizieguez ar Pautr-cos Richard.   Troet eus al levn
gallec B. Franklin.   Morlaix, imprimerie de Lédan. 1832.

Min. pp. 16.   202

₊*₊ Translated by A. L. Lédan. See No. 173.

1757. Way to Wealth. Besançon: 1833.
Principes elementaires de Morales . . . . . Par Etienne
Gabriel Peignot.   Suivis de la Science du Bonhomme
Richard.   Besançon: 1833.

12mo. pp. 199.   203

₊*₊ Title from *Swift*. See No. 151.

1757. Way to Wealth.   Coburg: 1833.
Alte Goldbriefe.   Neu herausg.   Zum Nutzen und Frommen der Jugend.   Coburg: Riemann.   1833.
12mo. pp.   204

₍*₎ Title from *Swift*.   He also mentions a "2te verm. Auflage" but without giving date or place of printing.

1757. Way to Wealth.   Paris: 1833.
Morceaux Choisis, comprenant La science du Bonhomme Richard, et autres écrits populaires, de Franklin.   Paris: Imprimerie de Carpentier-Méricourt.   1833.
Min. pp.   205

₍*₎ Title from *Swift*.

1757. Way to Wealth.   Paris: 1834.
Morceaux Choisis, / comprenant / la Science / du Bonhomme Richard, / et autres écrits populaires de / Benjamin Franklin. / Précédés / d'une Notice sur sa vie. / Paris / Rue Taranne, No. 12. / 1834.
Min. pp. 72, portrait.   206

1757. Way to Wealth.   New York: 1834.
Benjamin Franklin's / Way to Wealth; / and / William Penn's Maxims. / . . . . . ./ New-York: / Published by Daniel Cooledge, / . . . / West & Trow, Printers. / 1834.
Min. pp. 192, plate.   P. L. 207

1757. Way to Wealth.   Rochester: 1834.
The / Prompter: / [+149+] / To which is added, / the Way to Wealth. / By Benjamin Franklin. / Rochester: / Marshall & Dean, Printers. / 1834.
Min. pp. 143.   P. L. 208

1757. Way to Wealth.   Anneci: 1835.
La science du bonhomme Richard.   Anneci: A. Burdet. 1835.
8vo. pp. 24.   209

₍*₎ Title from *Swift*.

1757. Way to Wealth.   Venice: 1835.
Il cammino della fortuna, o la scienza del buon uomo

Riccardo. Traduzione. Almanacco per l'anno 1836. Venezia, dalla tipografia di G. Antonelli. 1835.

Min. pp. 48.   210

*** Title from *Swift*.

1757. Way to Wealth. Carlsruhe: 1836.

Handscriften 84 verschied; ein Lesebuch für Volks- und Gewerbeschulen, enthaltend Der arme Richard . . . . . Von B. Franklin. Carlsruhe: Wagner. 1836.

4to. pp.   211

1757. Way to Wealth. Northampton: 1837.

The Way to Wealth. Northampton: 1837.

o. pp.   212

*** Title from Boon's stock Catalogue of 1878.

1757. Way to Wealth. London: 1838.

The Apprentices' Pocket Guide . . . . . Franklin's Way to Wealth. London: 1838.

Min. pp.   213

1757. Way to Wealth. Teshen:? 1838.

Pokladnice Franklinowa . . . . . Wydana Frantessken K. Kampelijkem. W. Banské Bystrici. Tissen: Filippa Marcholda: 1838.

8vo. pp. v, 191.   214

*** See Jungmann's *Historie Litterature Cesk*é, 1272a.

1757. Way to Wealth. London: 1839.

Y / Ffordd I. Gaffael Cyfoeth; / neu, / Rhisiat Druan / yn ddinvrygiedig gan / Doctor Franklin, / yr en wog allironydd; / gydag ychwanegrad / y modd I. Wnenthur llawer o ychydig / gan B. Short. / Ac a gyfieithwyd idd y gymraeg / gan Thomas Roberts, / . . . / Llundain / Argraffedig dros y cyfiethhydd / 1839.

Min. pp. 36, portrait, covers.   P. H. S. 215

1757. Way to Wealth. Boston: [184–?]

Poor Richard illustrated. Lessons for the Young and Old on industry, temperance, frugality, &c. Engraved by O. Pelton. E. H. Clapp. Boston.

Folio. Broadside.   B. 216

1757. Way to Wealth. London: [184–?].
Poor Richard's Way to Wealth. / . . . . / London: Published by David Bogue, 86 Fleet Street.   Price Sixpence. Henry Vizetelly, Printer & Engraver, Gough Square, Fleet Street.

Folio. Broadside.   P. L. 217

1757. Way to Wealth. Faenza: 1840.
La maniera di farsi ricco, di Beniamino Franklin. Faenza. 1840.

8vo. pp.   218

₊*₊ Title from *Swift*.

1757. Way to Wealth. Erfurt: 1841.
Der Weg zum Reichthum.   Erfurt: Hennings und Hopf. 1841.

12mo. pp.   219

₊*₊ Title from *Swift*.

1757. Way to Wealth. Brussels: 1842.
Franklin / Le / Chemin de la Fortune, / ou / Science du Bonhomme Richard / et Œuvres diverses. / A Bruxelles, / et dans les principales Villes de l'Étranger, / Chez tous les Libraires. / 1842.

Min. pp. 158, 2, covers.   S. D. 220

1757. Way to Wealth. Vicenza: [1844.]
La maniera di farsi ricco, dono pel capo d'anno 1844. Aggiuntivi alcuni canti popolari vicentini.   Vicenza, tip. di Gaetano Longo. [1844.]

Min. pp. 40.   221

1757. Way to Wealth. Paris: 1845.
Almanach du bonhomme Richard; précédé d'une notice sur l'auteur . . . . Par A. J. Sanson.   Paris: Imprimerie de Boulé. 1845.

Min. pp.   222

₊*₊ Title from *Swift*.

1757. Way to Wealth. New York: 1848.
The / Way to Wealth. / By / Dr. Franklin / No. 2 / Published by the New-York Association for / Improving the

Condition of the Poor. / New-York: / Leavitt, Trow & Co., Printers, 49 Ann Street. / 1848.

12mo. pp. 8, covers.   B. 223

1757. Way to Wealth. Paris: 1848.

Conseils / pour faire Fortune / Avis d'un vieil ouvrier à un jeune ouvrier, / et / la Science du Bonhomme Richard / Par / Franklin / . . . . . / Paris, / Jules Renouard et Cie, Librairies, / rue de Tournon, 6 / 1848.

Min. pp. (4), 92.   224

1757. Way to Wealth. London: [185–?]

Way to Wealth. London. Henry Kent Causton. [1850.]

Broadside.   225

1757. Way to Wealth. London: 1850.

[The Way to Wealth.—In phonetic character.] [Bath printed.] London: Pitman. 1850.

12mo.   B. M., B. 226

1757. Way to Wealth. Paris: 1852.

La Science / du / Bonhomme Richard / Par Benjamin Franklin / l'Historie du Sifflet / et la Testament de Fortuné Ricard / Nouvelle Édition / Paris / P. H. Kreble, / Libraire-Éditeur / 12, rue de Savoie / 1852.

12mo. pp. 35.   227

1757. Way to Wealth. London: 1853.

[The Way to Wealth—In phonetic characters.] London: Pitman: 1853.

12mo. pp.   B. M., B. 228

1757. Way to Wealth. Caracas: 1858.

La Ciencia del Buen Ricardo ó el Camino de la Fortuna. Por Benjamin Franklin y Pensamientos sobre moral, politica, literatura, religion y costumbres par J. M. Samper. Carácas, 1858.

12mo. pp. 58.   B. M. 229

1757. Way to Wealth. London: [186–?]

Franklin's "Way to Wealth" / Maxims & Precepts for conduct in Life / and the first attainment of / Success in Business. / Compiled by B. Wells. Printed by Odell &

Ives, 18, Prince-Street, Cavendish Square, London, W.
Sold by Morrell, 13, Francis St. Bedford Square.

Folio. Broadside.   B., C.   230

1757. Way to Wealth. Berlin: 1864.

Der Weg zum Reichthum. Neu bearb. Nebst siner
Biographie des berühmten Berf Von G. A. B. Berlin:
Grothe. 1864.

Min. pp.   231

_**_* This and the next title are from Kayser's *Index Locupletissimus Librorum*, xiv.

1757. Way to Wealth. Berlin: 1864.

Des armen Richard Weg zum Reichthum. Aus dem
Engl. von C. F. Liebetreu. Berlin: A. Jonas.   1864.

8vo. pp.   232

1757. Way to Wealth. Bologna: 1864.

La maniera di farsi ricco; versione italiana di F. Z.
Bologna, tip. del Progresso. 1864.

8vo. pp. 39.   233

_**_* Title from *Swift.*

1757. Way to Wealth. Milano: 1864.

La maniera di farsi ricco, o la scienza del buon Riccardo, ed altri opuscoli di pratica economia volgarizzati
dal P. I., preceduta dalla biografia dell' autore.   Milano:
tip. Gernia. 1864.

Min. pp. 101.   234

_**_* Title from *Swift.*

1757. Way to Wealth. Paris: 1864.

Premières notions d'economie politique ou sociale, contenant la Science de Bonhomme Richard, par Franklin
. . . . . Par Joseph Garnier.   Paris: Guillaumin: 1864.

Min. pp.   235

_**_* Title from *Swift.*

1757. Way to Wealth. Paris: 1865.

Première Notions d'Économie politique ou sociale, contenant la Science du bonhomme Richard, par Benjamin
Franklin; . . . . . par Joseph Garnier.   Paris: Guillaumin. 1865.

Min. pp.   236

_**_* "C'est une nouvelle édition de l'ouvrage publié en 1858 sous le titre de 'Abrégé des éléments de l'économie politique.'" Title and note from Lorenz' *Catalogue de la Libraire Français*. See No. 245.

1757. Way to Wealth. Paris: 1865.

La science du bonhomme Richard . . . . . Paris: Jules Renouard. 1865.

Min, pp. (4), 32.   237

_**_* Title from *Sabin*.

1757. Way to Wealth. Paris: 1865.

Conseils / pour / Faire Fortune / Avis d'un vieil ouvrier à un jeune ouvrier / et / La Science de Bonhomme Richard / Par / Franklin. / Science Populaire de Claudius. / Paris / Vve. Jules Renouard, Libraire / 6, Rue de Tournon, 6. / 1865.

Min. pp. (4), 41, (1).   P. L.   238

1757. Way to Wealth. Dijon: 1866.

15 Centimes—La Douzaine: 1 fr. 50c. / Le Chemin / de / la Fortune / d'Après Franklin d'Amérique, Par T. Neuville / Professeur à la Faculté de Droit de Dijon. / Dijon: / Chez le Concierge de l'Ecole de Droit. / Se vend aussi chez / Lamarche et Maniere, libraire / Fevrier.   1866.

12mo. pp. 8, covers.   239

1757. Way to Wealth. Berlin: 1866.

Des Armen Richard Weg zum Reichthum. Aus dem engl. von. C. F. Liebetreu. Berlin, 1866. A. Jonas.

8vo. pp.   240

_**_* Title from *Swift*.

1757. Way to Wealth. St. Petersburg: 1869.

Hayka Dodprka Primapa . . . . . St. Petersbourg. 1869.

o. pp.   241

_**_* Title from Mejoff's *Histoire de la Litterature Russe*.

1757. Way to Wealth. London: 1869.

Money-Making for the Million: Comprising the Way to Wealth . . . London: 1869.

8vo. pp.   B. M.   242

1757. Way to Wealth.   Cincinnati: [*187–?*]
Practical Morality; or, a guide to men and manners;
[Containing] . . . . . Franklin's Way to Wealth . . .
. . Cincinnati: U. P. James. [187–?]

Min. pp.   243

 ₊₊ Title from Leypoldt's *American Catalogue.*

1757. Way to Wealth.   Paris: 1871.
Le Bonhomme Franklin / . . . . . / Trente centimes /
. . . . . / Mai 1871.

8vo. pp. 52, covers.   244

 ₊₊ This is the title on cover, the copy examined having no title-
page.

1757. Way to Wealth.   Paris: 1872.
Premières notions d'économie politique ou industrielle,
suivies . . . . . "la Science du Bonhomme Richard"
par Benjamin Franklin . . . . . 4e édition.   Paris:
Guillaumin et Cie.   1872.

12mo. pp.   245

 ₊₊ Title from Lorenz' *Catalogue de Libraire Français.* See No. 236.

1757. Way to Wealth.   Paris: 1872.
Bibliothèque Français / La Science / du / Bonhomme
Richard / par / Benjamin Franklin / Suivie / d'Extraits de
ses œuvres & de sa Correspondence / Avec des nombreuse
notes / et précédé de / La Jeunesse de Franklin / Par /
Édouard Laboulaye. / Paris / Libraire Franklin / Henry
Bellaire, Éditeur / . . . / 1872.

Min. pp. 113, (2), covers.   P. H. S.   246

1757. Way to Wealth.   Firenze: 1873.
La scienza del buon vecchio Riccardo, tradotta dal fran-
cese da Arturo Taranto.   Firenze: tip. Civelli.   1873.

Min. pp. 20.   247

1757. Way to Wealth. [*Boston: 1881.*]
Rand, Avery & Co.'s / Compliments to their friends and
patrons! / . . . . . / . . . We . . . / . . . / . . . offer
to the public a veritable treasure / in the reproduction of

the preface to / "Poor Richard's Almanac" / published by Benjamin Franklin in 1758. [Boston: 1881.]

Min. pp. (12), covers.   B. 248

1757. Way to Wealth. Milan: 1882.

Biblioteca de Popolo / Centesimi 15 il Volume / La Scienza / del / Buon Riccardo / ossia / il Cammino della Fortuna ed altri scritti sulti / di / Beniamino Franklin / . . . / da una particolareggiata / Vita dell' Autore / . . . . . / Milano / Edoardo Sonzogno, Editore / 14 Via Parquir & Co. 14 / 1882.

Min. pp. (62), 1.   249

1757. Way to Wealth. Peking: 1884.

La / Science / du / Bonhomme Richard / ou le / Chemin de la Fortune / Tel qu'il clairement indiqué dans un vieil Almanach de Pensylvanie intitulé / l'Almanach du Bonhomme Richard. / Imprimé / Au College de Tungwen / Peking. / 1884.

Min. pp. 15, (1), 18, covers.   S. D. 250

₊*₊ In French and Chinese.

1757. Way to Wealth. Boston: 1886.

Poor Richard's Almanac and other papers. By Benjamin Franklin. With Notes. Boston: Houghton, Mifflin & Co. 1886.

Min. pp.   251

1757. Way to Wealth. New London: n. d.

Father Abraham's Speech. New London: n. d.

o. pp.   252

₊*₊ Title from *Sabin*.

₊*₊ The piece has also been many times embodied in other books, of which the following is a partial list:

₊*₊ In English in:

Massachusetts Magazine, I, 484, 545.

American Museum, VII, 314.

Virtue made Easy. London: 1799.

A Right Pleasant and Famous Book of Histories. Newcastle: 1818.

The Whole Duty of Man. Georgetown: 1822.

Moral Tracts. Boston: 1820.

Stevens' Historical Nuggets. London: 1864.

Arber's English Garner. London: 1885.

*** In French in:

Tabletes d'un Curieux. Utrecht: 179–?

*** In German in:

Goldnes Schatzkastlein. v. d.

Sprüchwörter des alten Heinrich und Engels. Berlin: 1812.

*** In Italian in:

Strenna Populare. Milano: 1839.

*** In Polish in:

Foster's Dla hazdego kto 2 pracy zyje. Berlin: 1861.

Wybor pism moralnych. Warsaw: 1845.

*** The following is an index to the undated editions in the foregoing list, alphabetically arranged by the place in which they were printed:

Boston: B. Mecom.	107	Newcastle: J. Marshall.	153, 63
Boston: E. H. Clapp.	216	New Haven: T. & S. Green.	108
Boston: Rand, Avery & Co.	248	New London: ?	252
Cincinnati: U. P. James.	243	New York: S. Wood.	171*
Limoges: Ardant.	198	N. p. Montijon.	197
London: W. Darton.	156	N. p., n. d. Broadside.	119–20, 38
London: Darton & Clarke.	157	N. p., n. d. pp. 8.	112
London: J. Bailey.	170	N. p., n. d. pp. 16.	110–11
London: Sherwood, etc.	181	Nottingham: C. Sutton.	142
London: G. Cooke.	195	Nottingham: ?	146
London: H. Vizetelly.	217	Paris: A. Riom.	169
London: H. K. Causton.	225	Paris: Phillipart.	190
London: Odell & Ives.	230	Preston: G. Bateman.	172
Montroulez: Lédan.	173	Salem: T. C. Cushing.	141
Newburyport: W. Barrett.	128	Vicenza: G. Longo.	221

1759. Historical Review of Pennsylvania. London: 1759.
An / Historical Review / of the / Constitution and Government / of / Pensylvania, / From its Origin; / So far as regards the several Points of Controversy, / which have, from Time to Time, arisen / between / The several Governors of that Province, / and / Their several Assemblies. / Founded on Authentic Documents. / . . . / . . . / . . . / London: / Printed for R. Griffiths, in Paternoster-Row. / MDCCLIX.

8vo. pp. viii, (18), 444.   c., b. 253

*** This was included by Mr. Duane and Mr. Sparks in their editions of Franklin's writings, but the latter on discovering in Franklin's letter to Hume a positive denial of the authorship of the work, cancelled his

note and substituted in Volume x a new one, in which Franklin's statement is accepted as final.   In spite of this denial, however, I think
this work must still be treated as from Franklin's pen (though it is
clear that he deemed himself free to deny it), for Franklin was at that
time the only person in London who had the knowledge and material
for such a book; he was the only person interested in the writing of it,
and was indeed virtually sent to London for just such work; and he
was the person who paid the cost of publication, and distributed the
copies; but what is most conclusive is the statement of his son William
(then in London) that "My father has been much occupied of late with
putting together the materials for the work against the p—rs, but Mr.
Ralph is engaged to see it through the press, as he does not wish to
appear in the affair."   That Franklin did not succeed in this it is
hardly necessary to state, for the Reviews all treated it as from his pen,
and till Mr. Sparks printed the letter to Hume it was universally catalogued as by him.

1759. Historical Review.   Philadelphia: 1808.

An / Historical Review / of the / Constitution and Government / of / Pennsylvania, / from its Origin; / so far as
regards the several points of Controversy / which have
from time to time arisen / between / the several Governors
of Pennsylvania / and / their several Assemblies. / Founded
on Authentic Documents. / . . . / . . . / 1808, / reprinted
at Philadelphia / by Wm. Duane, / from the London edition of / 1759. /

8vo.   pp. (2), xv–xxxv, (1), 431.   C.   254

⁎⁎⁎ A reissue of Vol. II of Duane's edition of Franklin's writings.

1759. Historical Review.   Philadelphia: 1812.

An / Historical / Review of Pennsylvania, / from its Origin. / Embracing, among other subjects, the various points
of Contro- / versy which have arisen, from time to time,
between / the several Governors and the Assemblies. /
Founded on Authentic Documents. / By Benjamin Franklin, L. L. D. / (Originally published in London.) / Philadelphia: / Published by E. Olmsted and W. Power. /
1812.

8vo.   pp. (20), 444.   C., P. H. S.   255

⁎⁎⁎ This edition is not, as Mr. Sabin states, a reissue of No. 254, but
a reissue of the first edition, with a new title, and the omission of the
Dedication, and is part of the 500 copies sent by Franklin to America.

1759. Letter on Small Pox.

Some / Account / Of the Success of / Inoculation / for the / Small-Pox / in / England and America. / Together with / Plain Instructions, / By which any Person may be enabled to perform the Operation, / and conduct the Patient through the Distemper. / London: / Printed by W. Strahan, M, D, CCLIX.

4to.   pp. 8, 12.   c.   256

_**_* The "Account" is by Franklin; the Instructions by Dr. Archer.

1759. Parable against Persecution.   [London: 1759?]

1. And it came to pass after these / things that Abraham sat in the door of / his tent, about the going down of the sun. / . . . . . .

8vo.   2 ll.   P. L.   257

_**_* An imitation by Franklin of a chapter of the Bible, which he had privately printed and often read aloud to friends as Genesis LI, amusing himself by their comments thereon. This is the first version, lacking the last four paragraphs, and was printed before 1760, but Mr. C. R. Hildeburn and Mr. F. D. Stone both think it is not from a Pennsylvania press, so it was probably printed while Franklin was in England, between the years 1757–60. This version was the one printed by Lord Kames in his *History of Man* and by Vaughan in his edition of Franklin's writings, as well as in the so-called second edition, No. 260. To give the full history of this most curious skit herein would take more space than could be given to it; and it will be found at length in a (forthcoming) essay on it by the author of this list. Only one copy of each edition has come to the compiler's notice, and I question if more than a dozen copies of the first two issues were printed, as Franklin desired to keep it a secret. In Kayser's *Index Locupletissimus Librorum*, I find the following, which judging by the title seems to be an edition of this Parable, but the price (5 marks) would seem to indicate a work of greater size:

Franklin, B. *Gleichnitz von der Glaubers-Duldung. Dessau: 1855. Neubürger. 8vo.*   258

1759. Parable against Persecution.   [London: 176–?]

1. And it came to pass after these things, that / Abraham sat in the door of his tent, about / the going down of the sun. / . . . . .

12mo.   2 ll.   c.   259

_**_* This is the second version, with the supplementary four para-

graphs. It was certainly printed before April, 1764. The Stevens-Franklin Collection contains a copy.

1759. Parable against Persecution.   London: [1793.]

A / Parable / against / Persecution. / By Benjamin Franklin, LL. D., F. R. S. / The Second Edition. / Published by M. Gurney, No. 128, Holborn-Hill. / Price One Halfpenny; or 3s. per hundred. [London: 1793.]

12mo. pp. 3, (1).   P. L.   260

1759. State of Pennsylvania.

A / True and Impartial State / Of the Province of / Pennsylvania. / Containing, / An exact Account of the Nature of its Government; the Power / of the Proprietaries, and their Governors; as well those / which they derive under the Royal Grant, as those they have / assumed in manifest Violation thereof, their Father's Char- / ter, and the Rights of the People: Also, the Rights and / Privileges of the Assembly, and People, which they claim / under the said Grant, Charter, and Laws of their Country, / confirmed by the Royal Approbation. / With a true Narrative of the Dispute between the Governors / and Assemblies, respecting the Grants of Supplies so often / made by the Latter, and rejected by the Former.   In which / is demonstrated, by incontestable Vouchers, that arbitrary / Proprietary Instructions, have been the true and only Cause / of the Refusal of such Supplies, and the late defenceless State / of the Province. / The whole being a full Answer to the Pamphlets intitled A / Brief State, and A Brief View, &c. of the / Conduct of Pennsylvania. / . . . . . / Philadelphia: / Printed by W. Dunlap, at the Newest-Printing- / Office, M,DCC,LIX.

8vo. pp. (2), iv, 173, 34, (2).   P. H. S.   261

✱✱✱ "This tract was probably inspired, if not wholly written, by Franklin."—*Hildeburn*. Though I have been able to find nothing in support of Mr. Hildeburn's opinion, I consider that of sufficient authority to give the title a place in this list.

1760. Interest of Great Britain. London: 1760.

The / Interest / of / Great Britain / Considered, / With Regard to her / Colonies, / And the Acquisitions of / Canada and Guadaloupe. / To which are added, / Observations concerning the Increase of / Mankind, Peopling of Countries, &c. / London: / Printed for T. Becket, at Tully's Head, near / Surry-Street, in the Strand. / M DCC LX.

8vo. pp. (2), 58.   B. A., C.   262

₊*₊ W. T. Franklin stated that Franklin was assisted in this by Richard Jackson, and on its republication in Vaughan's edition of Franklin's writings, Baron Maseres wrote to Vaughan and claimed for the latter's share nearly ⅔ of the pamphlet, but was not able to satisfy Mr. Vaughan as to the accuracy of this division. On the contrary, Franklin in his outline autobiography and in his letter to Lord Kames writes of it as "my pamphlet," nor does he, in the "Errata" to Vaughan's edition, make any credit to Jackson beyond stating that he was "considerably assisted" by a "learned friend." It thus seems to me, that unless some statement by Jackson to the contrary is discovered, we shall do right in treating Franklin as the author. The pamphlet was in answer to William Burke's:

Remarks / on the / Letter / address'd to / Two Great Men. / In a Letter to the / Author of that Piece / . . . . . / London: / Printed for R. and J. Dodsley, in Pall-Mall. [1760.] 8vo. pp. 64.   263

₊*₊ To which Burke in turn replied in:

An Examination of the Commercial Principles of the late Negotiation between Great Britain and France In MDCCLXI, in which The System of that Negotiation with Regard to our Colonies and Commerce is Considered. London. R. and J. Dodsley. MDCCLXI. 8vo. pp. (2) 108.   264

₊*₊ "Penned with great good sense and moderation." *Monthly Review*, XXII, 432.

1760. Interest of Great Britain. London: 1761.

The / Interest / [₊262₊] / . . . &c. / The Second Edition. / London: / [₊262₊] / M DCC LXI.

8vo. pp. (2), 58.   C., B.   265

760. Interest of Great Britain. Boston: 760.

The Interest / [₊262₊] / With Regard to / Her Colonies / [₊262₊] / . . . &c. / As the very ingenious, useful, and worthy / Author of this Pamphlet (B . . . . n F . . . . n, LL.D.) is / well known, and much esteemed by principal

Gentlemen / in England and America; and seeing that his other Works / have been received with universal Applause; the present / Production needs no further Recommendation to a generous, / a free, an intelligent and publick-spirited People. / London, Printed.   MDCCLX. / Boston: Reprinted, by B. Mecom, / and Sold at the New Printing-Office, near the / Town-House.   1760. / (Price One Shilling.)

8vo.   pp. 59 (5).   B.   266

1760. Interest of Great Britain.   Boston: 1760.

The / Interest / [*266*] . . . . &c. / The second Boston Edition / . . . . . / London, Printed M,DCC,LX. / Boston, N. E.   Reprinted and Sold by B. Mecom, / at the New Printing-Office, near the Town-House. / 1760.

8vo.   pp. 64.   B.   267

1760. Interest of Great Britain.   Philadelphia: 1760.

The / Interest / [*262*] / Observations concerning the increase of Mankind, / Peopling of Countries, &c. / London Printed. / Philadelphia Re-printed, and Sold by William / Bradford, at the London-Coffee-House / MDCCLX.

8vo.   pp. 47.   P. H. S.   268

1760. Interest of Great Britain.   Dublin: 1760.

The Interest of Great Britain . . . . . Dublin: P. Wilson.   1760.

8vo.   pp. 60.   269

*** Title from *Sabin*.

1764. Cool Thoughts.   Philadelphia: 1764.

Cool Thoughts / on the / Present Situation / of our / Public Affairs. / In a Letter to a Friend in the Country. / Philadelphia: / Printed by W. Dunlap.   M,DCC,LXIV.

8vo.   pp. 22.   B., P. H. S.   270

*** Written in favor of sending a petition to England praying that the proprietary government might be changed to a crown government, and signed "A. B."   "First published as a Supplement to the *Pennsylvania Journal*, No. 1116, April 26, 1764."   *Hildeburn.*

1764. Cool Thoughts.   Philadelphia: 764.

Cool Thoughts / on the present / Situation / of our / Public Affairs. / In a Letter to a Friend in the Country, /

Philadelphia: / Printed by A. Stewart at the Bible-in- / Heart.   M,DCC,LXIV.

8vo. pp. 20.   N. 271

1764. Narrative of Massacre.

A / Narrative / of the late / Massacres, / in / Lancaster County, / of a / Number of Indians, / Friends of this Province, / By Persons Unknown. / With some Observations on the same. / [Philadelphia:] Printed [by Anthony Armbruster] in the Year M,DCC,LXIV.

8vo. pp. 31.   P. H. S. 272

₊*₊ A plain and simple statement of a most barbarous act. Owing to the heated condition of Pennsylvania, the massacre assumed political importance, and was the subject of many pamphlets, which will be found in Hildeburn's "*Issues of the Press in Pennsylvania,*" and all of which relate more or less to Franklin. The Narrative was reprinted in the *London Chronicle* of April 10, 1764, and in the *Gentleman's Magazine* (with a note signed J[ames] H[utton?]) of April, 1764, XXXIV, 173. It was answered by Thomas Barton in:

The / Conduct / of the / Paxton-Men, / impartially represented: / With some / Remarks / on the / Narrative. / Philadelphia: / Printed by Andrew Steuart. MDCCLXIV. Sm. 8vo. pp. (2), 24.   273

1764. Narrative of Massacre.

Historische / Nachricht / von dem / neulich in Lancaster County durch unbekannte / Personen ausgeführten / Blutbade / über eine / Anzahl Indianer, / welche Freunde dieser Provinz waren. / Mit einigen hinzugefügten / Anmerkungen. / Aus dem Englischen übersetzt. [Ephrata?] Gedruckt im Jahr 1764.

8vo. pp. 31.   274

1764. Petition to King.

[A Petition to the King, for changing the Proprietary Government of Pennsylvania into a Royal Government. Philadelphia: B. Franklin and D. Hall.   1764.]

o. pp.   275

₊*₊ Drafted by Franklin. "Hall says 300 were printed by the firm." *Hildeburn.*

1764. Remarks on a Protest.

Remarks / on a late / Protest / Against the Appointment of / Mr. Franklin an Agent / for this Province / [Philadelphia: Printed by B. Franklin and D. Hall.   1764.]

8vo. pp. 7.   P. H. S. 276

_**_* In the local elections of 1764, Franklin was defeated in his election to the Assembly. His friends, having control of that body, at once voted his appointment as agent of the Province to England. John Dickinson, David McCanaughy, John Montgomery, Isaac Saunders, George Taylor, William Allen, Thomas Willing, George Bryan, Amos Strettell, and Henry Keppele, at once united in a protest against this action, which was published in the *Pennsylvania Journal* of Nov. 1st, 1764, and more recently in Smith's *Life and Correspondence of William Smith*, from which it was reprinted as follows:

The Reasons / on which were founded, / The Protest / offered by certain members of the / Assembly to that Body / Concerning the Sending of Mr. Franklin to England as Assistant / to our Agent there. / (From the Pennsylvania Journal of March 1st, 1764.) / Reprinted / Philadelphia, 1878. 8vo. pp. 4.   P. L.   277

*_** This Franklin answered in his "Remarks," which was in turn replied to by the Rev. William Smith in:

An / Answer / to / Mr. Franklin's / Remarks / on a late / Protest. / Philadelphia: / Printed and Sold by William Bradford at his Book- / Store, in Market-street, adjoining the London Coffee-house. / M.DCC.- LXIV. 8vo. pp. 22.   P. H. S.   278

1764. Remarks on the Protest.

Proteſtation / gegen die Beſtellung / Herrn Benjamin Franklin's zu einem Agenten für / dieſe Provinz, / [Followed by] / Anmerkungen / über eine neuliche / Proteſtation / gegen die Beſtellung / Herrn Benjamin Franklin's zu einem Agenten für / dieſe Provinz / [Germantown: Christoph Saur. 1764.]

Folio. pp. (4.)   279

*_** "The Protest occupies the first page, the other three being filled with Franklin's Remarks upon it." Title and note from *Hildeburn*.

1764. Preface to Galloway's Speech. Philadelphia: 1764.

The / Speech / Of / Joseph Galloway, Esq; / One of the Members for Philadelphia County: / In Answer / To the Speech of John Dickinson, Esq; / Delivered in the House of Assembly, of the / Province of Pennsylvania, May 24, 1764. / On Occasion of a Petition drawn up by Order, and / then under the Consideration of the House; / praying his Majesty for a Royal, in lieu of / a Proprietary Government / . . . / Philadelphia: / Printed and Sold by W. Dunlap, in Market-street. / MDCCLXIV.

8vo. pp. xxxv, (3), 45.   B. A.   280

*** The "Preface" of 35 pages, was written by Franklin, and is a very bitter attack on the Penns and their partizans.

1764. Preface to Galloway's Speech.   Philadelphia: 1764.

The / Speech / [*280*] / A Proprietary Government / . . . / The Second Edition / Philadelphia: / Printed and sold by W. Dunlap, in Market-street. / MDCCLXIV.

8vo. pp. xxxv, (3), 45.   281

1764. Preface to Galloway's Speech.   London: 1765.

The / Speech / [*280*] / . . . A Proprietary Government. / With a Preface by a Member of the Assembly. / . . . / Philadelphia Printed; / London Reprinted, and sold by W. Nicoll, / in St. Paul's Church-Yard, MDCCLXV. / (Price Two Shillings).

8vo. pp. (2), 92.   B. 282

*** "We cannot but wonder that a man of Mr. Dickinson's abilities should, in his answer to Mr. Galloway, take no notice of the masterly Preface to the last-named Gentleman's Speech, by another Hand. This Preface, supposed to be written by Mr. F——n, is of itself a very considerable tract, of thirty-five pages, and exhibits a succinct view of this controversy." *Monthly Review*, XXXII, 67.

1764. Preface to Galloway's Speech.   Philadelphia: 1764.

Die / Rede / Herrn Joseph Galloway's, / eines der Mitglieder des Hauses für / Philadelphia County, / Zur Beantwortung / Der Rede welche Hr. John Dickinson / gehalten / im Hause der Assembly der Provinz / Pennsylvanien, am 24ten May, 1764, / Bei Gelegenheit einer Bittschrift, welche auf Befehl / des Hauses aufgesetzt, und damals in Ueberlegung genommen war, worin Seine Königliche Majestät um / ein Königliches anstatt des jetzigen Proprietors Gouvernements ersucht wird. / Mit einer Vorrede. / . . . / . . . / . . . / Aus dem Englischen übersetzt. / Philadelphia, Gedruckt und zu finden bey Henrich / Miller, in der Zweyten-strasse. [1764.]

8vo. pp. xliv, (4), 46.   283

1765. Emblematical Design.   London.

Magna Britannia; her Colonies Reduc'd. [London: 1765.]

Sm. 4to. 1 l.   P. 284

*** "During the disputes between the two countries, Dr. Franklin

invented a little *emblematical design*, intended to represent the supposed state of Great Britain and her colonies, should the former persist in her oppressive measures, restraining the latter's trade, and taxing their people by laws made by a legislature in which they were not represented. It was engraved on a copper plate. Dr. Franklin had many of them struck off on cards, on the back of which he occasionally wrote his notes. It was also printed on a half-sheet of paper, with the *explanation* and *moral.*" W. T. Franklin's *Memoirs of Franklin,* I, 219.

‎₊*₊ The plate was also engraved, with "Its Companion," for *The Political Register,* No. xxi, December, 1768. Of this issue I have only seen one impression.

‎₊*₊ The English plate measures 3¼ x 4⅞ inches, and is without the "explanation" added in the American edition. All three issues are of the greatest rarity.

1765. Emblematical Design. Philadelphia.

Magna Britannia; her Colonies Reduc'd. [Philadelphia: Engraved by Dawkins? 1766.]

Folio. 1 l. P. 285

‎₊*₊ The plate measures 4½ x 6½. An "Explanation" is added, but not by Franklin. This edition is reproduced in Franklin's, Duane's, and Sparks' editions of Franklin's writings.

1765. Emblematical Design. Amsterdam.

La Grande Bretagne inutilé. Das verstimuelte Britanien. / . . . . . / Amsterdam. [176–]

Oblong Folio. 1 l. 286

‎₊*₊ The engraver has made many changes in this Dutch edition from Franklin's idea. Great Britain is chained to a rock, which has been substituted for the globe, and a sailor has been added in the foreground. The only copy I have seen is through the courtesy of Mr. Charles R. Hildeburn, of Philadelphia, in whose collection it is.

1766. Examination in Parliament. [London: 1766.]

(1) / The / Examination / of / Doctor Benjamin Franklin, &c. / [London. J. Almon. 1766.]

8vo. pp. 50. P. L. 287

‎₊*₊ Owing to the secrecy of the proceedings in Parliament, this edition gives no clue either to where the examination was held, or when, and by whom it was printed, Almon evidently fearing prosecution, and the printers of most of the subsequent editions used much the same precautions. As no prosecution was instituted, Almon became bolder, and issued an edition (which is otherwise identical with the above), with a title as in No. 288.

₊*₊ The examination was before the House of Commons, and was held in April, 1766. "It was concerted that he should be interrogated on the whole merits of the question before the house of commons . . . Most of the questions propounded were already and skilfully arranged between him and the enemies of the act." Walsh in *Delaplaine's Repository*, 74.

₊*₊ "Some of my friends have thought that a publication of my *Examination* might answer some of the above purposes, by removing prejudices, refuting falsehoods, and demonstrating our merits with regard to this country. It is accordingly printed and has a great run." *Franklin to Galloway.*

₊*₊ "Your Friends received the highest gratification in the perusal of your Examination, and they anxiously looked for the arrival of the last packet, as they flattered themselves, they should have one they could print; but they are greatly disappointed. The one Mr. Hall has he has been very industrious, in the reading to different large companies; and the demand for it, from all parts of the Province, is beyond conception." *Letter to Franklin.*

₊*₊ See Delaplaine's *Repository*, 74, for a paper giving Franklin's account of the examination, and a list of the questioners; and the *Monthly Review*, xxxvii, 73; and *London Magazine*, xxxvi, 364, for reviews.

1766. Examination in Parliament.   London: 1767.

The / Examination / of / Doctor Benjamin Franklin, / Relative to the / Repeal / of the / American Stamp Act, / In MDCCLXVI. / [London: J. Almon.]   MDCCLXVII. / (Price One Shilling.)

8vo.   pp. (2), 50.   c.   288

1766. Examination in Parliament.   London: 1766.

The Examination of Dr. Benjamin Franklin before an Honourable Assembly, relative to the Repeal of the American Stamp Act, in 1766.   London: 1767.

8vo.   pp. 50.   289

₊*₊ This title is taken from Rich's *Bibliotheca Americana Nova*, and is I think untrustworthy. In the Stevens-Franklin Collection the same title is repeated, but on reference to the original pamphlet it proves to be a copy of No. 288.

1766. Examination in Parliament.   Philadelphia.

(1) / The Examination of Doctor / Benjamin Franklin, before an / August Assembly, relating to the Repeal of /

the Stamp-Act, &c. / [Philadelphia: Hall and Sellers. 1766.]

8vo. pp. 16.   c. 290

*** This and the following edition so closely resemble each other as to be easily confused. There are, however, minor differences as follows: The Philadelphia edition has a double line of even sized lines for a head piece, and the signatures are "A, A², A³, A⁴." In the New York edition the head lines are of uneven thickness; and the signatures are "A, A², B, B²."

1766. Examination in Parliament. New York.

(1) / The Examination of Doctor / Benjamin Franklin, before an / August Assembly, relating to the Repeal of / the Stamp-Act, &c. / [Reprinted by James Parker, Esq. in New York. September. 1766.]

8vo. pp. 16.   c. 291

*** The portion in brackets of the above title is a MS. note, in a contemporary handwriting, from a copy of the edition in the library of Gordon L. Ford, of Brooklyn, N. Y.

1766. Examination in Parliament. Boston.

(1) / The Examination / of Doctor Benjamin Franklin, / before an August Assembly, relating to the / Repeal of the Stamp-Act, &c. [Boston: 1766?]

8vo. pp. 23.   P., M. 292

1766. Examination in Parliament. Williamsburg.

The Examination of Dr. Benjamin Franklin, relative to the repeal of the American Stamp Act in 1766. Williamsburg.

4to.   B. A. 293

1766. Examination in Parliament. Boston.

The Examination of Benjamin Franklin, before the House of Commons, relating to the Stamp Act. Boston. 1766.

8vo. pp. 108.   294

*** Title from Thomas' and Haven's *"Catalogue of American Publications, 1639–1775."*

1766. Examination in Parliament. New London.

The New London Gazette . . . [extra] No. 132, for October 10, 1766. The Examination of Dr. Franklin be-

fore an August Assembly, relative to the repeal of the
Stamp Act. [New London. Timothy Green. 1766.]

Sm. Folio. pp. 2.   C. 295

1766. Examination in Parliament. Strasbourg.

Interrogatoire / de / Mr. Franklin / Deputé de Pensil-
vanie / au / Parlement / de la Grande Bretagne. / Traduit
de l'Anglois / par / Ch . . . D. H . . . / Maitre de la
langue Anglois à Strasbourg. / Prix 24 sols. / [colophon]
A Strasbourg: / de l'Imprimerie de Simon Kürsner. /
Avec Approbation. [1767?]

8vo. pp. 35.   C. 296

1766. Examination in Parliament. Philadelphia.

Die / Verhörung / Doctor Benjamin Franklin's / von der / Hohen
Versammlung / des / Hauses der Gemeinen / von Großbrittanien, / die
Stempel Act, ꝛc., betreffend. / Aus dem Englischen übersetzt. / Phil-
adelphia, Gedruckt und zu finden bey H. Miller, / in der
Zweyten-Strasse, 1766.

8vo. pp. 43.   P. H. S. 297

  ⁎ The Examination was also printed in: *A Collection of Tracts,
published in England and America on the subjects of Taxing the
American Colonies, and Regulating their Trade . . . London: 1770;
A Collection of Interesting Authentic Papers relative to the Dispute
between Great Britain and America . . . London: 1777; A Collection
of Scarce and Interesting Tracts . . . In Four Volumes . . . London:
1787;* In French in Nos. 113–116, 118, 326 and *Précis de l'État Actuel
des Colonies Angloises Dans l'Amérique Septentrionale. Par M. Dom-
inique de Blackford. A Milan: 1771;* and in German in *Sammlung
neuer Reisebeschreibungen . . . Franklin's Nachrichten von Nord
Amerika mit Köhler Anmerkungen begleitet. 1767; Herrn Hofrath
Achenwalls in Göttingen Anmerkungen über Nord Amerika und uber
dasige Grosbritannische Colonien aus mundlichen Nachrichten des
Herrn Franklin's. Frankfort und Leipzig: 1769;* and *Einige Anmerkungen über Nord-America und über dasige Grosbritannische
Colonien. Aus mündlichen Nachrichten des Herrn D. Franklin's
verfasst von Gottfried Achenwall . . Helmstedt: 1777.*

1766. Observations and Suppositions.

Physical and Meteorological / Observations, / and / Suppositions, / By Benjamin Franklin, LL. D. F. R. S. /

Read at the Royal Society, June 3, 1756. / London: / Printed in the Year M.DCC.LXVI.

4to. pp. 15.   c., p. h. s. 298

₊ Originally printed in the *Transactions of the Royal Society* for 1766, and the same forms used to print this separate issue. By an oversight this was omitted from its proper place in this list.

1768. Art of Swimming. London: 1816.

The / Art / of / Swimming / . . . . . / To which are added, / . . . . . / An Advice to Bathers, / by the / late Celebrated Dr. Benjamin Franklin. / London: / Orlando Hodgson, 21 Maiden Lane, Wood Street. / Price Sixpence. [1816?]

12mo. pp. 24, plate.   b. m. 299

1768. Art of Swimming. New-York: 1818.

The / Art of Swimming, / . . . . . / By J. Frost / . . . / To which is added, / Dr. Franklin's Treatise, / . . . . . / New-York: / Published by P. W. Gallaudet, Fulton-St. / Birch and Kelly, Printers. / 1818.

8vo. pp. xiv, 72, plates.   b. 300

1768. Art of Swimming. London: 1854.

The Swimmer's Handbook, with Dr. Franklin's Advice. London: 1854.

Min. pp.   b. m. 301

₊ Title from British Museum Catalogue.

₊ It is also included in *A Picture of Margate* . . . . . *London·1809.*

1768. American Discontents.

The Trve Sentiments of America: / Contained in a Collection of / Letters / . . . . . / London, Printed for I. [sic] Almon, in Piccadilly. / 1768.

8vo. pp. 158.   b. 302

₊ Contains Franklin's "Causes of the American Discontents before 1768," originally printed in the *London Chronicle* of Jan. 7, 1768. With the signature of F[ranklin's] S[eal.]

1768. Preface to Dickinson's Letters. London: 1768.

Letters / from a / Farmer in Pennsylvania, / to the / Inhabitants / of the / British Colonies. [By John Dickin-

son.] / London. / Printed for J. Almon, opposite Burlington-house, Piccadilly. / M DCC LXVIII.

8vo. (4), iii, (1), 118.   c. 303

*** Originally printed in Philadelphia, and reprinted in England at
the instance of Franklin, who added a Preface, dated "London, May
8, 1768," and signed "N. N."

*** "The *Farmer's Letters* were written by one Mr. Dickinson, of
Philadelphia, and not by me, as you seem to suppose. I only caused
them to be reprinted here with that little Preface, and had no other
hand in them, except that I see some of my sentiments formerly published are collected and interwoven with those of others and his own,
by the author." *Franklin to Le Roy.*

*** This preface is omitted in the later London edition of this
pamphlet, published in 1774.

1768. Preface to Dickinson's Letters. Paris: 1769.

Lettres d'un fermier de Pensylvanie aux habitants de
l'Amerique Septentrionale. Traduites de l'Anglois. Amsterdam [Paris:] M.DCC.LXIX.

8vo. pp. xxviii, 258.   H. 304

*** Translated by Barbeu Dubourg.

*** "I am just returned from France, where I found our dispute
much attended to, several of our pamphlets being translated and
printed there, among the rest my *Examination* and the *Farmer's
Letters*, with two of my pieces annexed, of which last I send you a
copy." *Franklin to Cooper.*

1769. "Curious" Note.

The Americans may be treated with as much equity,
and even / tenderness by the parliament of Great Britain
· · ·/ · · · · · [Hartford: 1880.]

Square 12mo. Broadside.   P. L. 305

*** This is an extract from *An Inquiry into the Nature and Causes
of the Present Disputes between the British Colonies and their Mother-
Country. London: 1769*, with Franklin's MS. note on the passage, and
an explanatory note by Mr. J. Hammond Trumbull of the "curious
illustration, in short-hand, which Mr. Sparks has *omitted.*" See
Brinley Catalogue, II, lot 3222. Only a few copies were printed for circulation among "the elect" at the Brinley auction sale. The volume
containing the original note is now in the Lenox Library.

1769. Electrical Experiments.

Experiments / and / Observations / On / Electricity, /

made at / Philadelphia in America, / By / Benjamin Franklin, L. L. D. and F. R. S. / To which are added, / Letters
and Papers / on / Philosophical Subjects. / The Whole corrected, methodized, improved, and now first col- / lected
into one Volume, / and / Illustrated with Copper Plates. /
London: / Printed for David Henry; and sold by Francis
Newbery, / at the Corner of St. Paul's Church-Yard. /
MDCCLXIX.

4to.   pp. (4), 496, (14), 5 plates.   c., P. H. S. 307

₊ The fourth edition of Franklin's *Experiments*. See Nos. 77, 93,
96 and 318.

1769. Letter to Philadelphia Committee.

Letters / To the Merchants Committee of Philadelphia,
/ Submitted to the Consideration of / The Public. / [Phila-
delphia: 1770.]

Folio.   Broadside.   P.   308

₊ Letters from Franklin (dated July 9, 1769) and John Neuville.

1771. Autobiography to 1731. See 1789.

1771. Letter to Humphrey Marshall.

London, April 22, 1771. / Sir / . . . . . / B. Franklin.
/ Entered according to the Act of Congress, in the Year
1865 by W. W. Cox.   In the / Clerk's Office of the District
Court of the District of Columbia. / Lith. of Charles Hart,
99 Fulton St. N. Y. [1865?]

Folio. pp. (4).   B.   309

₊ A lithographic copy of a letter not included in Sparks' or Bigelow's editions.

1771. Plan for New Countries.

[Plan for benefiting distant unprovided countries. By
Alexander Dalrymple and Benjamin Franklin. London:
1771?]

o. Broadside.   310

₊ "These proposals were printed on a sheet of paper some two or
three years ago, and distributed. The parts written by Dr. Franklin
and Mr. Dalrymple are easily distinguished." *Vaughan's edition of
Franklin's writings*, 37.

1772. Reply to Report on the Walpole Grant.

Report / of the / Lords Commissioner's for / Trade and

Plantations / on the / Petition / of the / Honourable Thomas Walpole, Benjamin / Franklin, John Sargent and Samuel / Wharton, Esquires and their Associ- / ates; / for / A Grant of Lands on the River Ohio, in North / America; for the purpose of Erecting a New / Government. / With / Observations and Remarks. / London: / Printed for J. Almon, opposite Burlington-House, in / Piccadilly / MDCCLXXII.

8vo. pp. 108, folding table.   c., N. 311

*** The Report (written by Lord Hillsborough) fills the first 34 pages; the remainder being the "Observations and Remarks" which were written by Franklin.

*** "Dr. Franklin's answer to the Report of the Board of Trade was intended to have been published, but Lord Hillsborough resigning, Dr. Franklin stopped the sale on the morning of the publication, when not above *five* copies had been disposed of." Almon's *Anecdotes*, II, 238.

*** Mr. Almon has, I believe, confused this pamphlet with No. 317, in the above statement, for this was advertised with a price, and reviewed in the *Monthly Review* (XLVII, 239) and in the *Critical Review* (XXXIV, 320), and though a rare pamphlet, the compiler has seen more than five copies, besides noting the existence of others.

*** The whole tract is reprinted in Almon's *Biographical, Literary and Political Anecdotes*, II, 200. See also No. 317.

1772. Letter on Toleration.

Two Letters, addressed to the Right Rev. Prelates, who a second Time rejected the Dissenters' Bill. London: Johnson. MDCCLXXII.

8vo. pp. 108.   312

*** The pamphlet is by E., Radcliff. The appendix contains Franklin's "Letter concerning persecutions in former Ages, the Maintenance of the Clergy, American Bishops, and the State of Toleration in Old England and New England compared," originally published in *The London Packet* of June 3, 1772.

*** "I now add . . . a spirited address to the bishops who oppos'd the Dissenter's petition. It is written by a dissenting minister at York. There is preserved at the end of it a little fugitive piece of mine, written on the same occasion." *Franklin to Mather.*

1773. Preface to Book of Common Prayer.

Abridgement / of / the Book of / Common Prayer, / And Administration of the / Sacraments, / and other / Rites and

Ceremonies / of the / Church, / According to the Use of / the Church of England: / together with the / Psalter, or Psalms / of / David, Printed as they are to be sung or said in Churches. / London: / Printed in the Year MDCC–LXXIII.

8vo.   76 ll.   c. 313

*** Franklin wrote the Preface, and abridged the Catechism and the Psalms.

*** "The Liturgy you mention was an abridgement of that made by a noble Lord of my acquaintance, who requested me to assist him by taking the rest of the book, viz., the Catechism and the reading and singing Psalms. These I abridged by retaining of the Catechism only the two questions, *What is your duty to God? What is your duty to your neighbour?* with answers. The Psalms were much contracted by leaving out the repetitions (of which I found more than I could have imagined), and the imprecations, which appeared not to suit well the Christian doctrine of forgiveness of injuries, and doing good to enemies. The book was printed for Wilkie, in St. Paul's Church Yard, but never much noticed. Some were given away, very few sold, and I suppose the bulk became waste paper." *Franklin to Sharp.*

*** "Printed at the expense of the late Lord Despencer at West Wycombe, Bucks; abridged by the late Sir Francis Dashwood, Bart. Dr. Dibdin, from whom this information was derived, said the late Earl of Bute shewed this abridgement to him in his library at Petersham." Martin's *Bibliographical Catalogue of Privately Printed Books,* 521.

*** Two misstatements in the above paragraph have led all succeeding cataloguers into error—one in stating that the volume was printed at West Wycombe, the other that it was abridged by Sir Francis Dashwood, *for* Lord Le-Despencer, for they were one and the same person. The volume is of the greatest rarity, neither the British Museum nor Bodleian Library possessing it. It is certainly a delicious bit of satire to find one of the most notorious of roués, assisted by a deist, reforming the Common Prayer, and then that volume made, to a certain extent, the basis of the "Proposed" prayer book of the "Church" in this country.

1773. Rules for Reducing a Great Empire.

Rules / for / Reducing / a / Great Empire / to / a / Small One. / By the late / Benjamin Franklin, L. L. D. F. R. S. / Dedicated / to the / Right Honourable / Alexander, Lord Loughborough. / To which is subjoined / The Declaration of Independence by the Representa- / tives of the United

States of America in / General Congress assembled. / London: / Printed for James Ridgway, No. 1, York Street / St. James Square. / 1793. / (Price Three Pence.)

8vo. pp. 16.   c. 314

_**_* Probably the cleverest political satire written by Franklin. It is a scathing review of the Ministry's methods for governing America, and is chiefly aimed at Lord Hillsborough, with whom Franklin certainly more than squares the accounts which the latter had opened by his treachery in the "Walpole Grant" affair.

_**_* Originally printed in October, 1773, in the *Public Advertiser*, and reprinted in the same paper a few weeks later by special request. It was also copied into several other papers, and into the *Gentleman's Magazine.* Reviewed in the *Monthly Review*, N. S. XII, 227.

_**_* This edition is dedicated by the English editor to Alexander, Lord Loughborough (Wedderburn), the author of the savage attack on Franklin in connection with the "Hutchinson and Oliver Letters" on the ground that "when I reflect on your Lordship's *magnanimous* conduct towards the author of the following *golden* Rules, there is, in my opinion, a peculiar propriety in dedicating this new edition of them to a nobleman, whose *talents* were so eminently useful in procuring the emancipation of our American brethren."

1773. Works Edited by Barbeu Dubourg.

Œuvres / de / M. Franklin, / Docteur ès Loix, / . . . / . . . / . . . / . . . / . . . / . . . / Traduites de l'Anglois sur la quatrieme Édition. / Par M. Barbeu Dubourg. / Avec des Additions Nouvelles / Et des Figures en Taille douce. / Tome Premier. / A Paris, / Chez Quillau l'aîné, Libraire, rue Christine, au Magasin Littéraire. / Esprit, Libraire de Mgr. le Duc de Chartres, au Palais Royal. / Et l'Auteur, rue de la Bucherie, aux Ecoles de Médecine. / M. DCC.-LXXIII. / Avec Approbation & Permission du Roi. /

2 Vols. 4to. pp. (4), xxii, (2), 338, portrait, 5 plates.—(4), xiii, (3), 318, (2), 7 Plates.   B. 315

_**_* My affection for the author has made me undertake the translation, and his friendship for me has caused him to draw from his portfolio many pieces, which have not before appeared, to enrich this French edition. *Preface.*

_**_* Brunet states that the translation was made by J. B. L'Écuy. The first volume is devoted entirely to electricity, being a reprint of the English editions, with the addition of several pieces not included in any former edition. The second volume includes his other scientific

writings; The Pennsylvania Fireplace; Observations on the Increase of Mankind; Letters to Shirley; Poor Richard (which in the translation, becomes "Le Pauvre Henri"); the Craven Street letters; and a number of letters from Franklin to the editor. See No. 321.

1773. Preface to Boston Proceedings.

The / Votes and Proceedings / of the / Freeholders and other Inhabitants / of the / Town of Boston, / In Town Meeting assembled, / According to Law. / (Published by Order of the Town) / . . . . / The whole containing a particular Enumeration of those / Grievances that have given Rise to the present alarming / Discontents in America. / Boston, Printed: / London, Reprinted and sold by J. Wilkie. / . . . / MDCCLXXIII.

8vo. pp. (4), viii, 43.   316

    ₊*₊ The "Preface of the English Editor" is by Franklin.

1774. Considerations on the Walpole Grant.

Considerations / on the / Agreement / of the / Lords Commissioners of His / Majesty's Treasury, / With / The Honourable Thomas Walpole and / his Associates, for Lands upon the River / Ohio, in North America. / In / A Letter to a Member of Parliament. / London, / MDCCLXXIV.

8vo. pp. (4), 46.   P. L. 317

    ₊*₊ Though this has never been referred to Franklin's pen, I think it written by him; for it relates to a scheme in which he was greatly interested, is signed "A. B." (a favorite pseudonym of his), and a copy in the library of Mr. Gordon L. Ford, of Brooklyn, N. Y., contains MSS. corrections, such as an author alone would make, in his writing.

    ₊*₊ "I discover the same adverse influence still at work on our land scheme. When it will remove its sphere of action to Philadelphia is unsettled—till then I can do little. I hear a pamphlet on the Grant was printed for him by Almon, but was withdrawn. Why I know not, as I cannot even get sight of a copy." *Arthur Lee to R. H. Lee*, Jan. 29, 1774.

    ₊*₊ From a comparison of this evidence it appears to me that Mr. Almon has confused this pamphlet with No. 311, and that his "anecdote" refers to this one. It is of the greatest rarity, being contained in no public library, mentioned in no bibliography, or noticed in any contemporary review, so far as I have been able to ascertain.

1774. Electrical Experiments.

Experiments / and / Observations / on / Electricity, / made at / Philadelphia in America, / By / Benjamin Franklin, L. L. D. and F. R. S. / . . . . . / To which are added, / Letters and Papers / on / Philosophical Subjects. / The Whole corrected, methodized, improved, and now collected into / one Volume, and illustrated with Copper Plates. / The Fifth Edition. / London: / Printed for F. Newbery, at the Corner of St. Paul's Church-Yard. / M. DCC. LXXIV.

4to.   pp. (2), vi, 514, (16), 7 plates.   c.   318

₊*₊ See Nos. 77, 93, 96 and 307.

1774. Oil on the Waters.

Of the / Stilling of Waves / by means of / Oil: / Extracted from / Sundry Letters / between / Benjamin Franklin, LL. D. F. R. S. / William Brownrigg, M. D., F. R. S. / and / The Reverend Mr. Parish. / Read at the Royal Society, June 2, 1774. / London, / Printed by W. Bowyer and J. Nichols, / M. DCC. LXXIV.

4to. pp. 18.   P. H. S.   319

1774. Notes on Trade.

Principles / of / Trade. / Fredom and Protection are its best Suport: / Industry, the only means to render / Manufactures cheap. / Of Coins; Exchange, and Bounties; / particularly the Bounty on Corn / By a Well-Wisher to his King and Country / With an Apendix / Containing Reflections on Gold, Silver, and / Paper pasing as Mony. / The Second Edition corrected and enlarg'd. / . . . . . / London, / Printed for Brotherton and Sewall in Cornhill. / MDCCLXXIV.

4to. pp. (6), 48, 16.   c.   320

₊*₊ The original edition was written by George Whately, and published in 1765 under the title of "The Laws and Policy of England, Relating to Trade, Examined By the Maxims and Principles of Trade in General; . . . . . By the Author of the Treatise on The Police of France, &c. London: Printed . . . by T. Harrison . . . . . MDCC-LXV." In this second edition, much is added in the form of notes; many of which were contributed by Franklin.

_**_* "It was originally published in 1774, and is the joint work of George Whately and Dr. Franklin. The original work was indeed written by the former, and communicated to the latter. The corrections and additions, which were made by Dr. Franklin, produced an amicable controversy between them, who had the best claim to call himself the author of it, which closed by a determination to publish it without any name." *Franklin's Memoirs of Franklin.*

*_** The above is plainly a misstatement, for Franklin and Whately both treat it as Whately's in their correspondence. In Vaughan's edition of the Writings of Franklin, the notes which were believed to have been written by Franklin are reprinted, probably correctly, for Franklin makes no correction for the "Errata" of that edition.

*_** "By good luck I find I have kept your original notes on "The Principles of Trade," those we agreed in, those I added, and those I dissented from, and were not published; moreover some other ideas you favored me with." *Whately to Franklin*, Nov. 1784.

*_** This edition makes many changes in the spelling of words, a specimen of which is given in the title, which were probably suggested by Franklin, and are severely handled in the *Monthly Review*.

*_** See *Monthly Review*, L, 490; *Critical Review*, XXXVII, 387, and Sparks' edition of Franklin's Writings, X, 132, 147.

1774. Writings.

Scelta di Lettere / E / di Opuscoli / del / Signor Beniano / Franklin / Tradotti / dall' Inglese / . . . . . / In Milano: MDCCLXXIV. / Nella Stamperia di Guiseppe Marelli. /

. . .

8vo.   pp. 99.   P. H. S.   321

*_** An abridgment of Dubourg's edition, made by Carlo Guiseppi Campi.

1775. Articles of Confederation.

Additions / to / Common Sense; / Addressed to the / Inhabitants of America. / Philadelphia, Printed: / London, Re-printed for J. Almon, opposite Burlington- / House, in Piccadilly. / 1776.

8vo.   pp. 47, (1).   C.   322

*_** Contains Franklin's "Proposals for a Confederation of the United Colonies," originally printed in the *Pennsylvania Evening Post*, April, 1776. This is not in the American editions of *Additions to Common Sense*. See Worthington C. Ford's letter in *The Nation*, March 28, 1889.

1775. Directions to Postmasters.

Directions to the Deputy Post-Masters, for keeping their

accounts . . . . . [signed] Benjamin Franklin. [Philadelphia: n. d.]

Folio.   Broadside.   P. H. S.   323

1775. Rates of Postage.

Tables of the Port of all Single Letters carried by Post in the Northern District of North America, / As Established by / Congress, / One Thousand Seven Hundred and Seventy-five / . . . . . / [signed] B. Franklin, / Post Master General. [Philadelphia: [n. d.]]

Folio.   Broadside.   S. D.   324

1776. Fictitious Ledger of Post Office.

The Ledger / of Doctor Benjamin Franklin, / . . . / B. Franklin / Postmaster General, 1776 / A Facsimile of the Original Manuscript / Now on file on the Records of the / Post Office Department / of the / United States. / Washington, D. C. / 1865. / Lith. in Fac-simile by Chas. Hart, 99 Fulton St. New York.

Folio.   60 ll.   C.   325

    *** The ledger is really that of Richard Bache.   See *The Critic* N. S. III, 159, and Washington *Star*, March 18, 1885.

    *** The title page of the copy in the Boston Public Library reads " / now on file in the office of the / Auditor of the Treasury for the / Post Office Department / "

1776. Affaires de l'Angleterre.   Paris: 1776–1779.

Affaires / de l'Angleterre / et de l'Amerique. / N°· 1ᵉʳ· / A Anvers. [Paris:] M.DCC.LXXVI.

15 vols. in 17.   8vo.   M., S. D.   326

    *** Barbier states that this rare periodical was edited by Franklin, Antoine Court de Gébelin, Jean Babtiste René Robinet and others. Though I can find nothing to verify this statement, the internal evidence shows that some one who received private information from America, was either editing or assisting the editors with private letters; and it deserves a place in this list merely for the writings it contains of Franklin's, which are as follows:

    "Extrait d'un discours prononcé par le docteur Franklin en l'honneur du Major-Genéral Warren."   II, 26.

    Letters to and from Lord Howe.   IV, cxxxvj.

    "Edit du Roi de Prusse."   IV, cxliv.

    "Comparaison des treize Etats-unis de l'Amérique avec la Grande-Bretagne, sur les facultés & le credit."   VI, cxliij.

"Mémoire sur l'origine de la querelle Américaine & sur l'état des affaires en Amerique jusqu'en Mars 1777."   VII, i.

Examination in Parliament.   VII, ccxj.

"Observations sur l'origine de la guerre civile des Colonies Améri-caines."   VII, cccxxij.

Correspondence on America with Strahan.   VII, cccxxvj.

"Raisons pour ne point taxer les Colonies."   VII, cccxl.

Means for reducing a great empire.   IX, lxxxviij.

** A full collation is contained in *The Pa. Mag. of History and Biography*, July, 1889.

1777. American Credit.

The following Paper is supposed to have been / written by a celebrated American Philo- / sopher (Doctor Benjamin Franklin) at / Paris; for the Purpose of borrowing Money / for the Use of the United States of Ame- / rica: / and it has had a wonderful Effect; / large sums having been lent, in consequence of the sound and irrefutable Facts and Argu-ments / contained in it.   It has been translated into the French and Dutch Languages and printed; / and it is now circulating in Holland, Flanders, / &c. [London: 1777.]

8vo. pp. 8.   c. 327

** *Swift* gives a title of *Comparison of Great Britain and the United States in regard to the basis of credit in the two countries 1777*, which I presume is taken from Sparks' list. I do not think it was ever issued in pamphlet with that title. It is also printed in Almon's *Re-membrancer*, 1777, 380, and in French in No. 326.

1777. Memorial.

Remarks / on / the Rescript / of the Court of Madrid, / and on / the Manifesto / of the Court of Versailles. / . . . . . / To which is added / an appendix, / Containing . . . / . . . / A Memorial of Dr. Franklyn [sic] / to the Court of Versailles. / . . . . . / London: / Printed for T. Cadell in the Strand. / MDCCLXXIX.

8vo. pp. (6), 91.   328

** This Memorial is not printed in any edition of Franklin's writ-ings, nor so far as I have been able to find, in any other work, though the author of the "Remarks" notes that "the passages between the inverted commas are left out by Almon in his publication of this Me-morial." As it is neither in Almon's *Remembrancer* nor Almon's *Parliamentary Register*, and as neither *Sabin, Rich*, nor the "monthly catalogues" in the *Monthly* and *Critical* reviews mention such a pamphlet, I am unable to find to what the above allusion refers.

1778. The Ephemera.

[The Ephemera; an emblem of Human Life. Passy: Private press of Franklin. 1778.]

o. pp.

329

　　*** See Sparks' edition of Franklin's writings, II, 179.

　　*** Of the bagatelles printed by Franklin on the press which he set up in his house at Passy, only one, so far as I can learn, has been preserved (No. 345), and so my authority for giving such editions of "The Ephemera," "The Whistle" (No. 330), "The Dialogue between Franklin and the Gout" (No. 344), and "Advice to those who would remove to America" (No. 348), is derived from the following statement of the editor in No. 135: "Des quatre pieces qui suivent, les trois premieres n'étoient point destinées à être publiques. Écrites sans aucune prétention, et comme bagatelles de société, elles n'ont été, dans le temps, imprimées qu'au nombe de quinze ou vingt exemplaires, et uniquement pour êtres distribuées parmi les personnes qui composoient la société choisie de Franklin."

1779. The Whistle.

[The Whistle. To Madame Brillon. Passy: Private press of Franklin. 1779.]

o. pp.

330

　　*** See Note to No. 329.

1779. The Whistle. Burlington: 1792.

The Prompter: To which has been added The Whistle. By Dr. Benjamin Franklin. I Have Seen and Not Seen. By Gov. Livingston. Remarkable Speech of Robert Pinder. A Vulgar Error. The Bee and the Drone, &c. Burlington, N. J. 1792.

12mo. pp.

331

　　*** Also printed in Nos. 135, 153, 163, 201 and 227.

1779. Morals of Chess.

Franklin's Game of Chess, with Anecdotes. [n. p. 1780?]

12mo. pp.

332

　　*** Title from John Camden Hotten's *Catalogue . . . of Books . . . relating to America*, Part 34.

1779. Morals of Chess. London: 1797.

Chess Made easy. / New and Comprehensive / Rules /

for playing the / Game of Chess; / . . . . . / to which is prefixed / . . . . . / . . . the Morals / of Chess, written by the / ingenious and learned / Dr. Franklin. / . . . . . / London: / Printed by H. D. Symonds, No. 20, Paternoster Row; / . . . . . [1797.]

Min. pp. 72.   B. M. 333

1779. Morals of Chess. London: 1799.

Chess made easy . . . . . to which is prefixed . . . . the Morals of Chess, written by the ingenious and learned Dr. Franklin . . . . . London: Printed for G. G. J. and J. Robinson. 1799.

o. pp.   334

1779. Morals of Chess. Philadelphia: 1802.

Chess made Easy. / To which is Prefixed / . . . . . / . . . the / Morals of Chess, / Written by the ingenious and learned / Dr. Franklin / . . . . . / Philadelphia: / Printed and Sold by James Humphreys, / . . . / 1802.

Min. pp. 97, (8) plates.   P. H. S. 335

1779. Morals of Chess. London: 1809.

An Easy Introduction to the Game of Chess . . . . . The Morals of Chess by Dr. Franklin. London: 1809.

12mo. pp.   B. M. 336

1779. Morals of Chess. London: 1816.

An Easy Introduction to the Game of Chess . . . . . With the Morals of Chess by Dr. Franklin. London: 1816.

8vo. pp.   B. M. 337

1779. Morals of Chess. London: 1820.

An Easy Introduction to the Game of Chess . . . . . With the Morals of Chess by Dr. Franklin. London: 1820.

12mo. pp.   B. M. 338

1779. Morals of Chess. 1821.

Il giuoco degli Scacchi . . . . . La Morale degli Scacchi, di B. Franklin. [n. p.] 1821.

8vo. pp.   B. M. 339

1779. Morals of Chess. Philadelphia: 1824.

An / Introduction / to the / Game of Chess; / To which

are added / . . . / The Morals of Chess, By Dr. Franklin; / Philadelphia: / Published by H. C. Carey & I. Lea, and Abraham Small; / New York: Bliss & White, and D. Mallory / Jesper Harding, Printer / 1824.

12mo. pp. 267, plate.   P. 340

1779. Morals of Chess.   Boston: 1841.

The Chess Player, / . . . / Containing / Franklin's Essay on the Morals of Chess, / . . . . . / Boston / Published by Nath'l Dearborn, / 1841. /

12mo. pp. 155.   B. 341

1779. Works edited by Vaughan.

Political, Miscellaneous, / and / Philosophical Pieces; / Arranged under the following Heads, and / Distinguished by Initial Letters in each Leaf: / (G. P.) General Politics; / (A. B. T.) American Politics before the Troubles; / (A. D. T.) American Politics during the Troubles; / (P. P.) Provincial or Colony Politics; and / (M. P.) Miscellaneous or Philosophical Pieces; / Written by / Benj. Franklin, LL. D. and F. R. S. / . . . . . / Now first collected, / With Explanatory Plates, Notes, / And an Index to the Whole. / . . . / London: / Printed for J. Johnson, No. 72, St. Paul's Church-Yard. / M DCC LXXIX.

4to. & 8vo. pp. xi, (1), 567, (7) Portrait, 3 plates, folding table. B., C. 342

⁎⁎ Edited by Benjamin Vaughan, who for many years was an intimate friend and correspondent of Franklin. The work is ably performed, many pieces being for the first time printed as Franklin's; and contains valuable notes. But what gives a special value to this collection is that it is the only edition of Franklin's writings (other than his scientific), which was printed during his life time; was done with Franklin's knowledge and consent, and contains an "errata" made by him for it.

⁎⁎ "Before you open this collection of your writings, I must entreat you to hear a few words of apology. My first idea was to collect into one body the several writings which I saw dispersed in different places, so as to form a manual to answer the purposes of the day. Consistently with *this* purpose, I thought I might add a few temporary notes. This idea lasted through the first 50 pages, and I was only checked in it by the sudden appearance of others of your pieces, which I had not before known. Then it was I saw that I had engaged in something

likely to be more than fugitive, and began to be more sparing of my own impertinences . . . Upon a review of the printed pages, I had decided to destroy the whole impression, and wrote Johnson to this effect; but as he told me that he could with the utmost ease cancel the exceptional pages . . . I determined to let the whole lie by me for some time." *Vaughan to Franklin.*

₊₊ Reviewed in *Monthly Review,* LXII, 194. See also Franklin's letter to Vaughan, Nov. 9, 1779.

1779. Works edited by Vaughan. Padova: 1783.

Opere Politiche / di / Beniamino Franklin, LL. D. F. R. S. / Nouvamente raccolte / e / dall' Originale Inglese / recate nella Lingua Italiana / Hominum Rerumque Repertor. / Virg. Œu. 12. / In Padova, MDCCLXXXIII. / Con licenza de' Superiori e Privilegio.

8vo. pp. viii, 287, portrait.   B., P. H. S.   343

1780. Dialogue with the Gout.

[Dialogue between the Gout and Franklin. Passy: Private press of Franklin. 1780.]

o. pp.   344

₊₊ See note to 329.

1780. Works.

Des / Herrn D. Benjamin Franklin's, / . . . / sämmtliche Werke. / Aus dem Englischen und Französischen übersetzt. / Nebst / des französischen Uebersetzers / des Herrn Barbey Dubourg, / Zusätzen, / und mit einigen Anmerkungen versehen / von / G. T. Wenzel. / Erster Band, mit Kupfern. / Dresden, 1780. / In der Waltherischen Hofbuchhandlung.

3 Vols. 8vo. pp. (12), 502, portrait, 5 plates—(12), 442, 9 plates—(12), 636.   P. H. S., B.   344*

₊₊ A union of Dubourg's and Vaughan's editions.

1782. Fictitious Supplement.

Volume VII. Number 1,095. / Supplement / To the Boston Chronicle / Monday, March 13, 1782. [Passy: Private press of Franklin. 1782.]

Folio. Broadside.   c.   345

₊₊ This is a skit on the Great British Public, being a close imitation of a Boston newspaper, with letter from Paul Jones, British Advertisements for Scalps, and account of bundles of Scalps of the Americans consigned by the Indians in British pay to Agents in London, all of which fell into the hands of the Yankees and hence this exposure in

the newspaper. This "Supplement" . . . is believed to be unique. *Henry Stevens.*

⁎ "Enclosed I send you a few copies of a paper that places in a striking light, the English barbarities in America, particularly those committed by the savages at their instigation. The FORM may perhaps not be genuine, but the *substance* is truth." *Franklin to Dumas.*

⁎ "Have you seen in the papers the excellent letter of Paul Jones to Sir Joseph York? *Elle nous dit bien des vérités.* I doubt poor Sir Joseph cannot answer them! Dr. Franklin himself, I should think, was the author. It is certainly from a first-rate pen, and not a common man-of-war." *Horace Walpole.*

1782. Fictitious Letters.

Two / Letters / from / Dr. Franklin, / to the / Earl of Shelburne / . . . / . . . / London: / Printed for M. Follingsby, Temple-Bar; and J. Debrett, / Piccadilly. [1782.]
　　　　　　　　　　8vo. pp. (4), 31.　　　　　　c. 346
⁎ Not by Franklin.

1782. Works.

Opere Filosofiche di Beniamino Franklin. Nuovamente raccolte, e dall, origine inglese recate in lingua italiana. Padova. 1783.
　　　　　　　　　　8vo.　　　　　　B. M. 347

1784. Autobiography. See 1789.

1784. Advice to Emigrants. Passy: 1784.

[Advice to such as would remove to America. Passy: Private press of Franklin. 1784.]
　　　　　　　　　　o. pp.　　　　　　348
⁎ See Note to No. 329. Franklin speaks of the English edition (No. 367) as "reprinted," proving that there was a prior edition. See *Monthly Review,* LXXI, 146.

1784. Advice to Emigrants. Paris: 1784.

Avis à ceux qui voudraient s'en aller en Amérique. [Translated from the English of B. Franklin.] 1784.
　　　　　　　　　　8vo. pp.　　　　　B. M. 349
⁎ Title from British Museum Catalogue.

1784. Advice to Emigrants. Hamburg: 1786.

Bericht für Diejenigen so sich nach Nordamerika begehen wollen: Aus dem Englischen, von Dr. B. Franklin. Hamburg: Herold. 1786.
　　　　　　　　　　8vo. pp.　　　　　　350

1784. Advice to Emigrants. London: 1794.

Information / to those / who would remove to / America /
By Dr. Benjamin Franklin. / London: / Sold by M. Gurney
. . . J. Johnson, / . . . D. I. Eaton, . . . R. / H. West-
ley, . . . and J. Ridgeway, . . . / 1794. / Price Six Pence.

8vo. pp. 23, (1).   c. 351

1784. Advice to Emigrants. London: 1796.

Information [+351+] London: Sold by M. Gurney . .
. . . 1796.

4to. pp.   352

1784. Advice to Emigrants. [n. p., 179–?]

Auszug / de / Anmerkungen / zum / Unterricht verjeni-
gen Europaer, / die sich in Amerika niederzulassen geson-
nen sind, / dem lektlich verstorbenen ber uhmten / Dr.
Franklin. / [n. p. n. d.]

12mo. pp. 8.   c. 353

⁎ Also printed in Nos. 122, 135, and 367–372.

1784. Exposure of Mesmerism. Paris: 1784.

Exposé / des Expériences / qui ont été faites pour l'Examen / du Magnétisme Animal. / Lu à l'Académie de
Sciences, par M. Bailly, / en son nom & au nom du MM.
Franklin, / Le Roy, De Borg & Lavoisier, / le 4 Septembre
1784 / Imprimé par ordre du Roi. / A Paris, / de l'Imprimerie Royale. / M.DCCLXXXIV.

Folio. pp. 15.   P. H. S. 354

⁎ The official edition, printed at the King's private press in the
Louvre.

1784. Exposure of Mesmerism. Paris: 1784.

Exposé / [⁎354⁎] / Imprimé par ordre du Roi, / Sur la
Copie imprimée au Louvre. / A Paris, / Chez Moutard,
Imprimeur-Libraire de la Reine / & de l'Academie Royale
des Sciences, Hotel de / Cluni, rue des Mathurins. /
M.DCC.LXXXIV.

8vo. pp. (2), 15.   P. H. S. 355

1784. Rainfall.

On the different Quantities of Rain which / fall, at different Heights over the same / Spot of Ground, with a Let-

ter from Benja- / min Franklin, LL. D.   By Thomas Per- / cival, M. D. &c.   Read January 21, 1784. [London: 1784.]

8vo.   pp. 8.   356

** Reprinted from the *Transactions* of the Royal Society.

1784. Report on Mesmerism. Paris: 1784.

Rapport / des / Commissaires / chargés par le Roi, / de l'Examen / du / Magnétisme Animal. / Imprimé par ordre du Roi. / A Paris, / de l'Imprimerie Royale. / M.DCC.-LXXXIV.

Sm. Folio.   pp. (2), 66.   P. H. S.   357

** Mesmer came to Paris in 1778 and began the practice of his pretended cure-all with so much success that by 1784 the delusion had reached a point which required official interference, and the king appointed a Commission to investigate his theory, of which Franklin was made a member, and though prevented by illness from witnessing the tests made by his fellow commissioners, yet he had a series of experiments made at Passy, and signed the adverse report they made to the king. The "Report" and the "Account" (No. 354) occasioned a very heated pamphlet discussion between Mesmer's supporters and opponents, all of which relate more or less to Franklin, but in view of the slight part Franklin took in the whole affair it has seemed unnecessary to give more than the following titles:

Observations / sur / les deux Rapport de MM. Les Commissaires / Nominées par son Majesté / pour l'Examen du Magnétisme Animal / Par M. D'Eslon / A Philadelphie ; / Et se trouve a Paris, Chez Clousier, · · · / · · · · · / 1784. Folio. (2).   pp. 31.   P. H. S.   358

Refléxions / Impartiales / sur / le Magnétisme Animal, / Faites après la publication du Rapport des / Commissaires, chargés par le Roi de l'Examen / de cette Decouverte. / A Geneve, Chez Barthelemie Chirot, · · · / · · · / · · · / · · · / 1784. 8vo.   pp. (2), 84.   P. H. S.   359

1784. Report on Mesmerism. Paris: 1784.

Rapport / [*357*] / Imprimé par ordre du Roi. / Sur la Copie imprimée au Louvre. / A Paris, / Chez Moutard, Imprimeur-Libraire de la Reine, & / de l'Academie Royale des Sciences, rue des Mathurins, / Hotel de Cluni. / M.DCC.LXXXIV.

8vo.   pp. (2), 80.   P. H. S., B.   360

1784. Report on Mesmerism. London: 1785.

Report / of / Dr. Benjamin Franklin, / and other / Commissioners, / charged by the / King of France, / with the

Examination of the / Animal Magnetism, / as now practised at Paris. / Translated from the French. / With an / Historical Introduction. / London: / Printed for J. Johnson, (No. 72) St. Paul's / Church-Yard.   1785.

8vo.   pp. xx, 108.   c. 361

1784. Report on Mesmerism.   Philadelphia: 1837.

Animal Magnetism. / Report of Dr. Franklin / and other Commissioners, / charged by the King of France with the Examination of the / Animal Magnetisms as practised at Paris. / Translated from the French. / With / an Historical Outline of the "Science." / . . . . . / Philadelphia: / Published by H. Perkins, Chestnut Street. / 1837.

8vo.   pp. (4), 58.   362

1784. Report on Mesmerism.   Philadelphia: 1837.

Animal Magnetism / [*362*] Second Edition. / Philadelphia: / Published by H. Perkins, Chestnut Street. / 1837.

8vo.   pp. (4), 58.   P. H. S. 363

1784. Remarks on the Savages.   Passy: 1784.

[Remarks concerning the Savages of North America. Passy: Private Press of Franklin.   1784.]

o. pp.   364

⁎⁎ "The following *Remarks*, written by Dr. Franklin, and printed by himself, for his own amusement, at his own house at Passy, near Paris." *Advertisement* to No. 365.

1784. Remarks on the Savages.   Birmingham: 1784.

Remarks concerning the Savages of North America. Birmingham: Printed by Pearson and Rollason.   1784.

8vo.   pp.   c. 365

⁎⁎ This title is from the *Monthly Review*, LXXI, 70, where it is followed by a critique. The "Advertisement" prefixed to this edition was probably by Joseph Priestley.

1784. Remarks on the Savages.   Paris: 1794.

Observations / sur / les Sauvages du Nord / de l'Amérique. / Par Franklin. / [Paris: A. A. Renouard.   1795.]

12mo. pp. 28.   c. 366

⁎⁎ See Note to 135.

1784. Two Tracts.   First edition.   London: 1784.

Two Tracts: / Information / to those / who would remove to / America / And, / Remarks / concerning the / Savages of North America / By / Dr. Benjamin Franklin. / London: / Printed for John Stockdale, opposite / Burlington-House, / Piccadilly. / MDCCLXXXIV.

8vo. pp. 39, (1).   B. 367

⁎⁎* For the original editions of these two pieces, see Nos. 348 and 364.

1784. Two Tracts.   Second Edition.   London: 1784.

Two Tracts: / [⁎367⁎] By Dr. Benjamin Franklin. / The Second Edition. / London: / [⁎367⁎] / MDCCLXXXIV.

8vo. pp. 39, (1).   c. 368

1784. Two Tracts.   Third Edition.   London: 1784.

Two Tracts: / [⁎367⁎] / The Third Edition. / London: / [⁎367⁎] / MDCCLXXXIV.

8vo. pp. 39, (1).   c. 369

1784. Two Tracts.   Dublin: 1784.

Two Tracts: / [⁎367⁎] / By / Benjamin Franklin. / Dublin: / Printed for L. White, No. 86, Dane-street, / MDCCLXXXIV.

8vo. pp. 40.   A. A. S. 370

1784. Two Tracts.   Padua: 1785.

Observazione / A Chiunque dersideri passare in / America; / E Riflessioni / Circa I Salvaggi dell' America settentrionale / Del Dre. Franklin / Dall' Originale Inglese regate / in Lingua Italiano / Da Pietro Antoricutti. / In Padova MDCCLXXV / Per Gio: Antonio Conzatti, A. S. Fermo. / Con Lic. de' Superiori.

12mo. pp. 38, (1).   c. 371

1785. Maritime Observations.   Philadelphia: 1786.

Maritime Observations: In a letter from Doctor Franklin, to Mr. Alphonsus Le Roy, member of several academies, at Paris.   Philadelphia, printed by Robert Aitken. M.DCC.LXXXVI.

4to. pp. 293–329, 2 plates.   c. 372

_**_* Reprinted from the *"Transactions of the American Philosoph-ical Society,"* Vol. II.   See *Monthly Review*, LVI, 467.

1785. Maritime Observations.   Paris: 1787.

Lettre de Monsieur Benjamin Franklin à Monsieur David Le Roy, Membre de Plusieurs Académies, &c. Contenant Observations sur la Marine.   Paris: 1787.

8vo. pp.   372

1785. Maritime Observations.   London: 1787.

Hydraulic and Nautical / Observations / on the Current / in the Atlantic Ocean, / forming an hypothetical Theo-rem / For Investigation. / With a Corresponding Chart of that Ocean. / Addressed to Navigators / By Governor Pownall, F. R. S. & F. S. A. / To which are annexed some notes / By Dr. Franklin. / London, / Printed for Robert Sayer, No. 53, Fleet-Street / MDCCLXXXVII.

4to. pp. 17, map.   c. 373

_**_* This only contains Franklin's "Observations" on the Gulf-stream.

1785. Smoky Chimneys.   Philadelphia: 1787.

Observations on the Causes and Cure of Smoky Chim-neys, By Benjamin Franklin.   In a letter to Dr. Ingen-Housz, Physician to the Emperor, at Vienna.   Philadel-phia: 1787.

8vo. pp.   374

_**_* Title from the David King auction catalogue.   A reprint from the *Transactions of the American Philosophical Society.*

1785. Smoky Chimneys.   London: 1787.

Observations / on the / Causes and Cure / of / Smoky Chimneys. / By his Excellency / Benjamin Franklin, LL. D. F. R. S. / . . . . . / In a / Letter to Dr. Ingen-Housz. / . . . / Illustrated by a copper-plate. / Philadelphia, Printed: / London: Reprinted for J. Debrett, / Opposite / Burlington-House, in Piccadilly; and J. Sewell, in Corn-hill. / M. DCC. LXXXVII.

8vo. pp. (4), 56, plate.   B. 375

1785. Smoky Chimneys.   London: 1787.

Observations / [_*375_*] / Illustrated by a copper-plate /

Second Edition / Philadelphia, Printed: / London: Reprinted for J. Debrett. / [*375*] M.DCC.LXXXVII.

8vo.   pp. (4), 56.   c.   376

1785. Smoky Chimneys.   London: 1793.

Observations / on / Smoky Chimneys, / their / Causes
and Cure; / with / Considerations on Fuel and Stoves. /
Illustrated with Proper Figures / By / Benjamin Franklin,
LL. D. / London: / Printed for I. and J. Taylor, at the
Architectural Library, / No. 56, opposite Great Turnstile,
Holburn. / M.DCC.XCIII. / (Price 2s.)

8vo.   pp. iv, 80, 2 plates.   Y. C.   377

1785. Letter on Privateering.

Observations on a late publication intituled Thoughts
on Executive Justice.   To which is added A Letter containing Remarks on the same work . . . London: I. Cadell.   M.DCC.LXXXVI.

Min.   pp. (4), 162.   c.   378

*** The Observations were written by Sir Samuel Romilly, in reply
to Dr. Madan's *Thoughts on Executive Justice*, and appended to it is
Franklin's reply to the same work, which is printed as "A Letter from
a Gentleman Abroad."

1787. Proclamation.

[Proclamation of the President [B. Franklin] and Executive Council, offering a Reward for the Apprehension
of Daniel Shays and others.   March 10, 1787.]

Folio.   Broadside.   379

*** Title from Massachusetts Historical Society Catalogue.

1787. Works edited by Bancroft.

Philosophical / and Miscellaneous Papers. / Lately written by / B. Franklin, L L. D. / . . . . . / London: /
Printed for C. Dilly, in the Poultry. / M.DCC.LXXXVII.

8vo.   pp. (6), 186, 4 plates.   B., C.   380

*** This includes Nos. 348, 364, 372, 374, 378, and "The Internal
State of America."   The volume was edited by Dr. Edward Bancroft,
who in the *advertisement* announces a second volume, but this was
never printed.

1789. Court of the Press?   Copenhagen: 1798.

Et Par Ord om Trykkefriheden. Ved B. Franklin.
Oversat af Jorg. Kierulf. Kjobenhavn. 1798.

o. pp.   381

_**_* Title from Brunn's *Bibliotheca Danica*.

1789. Fictitious Advice.

Avis / Aux Faiseurs / de / Constitutions. / Par M. Benjamin Franklin. / [Paris:] 1789.

8vo. pp. 12.   382

_**_* Barbier states that this was written by the Abbé Morellet, but
according to Morellet's *Mémoirs* it was by Franklin, and merely translated by the former. It was first printed in the *Federal Gazette*.

1789. Autobiography.   General Note.

_**_* The Autobiography of Franklin was written by him at four dif-
ferent periods:

I.   From 1706 to 1731 at Twyford in 1771.
II. For 1731 at Passy in 1784.
III. From 1731 to 1757 at Philadelphia in 1788.
IV. From 1757 to 1759 at Philadelphia in 1789.

_**_* Franklin's MS. of the first part fell into the hands of Abel
James, who sent to him a copy of it, which Franklin in turn sent to
Benjamin Vaughan; and other copies of this part of the life were in
the possession of Thomas Jefferson and Mathew Carey. A small continuation was added to the work at Passy in 1784, and a copy of this
second part, (and probably of the whole work), was left with some one
in France, when Franklin returned to America. In 1788, the third
part was written, and two copies of the three parts were made; one of
which he sent to Benjamin Vaughan in England, and the other to
Louis Le Veillard in France. In the next year he added the portion
with which the work concludes. Thus there were at least eight copies,
more or less complete, of the autobiography in MS. when Franklin
died.

_**_* In 1791, a translation in French of the first part was printed in
Paris, which was the first appearance of any portion of the autobiography in print; and a re-translation of this French translation has
practically become the "popular" edition of the Autobiography. The
second part was first printed in *La Decade* for February, 1798, and was
reprinted from that journal in Castéra's edition of Franklin's writings
published at Paris in 1798. In 1818, William Temple Franklin published the first edition as written by Franklin (which was also the first
appearance in print of the third part), from the MS. copy sent by
Franklin to Le Veillard. In 1828, the fourth and concluding part was

first printed in the French edition of his writings published in Paris by Renouard.   The complete work, as Franklin wrote it, was not printed till Mr. Bigelow's edition was issued.   It is a curious fact that of the four portions into which the autobiography was in a certain sense divided, three should have first appeared in the French language, from French presses.

.*. As the Autobiography, in its completest form, only comes to the year 1759, several of the editors of the various editions have written continuations.   The first was compiled by the editor of the Paris edition of 1791, from Wilmer's "Memoirs" of Franklin, and therefore was of necessity so valueless that it was never reprinted.   The second was by the editor of the "Private Life" of Franklin as printed in London in 1793, and like the first has never been reprinted.   The third was an appropriation of that part of Henry Stuber's biography of Franklin, (printed in the *Columbian Magazine*, 1790–91), which fitted on to the autobiography, and was first printed in the "Works" of Franklin, as edited by Benjamin Vaughan and published at London in 1793; and this "continuation" by Stuber has been that used in most of the "popular" editions of the autobiography.   The fourth "continuation" was printed in 1815 in a chap-book edition of Franklin's works, and was from the lively imagination of Mason Locke Weems.   The fifth was written by his grandson William Temple Franklin, and printed by him in his "Memoirs" of Franklin, published in London in 1818.   The sixth, from an unknown pen, was first printed in Chambers' edition of Franklin's writings as published at Edinburgh in 1838, and is of trifling value, being compiled almost wholly from Temple Franklin's "Memoirs."   The seventh was written by Jared Sparks and was first published in his edition of Franklin's writings in 1840.   The eighth was a re-hash of Mr. Sparks' continuation, from the pen of the Rev. Horatio Hastings Weld, and was added to the edition of the autobiography published in New York in 1848.   The ninth is a skillful dovetailing of Franklin's own writings, done by John Bigelow, and printed at Philadelphia in 1874.   The tenth is a very brief sketch added to the "Riverside Literature Series" edition of the autobiography, and was written by Horace E. Scudder.   The eleventh, by D. H. Montgomery, was prepared for the school-book edition of the autobiography published at Boston in 1888.   Other editors have added an occasional note or a new preface, but these eleven are all the "continuations" as yet printed.

.*. Thus there are four issues of the autobiography, differing in completeness, and seven differing in text, which with the translations, re-translations, and eleven continuations, make up a series of widely differing books, which are nevertheless all included for simplicity in one chronological list.   Many apparent editions of the autobiography are really classed under "Works," 1793.   The following is a list of the first editions of such issues of the autobiography as are necessary for the different texts and continuations:

Mémoires de la Vie . . . . . Paris: 1791.	No. 383
Private Life . . . . . London: 1793.	No. 386
Works . . . . . London: 1793.	No. 437
Vie . . . . . Paris: An VI [1799.]	No. 448
Life . . . . . Baltimore: 1815.	No. 476
Memoirs . . . . . London: 1818.	No. 562
Mémoires sur la Vie . . . . . Paris: 1828.	No. 403
Life . . . . . Edinburgh: 1838.	No. 517
Life . . . . . Boston: 1844.	No. 407
Autobiography . . . . . New York: 1849.	No. 413
Autobiography . . . . . Philadelphia: 1868.	No. 423
Life . . . . . Philadelphia: 1874.	No. 424
Autobiography . . . . . Boston: 1886.	No. 430
Life . . . . . Boston: 1888.	No. 435

*** See Dr. S. A. Green's *Story of a Famous Book*, Mr. Bigelow's preface to his edition of the Autobiography, Mr. McMaster's *Benjamin Franklin*, and the introduction infra, for more concerning this work.

1789. Autobiography edited by Gibelin. Paris: 1791.

Mémoires / de la Vie Privée / de Benjamin Franklin, / Écrits par lui-même, / et Adressés a son fils; / Suivis d'un Précis historique de sa Vie / politique, et de plusieurs Pièces, relatives / à ce Père de la Liberté. / A Paris, / Chez Buisson, Libraire, rue Haute-feuille, no. 20. / 1791.

8vo. pp. (2) vi, 156, 363 [for 207].   C., B. 383

*** The first edition of Franklin's Autobiography. *Quérard* attributes the translation to Dr. Jacques Gibelin. The portion written by Franklin is only to the year 1731, and the remainder of his life is a translation from Wilmer's *Memoirs* of Franklin, with the most objectionable statements omitted.

*** It is still an unsolved question where Buisson obtained the MS. from which this edition was printed. It was, to judge from Buisson's willingness to prove its authenticity by showing the MS., in Franklin's handwriting; yet we have Mr. Veillard's statement that his copy was not used, which is confirmed by the printing only to the year 1731, and this also is fair proof that the copy mentioned in the preliminary note, with the second part, was not used. The only explanations seem to be either the use of the copy in the possession of Abel James, of Philadelphia, or the existence of an unknown copy in Franklin's autograph. Owing to William Temple Franklin's delay in the publication of the autobiography in English, this edition was twice translated into that language, the first in No. 386, and the second in the "Works" of Franklin as published by Benjamin Vaughan in 1793, No. 437.

1789. Autobiography. Berlin: 1792.

Benjamin Franklin's / Jugendjahre, / von ihm selbst / für seinen Sohn beschrieben / und übersetzt / von / Gottfried August Bürger. / Berlin, 1792. / Bey Heinrich August Rottman.

12mo. pp. 214.   C., B., P. H. S.   384

** Contains only the first part, without continuation.

1789. Autobiography. Stockholm: 1792.

Benjamin / Franklins / Enskildta Lefwerne / upsatt af honom sielf och / staldt til hans Son. / Hwartil aro bifogade arskillige Han- / delser och omdomen, som anga denne store Man. / Ofwersattning / Stockholm, / Tryckt hos Anders Jac. Nordstrom, 1792.

8vo. pp. 218, (4), portrait.   c.   385

1789. Autobiography. London: 1793.

The / Private Life / of the late / Benjamin Franklin, LL. D. / late Minister Plenipotentiary from the United / States of America to France, &c., &c., &c. / Originally written by Himself, / and now translated from the French. / To which are added, / some account of his Public Life, a variety of / Anecdotes concerning him, by M.M. Brissot, / Condorcet, Rochefoucault, Le Roy, &c., &c. / and the Eulogium of M. Fauchet, / Constitutional Bishop of the Department of Calvados, / and a Member of the National Convention. / . . . / . . . / . . . / London: / Printed for J. Parsons, No. 21 Pater-Noster Row. / 1793.

8vo. pp, xvi, 324.   c.   386

** A wretched re-translation from the Paris edition (No. 383) with a continuation by the English editor, whose knowledge of Franklin and French are about equal. Though "Grub street" is apparent in the whole volume, it must nevertheless always be of interest as the first version of Franklin's autobiography which appeared in English. It is reviewed in the *Monthly Review*, N. S. XII, 307.

1789. Autobiography. New York: 1794.

The / Life / of / Dr. Benjamin Franklin. / Written by himself. / Second American Edition. / Philadelphia: / Printed for Benjamin Johnson, / No. 147 High-Street / M,DCC,XCIV.

12mo.   pp. 192, (2).   c. 387

*** There is also apparently a variation of this edition, pp. 197, (3). It is Vaughan's translation (No. 437), from the French edition (No. 383), as are all the following English editions, except as noted. The first American edition is described under 1793, (No. 446).

1789. Autobiography.   New York: 1794.

The Life of Benjamin Franklin. Written by Himself. Third American Edition. New York: Printed and sold by T. and J. Swords. 1794.

Min.   pp. 214, portrait.   388

*** Title from Stevens' *Historical Nuggets.*

1789. Autobiography.   Danbury: 1795.

The / Life / of / Dr. Benjamin Franklin. / Written by himself. / Fourth American Edition. / Danbury: / Printed and sold by N. Douglas. / M.DCC.XCV.

Min.   pp. 207, (4), portrait.   389

1789. Autobiography.   Tubingen: 1795.

D. Benjamin Franklin's Leben.   Tubingen: 1795.

8vo.   pp.   390

*** Vol. I of "Biographien für die Jugend." Title from *Sabin.*

1789. Autobiography.   Salem: 1796.

The / Life / of / Dr. Benjamin Franklin / Written by himself. / Salem: / Printed for Cushing and Carlton, at the / Bible and Heart. / 1796.

12mo.   pp. 132.   A. A. S.   391

1789. Autobiography.   Albany: 1797.

The / Life / of / Dr. Benjamin Franklin. / Written by himself. / First Albany Edition. / Albany: / Printed and sold by / Barber & Southwick / Faust's Statue below the Dutch Church, / State Street. / 1797.

12mo.   pp. 177, (3).   P. L.   392

1789. Autobiography.   Madrid: 1798.

Vida del Dr. Benjamin Franklin, sacada de documentos auténticos.   Madrid: Imprenta de P. Aznar.   1798.

8vo.   pp. xxii, 216.   393

*** Title from *Swift.*

1789. Autobiography.   Wilmington: 1799.

The / Life / of / Doctor / Benjamin Franklin. / Written by himself. / Fourth American Edition. / Wilmington: / Printed and sold by Peter Brynburg / 1799.

Min. pp. 178, (1).   c. 394

1789. Autobiography.   Montpelier: 1809.

The / Life / of / Dr. Benjamin Franklin / written by Himself. / Montpelier: / Printed by Samuel Gross / for Josiah Parks. / 1809.

12mo. pp. 202.   c. 395

⁎ Contains a preface by the publisher.

1789. Autobiography.   North Shields: 1809.

The / Life / of / Dr. Benj. Franklin. / Written / by himself. / And / continued / By Dr. Stuber. / . . . . . / North Shields: / Printed by T. Appleby, / . . . . . / 1809.

12mo. pp. 194.   P. H. S. 396

⁎ Contains the preface prefixed to Vaughan's edition. The date on the board cover is 1810.

1789. Autobiography.   Poughnill: [181–?]

The Life of Benjamin Franklin, LL. D. [Portrait.] Printed and sold by George Nicholson, Poughnill, near Ludlow, sold in London by T. Conder, 30 Bucklersbury, Champante and Whitrow, 4 Jewry Street, Aldgate, R. Bickerstaff, 210 Strand, and all other Booksellers. [181–?]

12mo. pp. (2), 56.   397

⁎ Title from Stevens' *Historical Nuggets*.

1789. Autobiography.   Philadelphia: 1811.

The / Life / of / the late Doctor / Benjamin Franklin. / Written by Himself. / Philadelphia: / Published by Johnson & Warner, No. 147, / Market Street. / 1811. / W. M'Culloch, Printer.

Min. pp. 104, (4).   P. H. S. 398

1789. Autobiography.   New York: 1813.

The / Life / of the late / Dr. Benjamin Franklin. / Written by Himself. / New York: / Published by Evert Duyckinck, / No. 102 Pearl-Street. / J. C. Totten, Printer / 1813.

Min. pp. 104.   P. L. 399

1789. Autobiography. Reading: 1820.

Der / Weg zum Glück, / oder / Leben und Meynungen / des / Dr. Benjamin Franklin. / Von ihm selbst geschrieben. / Reading, / gedruckt und zu haben bey Heinrich B. Gage, / 1820.

Min. pp. 128.   c. 400

1789. Autobiography. New York: 1824.

The / Life / of / Dr. Benjamin Franklin. / Written by Himself. / New-York: / Printed by Clayton & Van Norden, / No. 64 Pine-street. / 1824.

Min. pp. (2), 90, portrait.   B. 401

⁎*⁎ The engraved title is: "The / Life of / Benjamin Franklin, / written by himself. / S. King. / New York. / 1824."

1789. Autobiography. New York: 1825.

The / Life / of / Dr. Benjamin Franklin. / Written by himself. / New-York: / Printed by Hopkins & Morris, / No. 48 Pine-street. / 1825.

Min. pp. (2), 192, portrait.   P. 402

⁎*⁎ The engraved title is: "The / Life of / Benjamin Franklin, / written by himself. / D. Mallory. / New-York / 1825."

1789. Autobiography. Paris: 1828.

Mémoires / sur la Vie / de / Benjamin Franklin, / Écrits par lui-même. / Traduction nouvelle. / Tome premier. / Paris. / Jules Renouard, Libraire, / Rue de Tournon, No. 6. / MDCCCXXVIII.

2 Vols. Min. pp. viij, 346 (1), portrait—(4), 257, (2), portrait. B., C. 403

⁎*⁎ This is a new translation of the autobiography, made by A. C. Renouard, from the Le Veillard MS. It contains the fourth part of the autobiography, and was the first appearance in print of it.

1789. Autobiography. Cincinnati: 1830.

The / Life / of / Dr. Benjamin Franklin / Written by himself. / Cincinnati: / Published by Morgan & Sanxay and / Robinson & Fairbanks / 1830.

Min. pp. (2), 192, portrait.   403*

⁎*⁎ The engraved title is "The / Life of / Benjamin Franklin / written by Himself. / Robinson and Wright. / Cincinnati / 1828."

1789. Autobiography. London: 1833.
The Life of Benjamin Franklin, written by himself.
London: 1833.

8vo. pp.   B. M. 404

1789. Autobiography. Copenhagen: 1837.
Bogtrykeren / Benjamin Franklin's / Liv og Levnet /
Af / J. W. Marckmann / Ordineret Katechtved True Kirche
/ . . . / Priis overalt / Denmark 28 hestet. / Kjobenhavn
/ . . . / 1837.

Min. pp. iv, 159, (5).   C. 405

1789. Autobiography. Leipsic: 1839.
Leben / des / Benjamin Franklin / von / ihm selbst
geschrieben. / Leipsic, Verlag von Georg Wigand. [1839.]

Min. pp. 158.   406

_*[*]_* This is the Temple Franklin text.

1789. Autobiography. Edinburgh: 1839.
Life of Benjamin Franklin. Edinburgh: 1839.

o. pp.   407

_*[*]_* Title from *Sabin.*

1789. Autobiography. Boston: 1844.
The / Life / of / Benjamin Franklin. / Containing / the
Autobiography with notes, / and / A Continuation. / By
Jared Sparks. / . . . . . / Boston: / Published by Tappan
and Dement. / 1844.

8vo. pp. xv, (5), 612, 6 plates.   409

_*[*]_* A separate issue of Vol. 1 of the writings of Franklin as edited
by Jared Sparks and published in 1840. It is the Temple Franklin
text.

1789. Autobiography. Boston: 1845.
The / Life / [_*408_*] / Boston: / Published by Charles
Tappan. / 1845.

8vo. pp. xv, (5), 612, 6 plates.   410

1789. Autobiography. Philadelphia: 1846.
The Life of Benjamin Franklin. Philadelphia: 1846.

Min. pp.   411

_*[*]_* Title from *Swift.*

1789. Autobiography. Leipzic: 1848.

Leben des Benjamin Franklin von ihm selbst geschrieben. Leipzig: 1848.

Min. pp.   B. M.   412

⁎*⁎ Vol. II of "Geschichts-Bibliothek für Volk."

1789. Autobiography. New York: 1849.

Benjamin Franklin: / his / Autobiography; / with a Narrative of / his public life and services. / By Rev. H. Hastings Weld. / With numerous designs by J. G. Chapman. / New York: / Harper & Brothers, Publishers, / 82 Cliff street.

8vo.   pp. xvi, (2), 549, portrait.   B.   413

⁎*⁎ The Temple Franklin text of the autobiography, with a continuation purporting to be by Weld, but which is really a re-hash of Mr. Sparks' continuation.

⁎*⁎ The engraved title is: "Autobiography / of / B. Franklin / New York: / Harper and Brothers / MDCCCXLIX." There are copies with the imprint: "New York: / Harper and Brothers / MDCCCXLIX. / London: Sampson Low, 169, Fleet Street." and the work was originally issued in eight parts, with the following title on the covers:

Part I. 25 cents / Benjamin Franklin: / His Autobiography, / and a narrative of / His Public Life and Services / Splendidly Embellished / by numerous exquisite Designs / by Chapman / New York: / Harper Brothers. / MDCCCXLIX.

1789. Autobiography. London: 1850.

The / Autobiography / of / Benjamin Franklin. / Published verbatim from the original Manuscript, / by his grandson, / William Temple Franklin, / Edited by / Jared Sparks, / . . . / London: / Henry G. Bohn, York Street, Covent Garden. / 1850.

12mo.   pp. vi, 154.   P. L.   414

⁎*⁎ This edition does not contain Sparks' continuation. The title on the board cover is:

Bohn's / Shilling Series. / The Genuine / Autobiography of / Benjamin Franklin / Complete / in / One Volume / London. / Henry Bohn, . . . / 1850.

1789. Autobiography. Dessau: 1854.

The Life / of / Benjamin, Franklin / Vol. I / B. Franklin's Autobiography / with an Appendix / Authorized Edition. / Dessau: / Katz Brothers / 1854.

2 vols. 12mo. pp. x, 239, fac simile.—xii, 243.   415

_**_* The half-title is: "Standard / American Authors / published under the Superintendence / of / Dr. Karl Elze . . . / Vol. II" and the title of Vol. II is: "The Life / of / Benjamin Franklin / Vol. II. / A Continuation / To B. Franklin's Autobiography. / By Jared Sparks / . . . / Dessau: / Katz Brothers. / 1854." Sabin also mentions this work with the imprint. "Leipzig. A. Dürr. [185–?]"

1789. Autobiography. Boston: 1856.

The / Life / [_*408_*] / Boston: / Whittemore, Niles, and Hall. / Milwaukee: A. Whittemore & Co. / 1856.

8vo. pp. xv, (2), 612.   B.   416

1789. Autobiography. Brussels: 1856.

Mémoires / de / Benjamin Franklin, / Avec un Autographe, / Traduits de l'Anglais / par / F. Lancelot, Avocat / Tome I. / Bruxelles, / Librairie Polytechnique de Aug. Decq, / 9, rue de la Madeleine. / 1856.

2 Vols. 12mo. pp. (4), iv, 263, facsimile.   417

1789. Autobiography. Leipsic: 1859.

Benjamin Franklin's Autobiography. Im Auszuge und mit anmerkungen hrsg. Leipzig: Gerhard. 1859.

2 Vols. 8vo.   418

_**_* Title from *Kayser*. It contains Sparks' continuation, and is part of "Bibliothek der Englischen literatur für Schule und Haus."

1789. Autobiography. London: 1860.

The / Autobiography / [_*414_*] / London: / [_*414_*] / 1860.

12mo. pp. vi, 154, covers.   B.   419

1789. Autobiography. Paris: 1866.

Mémoires [+417+] Paris: Libraire central. 1866.

12mo. pp.   420

_**_* Title from *Lorenz*.

1789. Autobiography. Paris: 1866.

Mémoires / de / Benjamin Franklin / Écrits par lui-même / Traduits de l'Anglais, et annotés / par / Édouard Laboulaye. / . . . . . / Paris / Librairie de L. Hachette et Cie. / . . . / 1866. / . . .

12mo. pp. (4), 400.   421

_**_* This is really Vol. I of a four-volume collection of the writings of Franklin. See under 1867.

1789. Autobiography.   Paris: 1866.

Mémoires / [*421*] / Edouard Laboulaye / . . . . . /
Deuxième Édition / Paris / [*421*]. / 1866 / . . .

12mo.   pp. (4), 400.   422

1789. Autobiography.   Philadelphia: 1868.

Autobiography / of / Benjamin Franklin. / Edited from
his Manuscript, with Notes / and an Introduction, / By /
John Bigelow / . . . . . / Philadelphia: / J. B. Lippincott
& Co. / London: Trübner & Co. / 1868.

Rl. 8vo. & 8vo.   pp. 409, portrait.   423

✱*✱ This is not only the first appearance of the autobiography from
Franklin's own copy, but also the first publication in English of the
four parts, and the first publication of the very important "outline"
autobiography.   It is therefore the first edition of *the* autobiography,
and all references to that work in this volume must be understood to
refer to this edition except as noted.

✱*✱ Mr. Bigelow has so thoroughly told the story of the history and
recovery of this original MS. of Franklin, in the preface to this work
and in Vol. 1 of his edition of Franklin's writings, that nothing is left
to say.   This edition is reviewed in *The Athenæum*, No. 2128, August
8, 1868; *International Review*, II, 692; by Henri Moreau in *Revue
Contemporaine* (Paris), 1868; *The Nation*, July 9, 1868; *Saturday Review* (London), 1868; *Boston Advertiser*, May 16, 1868; *National Intelligencer*, Aug. 29, 1868; *New York World*, May 21, 1868; *Spring-
field Republican*, May 13, 1868; *New York Tribune*, 1868; *The New
Englander*, 1868; and *Harper's Magazine*, XXXVII, 274.

1789. Autobiography.   Philadelphia: 1874.

The Life / of / Benjamin Franklin, / written by himself.
/ Now first edited from original manuscripts / and from
his printed correspondence / and other writings, / by / John
Bigelow. / Vol. I. / . . . . . / Philadelphia: / J. B. Lippincott & Co. / 1874.

3 vols. 8vo.   pp. (2), 579, portrait.—(2), 549.—542.   424

✱*✱ This is the Bigelow text of the autobiography, with a continuation made up chiefly of extracts from Franklin's own letters and
writings.

✱*✱ Reviewed in *The Independent*, March 18, 1875; *New York
Tribune*, Oct. 13, 1875; *Christian Union*, March 27, 1875; *Boston
Traveller*, November 6, 1874, and by William Cullen Bryant in the
Evening Post (N. Y.), Oct. 13, 1874.   See also No. 427.

1789. Autobiography.   Stuttgart: 1876.

Benjamin Franklin. / Sein Leben / von ihm selbst beschrieben / Mit einer Vorwort / von / Berthold Auerbach / und einem historisch-politischen Einleitung / von / Friedrich Kapp. / Nebst dem Bildnisse Franklin's. / Stuttgart. / Verlag von Aug. Berth. Auerbach / 1876.

12mo.   pp. (2), 496, portrait.   425

1789. Autobiography.   Stuttgart: 1877.

Benjamin Franklin. / Sein Leben / [*425*] / Zweite unveränderte Auflage. / Stuttgart: [*425*] 1877.

12mo.   pp. (2), 496, portrait.   426

1789. Autobiography.   Philadelphia: 1879.

The Life / [*424*] / by / John Bigelow. / Second Edition, revised and corrected. / . . . . . / Philadelphia: / J. B. Lippincott & Co. / London: 16 Southampton St. Strand. / 1879.

3 Vols. 8vo.   pp. (2), 579, portrait.—(2), 549–542.   427

₊*₊ Reviewed in the *Edinburgh Review*, CLI, 321; *London Athenæum*, July 19, 1879; *Lippincott's Magazine*, July, 1879; *Chicago Tribune*, Dec. 13, 1879; and by Thomas Hughes in the *Contemporary Review* (London), XXXV, 581.

1789. Autobiography.   London: [1881.]

Faith, Doubt, and Evidence, by G. B. Cheever . . . with critical illustrations from the autobiography of Dr. Franklin. London: [1881.]

8vo. pp.   B. M.   428

1789. Autobiography.   London and New York: 1886.

Cassell's National Library. / The / Autobiography / of / Benjamin Franklin. / Cassell & Company, Limited: / 739 & 741 Broadway, New York.

Min.   pp. 192, covers.   B. M.   429

₊*₊ Contains an introduction signed H[enry] M[orley.] It is also issued in London with that place in the imprint. It is the Temple Franklin text.

₊*₊ The title on cover is:

Vol I, No. 3. Subscription price per year, $5.00. Feb. 13, 1886. / Autobiography / of / Benjamin Franklin. / Cassell's / National / Library / Edited by / Professor / Henry Morley / Ten Cents / Cassell &

Company / Limited / 739–741 Broadway, N. Y. / Entered at the Post Office, New York, N. Y., as second-class matter. / Copyright 1886, by O. M. Dunham . . .

1789. Autobiography.. Boston: 1886.

The Riverside Literature Series. / The Autobiography of Benjamin Franklin / with notes and a chapter completing the / story of his life / Part I. / From his birth in 1706 to the publication of the / first number of Poor Richard's / Almanac in 1732 / Houghton, Mifflin and Company / Boston: 4 Park Street; New York: 11 East Seventeenth Street / The Riverside Press, Cambridge / 1886.

2 Vols. 12mo. pp. 114, covers.—(2), 115–238, covers.   430

⁎ Contains an introductory note and a short continuation by Horace E. Scudder.

⁎ The title on the covers is:

Issued Monthly Number 19 [20] September, 1886 / The Autobiography / of / Benjamin Franklin / with notes and a chapter / completing the story / of his Life / Part I / From his birth in 1706 to the / publication of the first num- / ber of Poor Richard's Al- / manac in / 1732 / [Part II / From 1732; with a sketch of / Franklin's Life from the point / at which his autobiography / ends, chiefly drawn from his letters] Houghton, Mifflin and Company / Boston: 4 Park Street / . . . / The Riverside Press, Cambridge / . . . / Single Numbers Fifteen Cents. Yearly Subscription (9 Numbers), $1.25.

1789. Autobiography.   New York: 1886.

The Autobiography / of / Benjamin Franklin / New York: / George Munro, Publisher / 17 to 27 Vandewater Street.

12mo. pp. 155, covers.   431

⁎ A literary piracy of No. 429. The title on cover is:

No. 730. Single Number. Price 10 Cents / The / Seaside Library / Pocket Edition. / The Autobiography / of / Benjamin Franklin. / 17 to 27 Vandewater St. / New York / George Munro / Publisher / . . . / Copyrighted 1886 . . .

1789. Autobiography.   London: 1887.

The Life of Benjamin Franklin . . . . . London: Chambers.   1887.

o. pp.   432

⁎ Title from the *English Catalogue* of Books.

1789. Autobiography. Paris: 1887.

Autobiographie.   Traduction francaise par Edouard
Laboulaye.   Paris: Hachette et Cie.   1887.

Min. pp. (3), 156.   B. 433

1789. Autobiography. Leipsic: [1888.]

The Autobiography of Benjamin Franklin.   Leipzig:
Gressner & Schramm [1888.]

Min. pp. 192.   B. 434

1789. Autobiography. Boston: 1888.

Benjamin Franklin; / His Life / written by himself. /
Edited for school use, with notes and a / continuation of
his life, / by / D. H. Montgomery. / Boston: / Published
by Ginn and Company. / 1888.

12mo. pp. v, (2), 311, 4 plates.   B. 435

$*_*^*$ This is the Bigelow text, with a brief continuation. The title
on the board cover is: "Classics for Children / Franklin / his life by
himself / Montgomery. / Ginn & Company."

1789. Autobiography. Boston: [n. d.]

Old South Leaflets. / Franklin's Boyhood, / From his
Autobiography. [colophon] Beacon Press, Thomas Tod,
Congregational House, Boston. [n. d.]

12mo. pp. 8.   436

1793. Works. London: 1793.

Works / of the late / Doctor Benjamin Franklin: / Con-
sisting of / His Life Written by Himself, / together with /
Essays, Humorous, Moral, & Literary, / Chiefly in the
Manner of / The Spectator. / In Two Volumes. / Vol. I. /
[Vignette portrait] / London: / Printed for G. G. J. and J.
Robinson, / Pater-noster Row. / 1793.

2 Vols. 12mo. pp. ix, (3), 317.—6, 268. P. H. S., C.   437

$*_*^*$ A collection of the "popular" pieces of Franklin, together
with a re-translation of the autobiography from the French translation
of Gibelin (No. 383), and Stuber's continuation. The editing was done
by Benjamin Vaughan, who has clearly made use of his MS. copy of
the autobiography in the re-translation. The work was prepared for
publication in 1791, but withheld on account of Temple Franklin's an-
nouncement of an edition of his grandfather's writings. An additional volume of Franklin's scientific writings was also announced,

but never printed. It is reviewed in the *Monthly Review*, N. s. xiii, 304.

_**_* The first issue of this edition contains an "erratum." There is a second issue in which these errors were corrected.

_**_* Owing to the non-appearance of Temple Franklin's edition, this re-translation of the autobiography and the collection of essays has become the "popular" and one might almost say "chap-book" edition of Franklin's "Life and Writings," and though some few changes have been made by the editors and publishers of certain issues, the following list of editions are practically reproductions of this work.

1793. Works. London: 1793.

Works / [_*437_*] / In Two Volumes / Second Edition / Vol. I. / London: / [_*437_*] · 1793.

> 2 Vols. 12mo. pp. ix, (3), 317.—vi, 290. P. H. S., C.   438
> _**_* Contains three essays not in the first edition. There are also copies without date or title.

1793. Works. Dublin: 1793.

Works / [_*437_*] / The Spectator. / Dublin: / Printed for W. Wogan, P. Byrne, J. Moore, / and W. Jones. / 1793.

> 8vo. pp. vi, (2), 303, portrait.   c.   439

1793. Works. London: 1794.

Works / [_*437_*] In Two Volumes. / Third Edition. / Vol. I / London: / [_*437_*] / 1794.

> 2 Vols. 12mo. pp. ix, (3), 317.—vi, 290.   c.   440
> _**_* There are also copies without date on title.

1793. Works. New York: 1794.

The / Works / of the late / Dr. Benjamin Franklin / Consisting of / His Life / Written by himself / Together with / Essays / Humorous, Moral, & Literary, / chiefly in the manner of the / Spectator. / New-York / Printed by Tiebout & Obrian for / H. Gain, V. Nutter, R. McGill, T. Allen, / J. Read, E. Duyckinck, & Co. and / Edward Mitchell, No. 9, Maiden Lane. / Engraved by P. R. Maverick, 65 Liberty Street.

> Min. pp. 174, 3–139, (3), portrait.   c.   441
> _**_* A reprint of the first London edition. Though paged for two volumes, there is no title to the second part, and they were always bound together.

1793. Works. New York: 1794.

Works / of the late / Dr. Benjamin Franklin; / Consisting of / His Life, Written by Himself, / together with / Essays, Humourous, Moral & Literary; / chiefly in the manner of / The Spectator. / In Two Volumes. / Vol. I. / New-York: / Printed by Samuel Campbell, / No. 37, Hanover-Square. / M,DCC,XCIV.

2 Vols.   12mo.   pp. 206, portrait.—142.   442

1793. Works. New York: 1794.

Works / [*442*] / Vol. I. / The Second American Edition. / Printed by / Samuel Campbell, Bookseller, / No. 124, Pearl Street, New-York. / 1794.

2 Vols.   12mo.   pp. 206, portrait.—142.   443

1793. Works. Weimar: 1794.

Benjamin Franklins / Kleine Schriften / meist in der / Manier des Zuschauers, / nebst seinem Leben. / Aus dem englischen / von / G. Schatz / Mit Franklins doppeltem Bildniße. / Erster Theil. / Weimar, / Im Verlage des Industrei-Comptoirs. / 1794.

2 Vols.   12mo.   pp.   444

1793. Works. London: 1796.

Works / of the late / Doctor Benjamin Franklin, / Consisting of / His Life written by himself; / Together with / Essays, / Humorous, Moral, & Literary, / Chiefly in the manner of / the Spectator / In Two volumes / Vol. I. / London, / Printed for C. Dilly, near the Mansion-house / M,DCC,XCVI.

2 Vols.   12mo.   pp. (2), 232, (4), 227.   P. H. S.   445

1793. Works. Dundee: 1796.

The Works of the late Dr. Franklin, consisting of his Life written by himself: together with Essays, humorous, moral and literary, chiefly in the Manner of the Spectator. In Two Volumes. Vol. I. Dundee, Printed by G. Miller. 1796.

2 Vols.   12mo.   pp.   B. M.   446

1793. Works. New York: 1797.

The / Works / of the late / Dr. Benjamin Franklin / consisting of / his Life / written by himself / together with / Essays / Humourous, Moral and Literary; / Chiefly in the manner of the / Spectator. / New-York: / Printed for Phillip Arnold. / 1797.

12mo. pp. 182, 104, (2), portrait.   447

1793. Works. Paris: 1798.

Vie / de / Benjamin Franklin, / Écrite par lui-même, / suivie / de ses Œuvres / Morales, Politiques / et Littéraires, / Dont la plus grande partie n'avoit pas encore été publiée. / Traduit de l'Anglais, Avec des Notes, / Par J. Castéra. / . . . / Tome Premier. / A Paris, / Chez F. Buisson, Imp.-Lib. rue Hautefeuille, No. 20. / An VI de la Republique.

2 Vols. 8vo. pp. (4) viij, 382, portrait.—(4), 438.   c.   448

* The autobiography is a translation from the English re-translation of the French translation of Gibelin (No. 383), with the exception of the portion for 1731, which is reprinted from *La Decade*, and is first added to the heretofore published portion of the autobiography in this edition.

1793. Works. Charlestown: 1798.

The / Works / of the late / Dr. B. Franklin. / Consisting of his / Life, / written by himself. / Together with / Essays / Humorous, Moral and Literary, / chiefly in the manner of the / Spectator. / Charlestown: / Printed by John Lamson, / for the principal booksellers / in Boston, / 1798.

12mo. pp. 300, portrait.   A. A. S.   449

1793. Works. Gronigen: 1798.

Het Leven / van / Benjamin Franklin, / door hem zelven beschreven. / Benevers / Deszelfs Zede-, Stat-, / Letterkundige / en / Geestige Schriften. / Uit het Engelsch. / . . . / Eerste Deel. / Te Gronigen, / Bij W. Zuidama / 1798 [–1800].

2 Vols. 8vo. pp. xi, (1), 258, (2).—(8), 432.   c.   450

1793. Works. Fairhaven: 1798.

Works of the late Dr. Benjamin Franklin; consisting of his life, written by himself, together with Essays, Humorous, Moral & Literary; chiefly in the manner of the Spectator. Fairhaven, Vt.: J. Lyon. 1798.

12mo. pp. 254.   451

1793. Works. New London: 1798.

The / Life / of / Doctor Benjamin Franklin; / written by himself: / Together with / Essays, / humorous, moral, and literary, / . . . / The Seventh American Edition. / New-London: / Printed for Charles Holt. / 1798.

12mo. pp. 200, (4), portrait.   P. H. S.   452

1763. Works. New York: 1798.

The / Works / of the Late / Dr. Benjamin Franklin; / Consisting of / his Life, / written by himself: / together with / Essays, / humorous, moral, and literary; / chiefly in the manner of the / Spectator. / New-York: / Printed by John Tiebout, No. 358 / Pearl-Street. / 1798.

Min. pp. 174, 139 (3), portrait.   B., P. H. S.   453

1793. Works. London: 1799.

Works / of the late / Doctor Benjamin Franklin. / Consisting of / his Life written by himself; / together with / Essays / humorous, moral, and literary, / chiefly in the manner of / The Spectator. / In Two Volumes. / Vol. I. / London: / Printed for A. Millar, Strand / 1799.

2 Vols. Min. pp. vi, (2), 207, portrait.—vi, 201.   P. H. S.   454

1793. Works. Dundee: 1800.

Works / of the late / Doctor Benjamin Franklin. / Consisting of / his life written by himself; / Together with / Essays, / Humourous, Moral and Literary, / chiefly in the manner of / The Spectator. / In Two Volumes. / Vol. I. / Dundee: / Printed for J. Chalmers, for W. Chalmers . . . / . . . . . / 1800.

2 Vols. Min. pp. ix, (1), 201.—(6), 194.   P. H. S.   455

1793. Works. Huntingdon: 1800.

Works / of the late / Dr. Benjamin Franklin: / Consisting of / his Life written by Himself, / Together with / Essays, Humourous, Moral and / Literary. / Chiefly in the Manner of / the Spectator / In Two Volumes / Volume I. / Huntingdon: / Printed for the Proprietor / M.DCCC.

2 Vols.   12mo.   pp. 156.—119.   P. H. S.   456

1793. Works. Philadelphia: 1801.

Works / of the late / Dr. Benjamin Franklin; / consisting of his / Life, / written by himself. / Together with / Essays / Humorous, Moral, and Literary / Chiefly in the manner of the / Spectator. / To which is added, not in any other Edition, / An Examination, before the British House of / Lords, respecting the / Stamp-Act. / Two Volumes in one. / Philadelphia: / Printed and Published by Wm. W. Woodward, / No. 17, Chestnut Street. / 1801.

12mo.   321, (11), portrait.   P. H. S., C.   457

1793. Works. Weimar: 1802.

B. Franklin's / Kleine Schriften / meist in der Manier des Zuschauers, / nebst seinem Leben. / Aus dem Englischen / von / G. Schatz. / Erster Theil / mit Franklin's Bildnisse: / Zweyte Auflage / Weimar / im Verlag des Landes-Industrie-Comptoirs, 1802.

2 Vols.   8vo.   pp. xii, 188, portrait.—(2) 228.   C.   458

1793. Works. Dublin: 1802.

Works / of the late / Doctor Benjamin Franklin: / Consisting of / his Life, written by Himself, / together with / Essays, humorous, moral / and literary, / chiefly in the manner of / the Spectator. / Dublin: / Printed by P. Wogan, 23, old Bridge. / 1802.

12mo.   pp. viii, 316.   B. M.   459

1793. Works. London: 1802.

Works / of the late / Dr. Benjamin Franklin; / Consisting of / his Life written by himself; / together with / Essays, / Humorous, Moral, and Literary, / chiefly in the manner of / The Spectator. / . . . / . . . / . . . / . . . /

In two Volumes. / Vol. I. / London: / Printed by J. Cundee, ivy-lane, / for J. Jones, Paternoster-Row. / 1802.

> 2 Vols. 12mo. pp. vii, (1), 182, portrait—(4), 188.   c.   460
> *** The imprint of a variation of this edition is as follows: "London: / Printed by J. Cundee, Ivy lane, / for M. Jones, Paternoster Row; / And sold by / J. Hatchard, Bookseller to her Majesty, Piccadilly. / 1802.   P. H. S.   461

1793. Works. Edinburgh: 1803.

Works / of the Late / Dr. Benjamin Franklin: / consisting of / his Life; / together with / Essays, / humorous, moral, and literary. / Vol. I. / Edinburgh: / Printed by D. Shaw & Sons, Lawnmarket; / and sold by the Booksellers. 1803.

> 2 Vols. Min. pp. x, 199.—ix, 196.   c.   462
> 2 Vols. Min. pp. viii, 199.—iv, 196.   P. H. S.   463

1793. Works. London: 1806.

Works / of the late / Dr. Benjamin Franklin; / consisting of / his Life written by himself; / together with / Essays / Humorous, Moral, and Literary, / chiefly in the Manner of / The Spectator / . . . . . / In Two Volumes. / Vol. I. / London: / Printed for Longman, Hurst, Rees and / Orme, Paternoster-Row. / 1806.

> 12mo.   pp. vii, (1), 206, (2), portrait. — ?   c.   464

1793. Works. New York: 1807.

The / Works / of the late / Dr. Benjamin Franklin; / consisting of His / Life, / written by Himself. / Together with / Humourous, Moral, and Literary / Essays, / chiefly in the Manner of the / Spectator. / Among which are several not inserted in any Ameri- / can edition, / New-York: / Published by E. Duyckinck. / 1807. / J. C. Totten, printer.

> 12mo. pp. 295, (3), portrait.   P. L.   465

1793. Works. Edinburgh: 1809.

Works / of the late / Dr. Benjamin Franklin, / consisting of / his Life, / written by himself; / together with / Essays, Humorous, Moral, and Literary. / Vol. I. / Edinburgh: / Printed by D. Shaw & Son; / and Sold by the Booksellers. / 1809.

> 2 Vols. 12mo. (4), 203, iv, 186.   P. H. S.   466

1793. Works. London: 1809.

The / Works / of / Dr. Benjamin Franklin. / London. / Published by W. Suttaby: / . . . . . / 1809 / C. & R. Baldwin, Printers.

Min.   pp. (2), xvi, 454, 10, plate.   B. 467

⁎ Contains an introduction signed "G. D." It is one of "Suttaby's Miniature Library."

1794. Works. Easton: 1810.

Works / of the late / Dr. Benjamin Franklin. / Consisting of / Memoirs of his Early life, / written by himself; / together with a collection of his / Essays / humorous, moral and literary, / chiefly in the manner of / The Spectator. / A new edition revised and enlarged. / Easton: / Published by Henry W. Gibbs. / James St. John, Printer. / 1810.

12mo.   pp. 274.   P. H. S.   468

⁎ With a preliminary note by the publisher.

1793. Works. Edinburgh: 1812.

The / Works / of the late / Dr. Benjamin Franklin, / In two Volumes; / Consisting of / his life and essays / with various pieces / which have never appeared in any Edition of this size. / Vol. I. / Edinburgh: / Published by Oliver & Boyd, Caledonia Press, / Netherbow. / 1812.

2 Vols. 12mo.   pp. 204, portrait.—228, front.   P. H. S.   469

1793. Works. Philadelphia: 1812.

The / Works / of the late / Dr. Benjamin Franklin / consisting of his / Life, / written by himself. / Together with / humorous, moral, and literary / Essays / chiefly in the manner of the Spectator. / Among which are several not inserted in any American / Edition. / Philadelphia: / Printed by Edward Parke, / No. 178, Market Street. / 1812 / William Brown, Printer.

12mo.   pp. 301, portrait.   C.   470

⁎ Also issued with the imprint of "Philadelphia: / Published by David Abbott. / 1812 / William Brown, Printer."   P. H. S.   471

1793. Works. Philadelphia: 1812.

The / Life and Essays / of / the late Doctor / Benjamin

Franklin. / Written by Himself. / Philadelphia: / Published by Johnson and Warner, / No. 147, Market Street, / And sold at their Book stores in Philadelphia and in / Richmond, Virginia. / Griggs and Dickinson, Printers. / 1812.

Min. pp. 324.   P. H. S.   472

1793. Works. Easton: 1812.

Works of the late Dr. Benjamin Franklin, Consisting of Memoirs of his early life, Written by Himself. Easton: 1812.

12mo. pp.   473

*** Title from the auction catalogue of W. H. Corner. See 468.

1793. Works. Pittsburg: 1813.

The Life of Dr. Benjamin Franklin, written by himself, with his Essays. Pittsburg: 1813.

12mo. pp.   474

1793. Works. Edinburgh: 1814.

Works / of the late / Dr. Benjamin Franklin; / consisting of / his Life, / written by himself: / together with / Essays, Humorous, Moral, and Literary. / Vol. I. / Edinburgh: / Printed by D. Shaw and Son; / And sold by the Booksellers. / 1814.

2 Vols. 12mo. pp. (4), 203.—iv, 188.   P. H. S.   475

1793. Works. Brattleborough: 1814.

The / Life and Essays / of / the late Doctor / Benjamin Franklin. / Written by Himself. / Brattleborough: / Published by William Fessenden. / 1814.

12mo. pp. 322.   476

1793. Works. Baltimore: 1815.

The / Life / of / Doctor Benjamin Franklin, / Written chiefly by himself; / with a Collection / Of his finest Essays, / Humorous, Moral, and Literary. / A new edition, revised and enlarged / By Mason L. Weems, / of Lodge No. 50, Dumfries. / Baltimore: / Printed by Ralph W. Pomeroy, & Co. / No. 12, Light street. / 1815.

12mo. pp. 264.   477

*** Though this varies in many respects from No. 437, it is nevertheless based on that collection, so I have included the editions of it in this list. Not satisfied with Stuber's continuation of the autobiography, the editor has added a new one "by one of his [Franklin's] friends," which is about as accurate a description of Mr. Weems as his other title of "Washington's pastor." Having invented half a life of Franklin in this work, the editor printed three editions and then from his imagination wrote the whole life, editions of which are given in the fifth part, and which should not be confused with this edition of the autobiography. See Nos. 383 and 385.

1793. Works. Boston: 1815.

The / Life / of / Dr. Benjamin Franklin; / Written by himself, / with / Essays, / Humorous, Moral, and Literary. / Boston: / Published by I. Thomas, Jun. and J. T. Buckingham. / J. T. Buckingham, Printer. / 1815.

Min. pp. 168, portrait.   478

1793. Works. Bungay: [1815.]

The / Life and Works / of / Dr. Benjamin Franklin. / [vignette] / Bungay: / Printed and Published / by / Brightly & Childs.

8vo. pp. (2), viii, 476, portrait.   c. 479

_**_* The preface is dated 1815.

1793. Works. Philadelphia: 1815.

The / Works / of the late / Dr. Benjamin Franklin; / consisting of his / Life / written by himself. / Together with / Humorous, Moral and Literary / Essays, / Chiefly in the manner of the / Spectator. / Among which are several not in any American Edition. / Philadelphia: / Published by William McCarty, / 1815. / A. Griggs & K. Dickinson,—Printers, Whitehall.

12mo. pp. 324, (2), portrait.   P. H. S. 480

1793. Works. London: 1816.

The / Life and Essays / of / Dr. Franklin. / [Vignette] / London, Published Augst 1st, 1816 by T. Kinnersley.

8vo. pp. viii, 464, portrait.   S. D. 481

1793. Works. London: [1816 ?]

The Works of Dr. Benjamin Franklin, consisting of Essays, humorous, moral and literary; with his Life written by himself. London: J. F. Dove.

Min. pp. (2), 263.   482

_**_* See No. 495.

1793. Works. Philadelphia: 1817.

The / Life / of / Benjamin Franklin, / Written chiefly by Himself; / with a / Collection of his best Essays / Humorous, Moral, and Literary. / A New Edition, / Revised and Enlarged. / By Mason L. Weems, / of Lodge No. 50, Dumfries / . . . . . / Philadelphia: / Published by M. Carey. / 1817.

12mo. pp. 264, portrait.   483

⁎⁎⁎ See Nos. 476 and 485. Reviewed in the *Analectic Magazine,* IX, 389.

1793. Works. Harlem: 1817.

Gedenkshriften / van / Benjamin Franklin; / Bestaande in / Uitgelezen Brieven. / Naar het Engelsch. / Te Haarlem, / Bij A Loosjes Pz. / MDCCCXVII.

8vo. pp. viii, 338.   484

1793. Works. Hagerstown: 1818.

The Life of Benjamin Franklin, ... Third Edition. Revised and enlarged. By Mason L. Weems. Hagerstown: 1818.

12mo. pp.   485

1793. Works. Philadelphia: 1818.

The / Works / of / Benjamin Franklin / . . . / Philadelphia: / Published by B. C. Busby, North 3rd St. / 1818.

Min. pp. (2), 402, plate.   P. 486

1793. Works. Edinburgh: 1818.

Works . . . . . Edinburgh: Oliver & Boyd. 1818.

2 Vols. 12mo. pp.   487

⁎⁎⁎ Title from *Swift*. See No. 469.

1793. Works. Glasgow: 1819.

The / Works / of the late / Dr. Benjamin Franklin, / containing / his life / with / Letters illustrative of his Manners and Character, / and / Essays, / Humorous, Moral and Literary. / . . . . . / Glasgow: / Printed by W. Falconer, High-Street. / 1819.

12mo. pp. 288.   488

1793. Works.   London: 1819.

The / Works / of / Dr. Benjamin Franklin; / consisting of / Essays, / humorous, moral and literary: / with / his life, written by himself. / London: / Printed for J. Walker, . . . / . . . . . / 1819.

Min.   pp. (2), xi, 310, plate.   P. H. S.   489

_**_* The engraved title is:

The Works of / Dr. Franklin, / with his life / (written by Himself.) / . . . / . . . / London: / Published by J. Walker / and the other Proprietors. / 1819.

1793. Works.   Philadelphia: 1821.

The / Works / of the late / Dr. B. Franklin; / Consisting of his / Life, / written by himself. / Together with / humorous, moral and literary / Essays, / . . . Among which are several not inserted in any American / Edition. / Philadelphia: / Printed by Edward Parker, / No. 178 Market Street. / 1821.

8vo. pp. 294.   490

1793. Works.   Rottweil: 1822.

Kleine Schriften und Engels-Lebensweisheit d. alten Witt. Rottweil. Herder. 1822.

8vo. pp.   491

_**_* Title from *Swift.*

1793. Works.   Middletown: 1823.

The / Life / of the late / Dr. Benjamin Franklin, / written by himself. / Together with a number of his / Essays / chiefly in the manner of the Spectator. / Middletown. / Printed and published by Starr & Niles. / 1823.

12mo. pp. 300.   C.   492

1793. Works.   Paisley: 1823.

Works / of the late / Dr. Benjamin Franklin: / consisting of his / Life / written by himself, / together with / Essays, / Humorous, Moral, and Literary / chiefly in the manner of / The Spectator / In Two Volumes / Vol. I. / Paisley: / Printed by J. Neilson. / 1823.

2 Vols. Min. pp. 215.—216.   P. H. S.   493

1793. Works.   London: 1824.

The / Works / of / Dr. Benjamin Franklin: / consisting of / Essays, / Humorous, Moral, and Literary / with his life / written by himself. / London: / Printed and published by J. Limburd, / 143 Strand, / Near Somerset House. / 1824.

12mo.   pp. (2), 109, covers.   P. H. S.   494

∗∗∗ The title on cover is:

Part II / Limburd's British Classics: / Containing / the Essays / of Dr. Franklin / Embellished / With Engravings on Wood. / London: / Printed and Published by J. Limburd / . . . . . / 1824.

1793. Works.   London: 1824.

The Works of Dr. Benjamin Franklin, consisting of Essays, humorous, moral and literary; with his Life, written by himself.   London: J. F. Dove, English Classics. 1824.

Min.   pp. (2), viii, 288, portrait.   C.   495

∗∗∗ See No. 482. Nos. 511, 521, 530, 531, 536 and 542 are apparently from the same plates.

1793. Works.   London: 1824.

The / Works / of / Dr. Benjamin Franklin: / Consisting of / Essays / Humorous, Moral, and Literary / with / his life, written by himself. / London: / W. Baynes and Son, Paternoster Row; . . . / . . . . . / 1824.

12mo.   pp. (2), 260.   P. H. S.   466

∗∗∗ The engraved title is:

The / Works / of / Dr. Benjamin Franklin, / with his life / . . . / . . . / . . . / . . . / London: / For the Proprietors of the English Classics.

1793. Works.   Chiswick: 1824.

The / Works / of / Dr. Benjamin Franklin; / Consisting of / Essays, / Humorous, Moral, and Literary: / With / his Life, written by himself. / Chiswick: / From the Press of C. Whittingham, / College House. / . . . . . / 1824.

Min.   pp. (2), viii, 295.   C.   497

∗∗∗ The engraved title is:

The Works of / Dr. Benjamin Franklin. / Chiswick. / Printed by C. Whittingham / for Thomas Tegg . . . / . . . / March, 1824.

1793. Works. New York: 1825.

The / Works / of / Dr. Benjamin Franklin, / consisting of / Essays, / Humorous, Moral, and Literary / with / His Life, / written by himself. / New-York: / Printed and published by W. Van Norden. / No. 393 Water Street. / 1825.

Min. pp. 290, portrait.   498

⁎⁎⁎ This edition was issued with three different engraved titles, as follows:

The Life of Benjamin Franklin, / written by himself. / G. G. Sickles. / New-York. / 1829.   P. L. 499

The / Life of / Benjamin Franklin. / Written by Himself. / D. Mallory. / New-York. / 1825.   S. D. 500

The / Life and Essays / of / Benjamin Franklin. / Written by himself. / New York: / Printed by Johnstone & Van Norden.   P. L. 501

1793. Works. Boston: 1825.

The / Works / of / Dr. Benjamin Franklin; / Consisting of / Essays, / Humorous, Moral, and Literary: / with / His Life, written by Himself. / Stereotyped by T. H. Carter & Co. / Boston: / Published by T. Bedlington, / No. 31, Washington-Street. / 1825.

12mo. pp. (2), 303, portrait.   A. A. S. 502

⁎⁎⁎ The engraved title is:

Life / of / Benjn Franklin. / To which are added / Essays, &c. / Boston. / Timothy Bedlington. / 1828.

1793. Works. London: 1826.

The / Works / of / Dr. Benjamin Franklin. / Consisting of / Essays, / Humorous, Moral, and Literary; / with / his Life; Written by Himself. / London: / Printed for T. and J. Allman, / . . . / John Anderson, Jun, Edinburgh; and / John Cummings, Dublin. / 1826.

Min. pp. (2), 362, portrait.   503

⁎⁎⁎ The engraved title is:

The Works of / Dr. Franklin. / With his Life / . . . / London: / Printed for T. and J. Allman, Gt. Queen Street. Lincoln's Inn Fields.

1793. Works. Middletown: 1826.

Life and Essays of Benjamin Franklin . . . . . Middletown: 1826.

12mo. pp.   504

⁎⁎⁎ Title from *Swift*.

1793. Works. Boston: 1828. See No. 502.
1793. Works. New York: 1828. See No. 501.
1793. Works. New York: 1829. See No. 499.
1793. Works. New York: 1830.

Life and Essays of Benjamin Franklin . . . . . New York: 1830.

12mo. pp.   505

 ₓ*ₓ Title from *Swift.*

1793. Works. New York: 1830.

The / Works / of / Dr. Benjamin Franklin, / Consisting of / Essays, / humorous, moral, and literary / with / his Life / written by himself. / New-York: / George G. Sickles, publisher. / 1830.

18mo. pp. 290, portrait.   A. A. S.   506

 ₓ*ₓ The engraved title is:
  The Life and Writings / of / Benjamin Franklin. / Written by Himself. / New York / Published by G. G. Sickles. / 1831.

1793. Works. New York: 1831. See No. 506.
1793. Works. New York: 1834.

The / Works / of / Dr. Benjamin Franklin, / Consisting of / Essays, / humorous, moral, and literary. / With / his Life, / written by himself. / New-York. / Mahlon Day, / 374 Pearl Street.

24mo. pp. 290, portrait.   507

 ₓ*ₓ The engraved title is:
  The / Life & Writings / of / Benjamin Franklin. / Written by Himself / New York / Published by Mahlon Day, / 374 Pearl Street. / 1834.

1793. Works. Peekskill: 1834.

The / Works / of / Dr. Benjamin Franklin, / Consisting of / Essays, / Humorous, Moral, and Literary; / with His Life, / written by Himself. / Peekskill, N. Y. / Printed and Published by S. Marks / 1834.

Min. pp. 290.   508

1793. Works. Exeter: 1834.

The / Works / of / Dr. Benj. Franklin, / Consisting of / Essays / Humorous, Moral and Literary: / with / his life, written by himself. / Exeter: / J. & B. Williams. / 1834.

Min. pp. 256.   509

1793. Works. London: 1835.

The / Works / of / Dr. Benjamin Franklin, / Consisting of / Essays, / Humorous, Moral and Literary: / with his Life written by himself. / London: / Printed for Scott, Webster, and Geary, (Successors to Mr. Dove) / 36 Charterhouse Square. / MDCCCXXXV.

Min. pp. (2), viii, 288, portrait.   P. H. S.   511

⁎⁎ See No. 495.

1793. Works. London: 1835.

The / Works / of / Dr. Benjamin Franklin: / Consisting of / Essays, / Humorous, Moral, and Literary: / with / his Life / written by himself. / London: / T. Allman, Holborn hill / and / E. Spettegue, / Guilford Place, Spa-fields. / 1835.

Min. pp. (2), 224, portrait.   P. H. S.   512

⁎⁎ The engraved title is:
The Works of / Dr. Franklin / with his Life / London / Published by Thos. Allman / . . . / 1835. See No. 526.

1793. Works. Exeter: 1835.

The / Works / [⁎509⁎] / 1835.

Min. pp. 224.   513

1793. Works. Nuremberg: [1835?]

The / Works / of / Dr. Benjamin Franklin / Campe's Edition / Nurnberg and New-York / Printed and Published by / Frederick Campe & Co.

12mo. pp. xii, 312.   B. M.   514

1793. Works. Baltimore: 1835.

The / Works / of / Dr. Benjamin Franklin: / Consisting of / Essays, / humorous, moral and literary: / with his / Life, written by himself. / Stereotyped by J. A. James. / Baltimore: / N. Hickman, Market Street. / 1835.

12mo. pp. 304, portrait.   515

⁎⁎ There is also an issue with the same title, lacking the date.

S. D.   516

1793. Works. Halifax: 1837.

The / Works / of / Dr. Benjamin Franklin: / Consisting of / Essays / Humorous, Moral and Literary, / with / His

Life / written by Himself. / Halifax: / Printed for H. Pohl-
man. / 1837.

Min. pp. vi, 328, plates.   P. H. S. 517

1793. Works. Edinburgh: 1838.

People's Edition / The Life / of / Benjamin Franklin /
Comprising the account of the early part of his Life, /
written by himself. / And a new and greatly extended
narrative in continuation / till his death. / The whole illustrated with letters and / biographical notes / Also / The
Miscellaneous Writings / of Franklin. / . . . . . / Edinburgh: / Published by William and Robert Chambers /
. . . . . / 1838.

8vo. pp. (2), 86, covers.   518

*** See No. 522.

1793. Works. Carlsruhe: 1838.

The Life / of / Dr. Benjamin Franklin, / Written by
himself; / to which are added / Essays / by the same author.
/ Mit einen Wörterbuche, Zum Schul und Privatgebrauchs.
/ Karlsruhe / William Creuzbauer. / 1838.

12mo. pp. (2), 186, 41, portrait.   P. H. S. 519

1793. Works. Leipsic: 1838.

Leben und ausgewählte Schriften. Leipzig: Wigand.
1838.

Min. pp.   520

*** Title from *Swift*. See No. 534.

1793. Works. London: 1838.

Works of Benjamin Franklin. London : Scott, Webster & Geary. 1838.

12mo. pp. viii, 288, front.   521

1793. Works. Edinburgh: 1839.

People's Edition. / The Life / and / Miscellaneous Writings / of / Benjamin Franklin / Greatly extended and improved / . . . . . / Edinburgh: / Published by William
and Robert Chambers; / . . . . .

8vo. pp. (2), 86, covers.   522

*** The cover title is:

The Life / . . . . . / Edinburgh: / Published by William and Robert Chambers; / and W. S. Orr and Company, London. / 1839.

1793. Works. Exeter: 1839.

The Works / of / Dr. Benjamin Franklin. / Consisting of Essays, / Humorous, Moral, and Literary: / With his Life, / written by himself. / Exeter:'/ Published by J. and B. Williams. / 1839.

Min. pp. 224.   523

*** See No. 509.

1793. Works. New York: 1839.

Memoirs / of / Benjamin Franklin; / written by himself / with his / most interesting Essays, Letters, and Miscella- / neous Writings; Familiar, Moral, Political, / Economical and Philosophical. / Selected with care / from all his published productions and comprising / whatever is most entertaining and valuable / to the general reader. / In Two Volumes. / Vol. I. / New-York: / Harper & Brothers, 82 Cliff Street. / 1839.

2 Vols. 12mo. pp. 287.—(2), 288.   c. 524

*** Also issues dated 1840, 1843, 1845 and 1847. It is the Temple Franklin text.

1793. Works. London: 1840.

The / Works / of / Dr. Benjamin Franklin; / Consisting of / Essays, Humorous, Moral, and Literary / with / His Life / Written by Himself. / London: / Published by the booksellers. / William Walker, Otley. / MDCCCXL.

Min. pp. 320, plate.   P. H. S. 525

1793. Works. New York: 1840. See No. 524.

1793. Works. New York: 1843. See No. 524.

1793. Works. Barcelona: 1843.

El libro del hombre de bien, opúsculos morales, económicos y políticos extractados de Benjamin Franklin. Barcelona. 1843.

Min. pp.   525*

*** Title from *Swift.*

1793. Works. London: 1843.

The / Works / of / Dr. Benjamin Franklin: / Consisting of / Essays, / Humorous, Moral, and Literary: / with / his

Life, / written by himself. / London: / T. Allman, Holborn Hill. / 1843.

Min. pp. (2), 238, (2), portrait.   P. H. S. 526

** The engraved title is:

The Works of / Dr. Franklin / with his Life. / London / Published by T. Allman.

1793. Works. Auburn: 1846.

Life / of / Benjamin Franklin, / written by himself. / Together / with his Essays, / Humorous, Moral and Literary. / Auburn, N. Y. / Published by J. C. Derby and Co. / Geneva: / Geo. H. Derby and Co. / H. Oliphant, Pr. / 1846.

Min. pp. 224.   527

1793. Works. Paris: 1843.

Mémoires / Complete / Œuvres Morales et Littéraire / de Benjamin Franklin / Traduction nouvelle d'après la dernièr traduction / publiée a New-York. / Paris / Libraire de Charles Gosselin / . . . . . / MDCCCXLIII.

12mo. pp. (2), 338, covers.   P. H. S. 527*

** The title on cover is:

Bibliothèque d'Élite / Memoires / . . . . . [as above.]

1793. Works. Hartford: 1846.

The / Works / of / Dr. Benjamin Franklin: / Consisting of / Essays, / Humorous, Moral, and Literary: / with his / Life, written by himself. / Stereotyped by J. A. James. / Hartford. / S. Andrus and Son. / 1846.

12mo. pp. 304.   528

** Also issues dated 1848 and 1851.

1793. Works. New York: 1847. See No. 524.

1793. Works. Auburn: 1848.

Life / [*527*] / Auburn, N. Y. Derby, Miller & Co. 1848.

Min. pp. 224.   529

** Also an issue dated 1853.

1793. Works. New York: 1848.

The / Works of / Dr. Benjamin Franklin; / Consisting of / Essays, / Humorous, Moral & Literary: / with his Life, written by himself. / New-York: / Leavitt, Trow & Co., 191 Broadway. / 1848.

12mo.   pp. viii, 288.

530

1793. Works. Hartford: 1848. See No. 528.

1793. Works. London: 1850. See No. 532.

1793. Works. Hartford: 1851. See No. 528.

1793. Works. Halifax: 1851.

The / Works / of / Dr. Benjamin Franklin; / Consisting of / Essays, / Humorous, Moral, and Literary: / with / his Life, written by himself. / Halifax: / Printed and published by Milner & Sowerby, / Cheapside. / MDCCCLI.

Min.   pp. (2), viii, 288, portrait.

531

₊*₊ The engraved title is:

The / Works / of / Dr. Benjamin Franklin / With His Life / . . .

. . / London: / Engraved for the English Classics, / Halifax. / Milner and Sowerby.

1793. Works. London: 1852.

The / Life and Essays / of / Dr. Franklin. / London: / Published by G. Kershaw & Son. / MDCCCLII.

2 Vols.   Min.   pp. (4), 11–147.—144.

B. 532

₊*₊ The title of the second volume is:

Essays: / Humorous, Moral and Literary. / By Dr. Franklin. / London: Published by J. S. Pratt. / MDCCCL.

1793. Works. Leipsic: 1853.

Benjamin Franklin's / Leben und Schriften. / Von / Theodor Ruprecht / Leipzig / Verlag von Otto Wigand. / 1853.

8vo.   pp. 274, cover.

B. 533

₊*₊ The title or cover is:

Bildungs-Halle / im / Sinne und Geiste unserer Zeit. / Für alle Stande. / . . .

. . . . / Fünfter Band : / Benjamin Franklin's Leben und Schriften. / Leipzig / Verlag von Otto Wigand / 1853.

1793. Works. Auburn: 1853. See No. 529.

1793. Works. New York: 1853.

The / Work, [sic] / of / Dr. Benjamin Franklin; / consisting of / Essays, / humorous, moral and literary: / with / his life, written by himself / New-York: / Published by Leavitt & Allen, / 27 Dey street. / 1853.

12mo.   pp. viii, 288.

534

1793. Works. London: 1853.

The / Life and Works / of / Dr. Benjamin Franklin /
. . . . . / London: / T. Nelson and Sons, Paternoster
Row; / and Edinburgh. / MDCCLIII.

Min. pp. (2), viii, 324, plate.   535

⁎⁎⁎ The engraved title is:

Franklin's / Life and Works / . . . . . / Edinburgh: Thomas Nelson.

1793. Works. London: 1855.

The / Works / of / Dr. Benjamin Franklin; / Consisting
of / Essays / Humorous, Moral and Literary: / with / His
Life, / Written by Himself. / Halifax: / Milner and Sowerby. / 1855.

8vo. pp. (2), viii, 288, plate.   536

⁎⁎⁎ See No. 531 for the engraved title. There are reissues, dated
1861 and 1864.

1793. Works. New York: 1858.

The Life / of / Benjamin Franklin / Written by Himself
/ to which is added / His Miscellaneous Essays. / New-
York: / C. M. Saxton, 25 Park Row. / 1858.

12mo. pp. 375, portrait.   A. A. S.   537

1793. Works. London: 1861.

The Life / and / Miscellaneous Writings / of / Benjamin
Franklin, / greatly extended and improved. / . . . . . /
William and Robert Chambers / London and Edinburgh.
1861.

Min. pp. viii, 344, portrait.   P. H. S.   538

1793. Works. Halifax: 1861. See No. 536.

1793. Works. Halifax: 1864. See No. 536.

1793. Works. Macon: [187–?]

Autobiography and Essays of Benjamin Franklin.
Macon: Albert. [187–?]

Min. pp.   539

⁎⁎⁎ Title from *American Catalogue.*

1793. Works. Philadelphia: 1871.

Autobiography and Essays of Benjamin Franklin.
Philadelphia: Claxton, Remsen & Haffelfinger. 1871.

Min. pp.   540

⁎⁎⁎ Title from the *American Catalogue.*

1793. Works. Carlsruhe: 1871.

The Life / of / Dr. Benjamin Franklin, / Written by Himself; / To which are added / Essays, / and some / Anecdotes / of or by the same Author. / Mit einer Wörtebuche / Zum Schul-und Privatgebrauch. / Zweite Auflage, / durchgisehen, vermehrt und Anmerkungen / von / Dr. D. Jüngling, / . . . / Carlsruhe, William Creuzbauer. 1871.

12mo. pp. xv, 194, 45.   541

1793. Works. New York: 1880.

Autobiography / of Benjamin Franklin. / New York: / R. Worthington, 750 Broadway. / MDCCCLXXX.

Min. pp. viii, 288, portrait.   P. 542

1793. Works. New York: [1881.]

Autobiography / of / Benjamin Franklin: / with his Essays and Will. / New York: / The Arundel Print.

12mo. pp. 307, portrait.   543

1793. Works. Philadelphia: 1884.

The / Autobiography and Essays / of / Dr. Benjamin Franklin / Complete in one volume. / Philadelphia / E. Claxton & Company. / 930 Market Street. / 1884.

12mo. pp. 231, portrait.   544

1793. Works. Philadelphia: [188–?]

The / Life and Essays / of / Dr. Benjamin Franklin. / Comprised in one volume. / Philadelphia. / Published by Leary & Getz / 138 North Second St.

Min. pp. 231, portrait.   H. 545

1793. Works. New York: [187–?]

Autobiography and Essays of Benjamin Franklin, with letters and miscellaneous writings. New York: Harper & Brothers.

2 Vols. Min.   546

** Title from the *American Catalogue.* Probably a reissue of No. 524.

1801. Essays.

Select Pieces / by / Benj. Franklin, L. L. D. / Published

Mar. 1, 1801, by George Nicholson, Poughnill, near Ludlow / Sold in London by T. Conder . . ./ . . . . .

Min. pp. 59, (1).   P. H. S.   547

1805. Essays. London: 1805.

A / Present / for an / Apprentice; / . . . . . / And / two Essays / By Dr. Benjamin Franklin. / London: / Printed for the Booksellers, / By W. Turner, Hull, 1805.

Min. pp. (iv), 109, 4, 2.   P. H. S.   548

1805. Essays. Boston: 1808.

A / Monitor / for an / Apprentice; / . . . . . / To which is added, / . . . . . / Two Essays / By Dr. Benj. Franklin. / First American from the Sixth London Edition. / Boston: / Published by Jarrand, Mallory & Co. / . . . . . / 1808.

12mo. pp. (4), 9–120.   B.   549

1806. Works edited by Marshall.

The / Complete / Works / in / Philosophy, Politics, and Morals, / of the late / Dr. Benjamin Franklin, / now first collected and arranged; / with / Memoirs of his early life, / written by himself. / In Three Volumes. / Vol. I. / London: / Printed for J. Johnson, St. Paul's Church-Yard; / and Longman, Hurst, Rees, and Orme, / Paternoster-Row. / 1806.

3 Vols. 8vo. pp. xiv, (2), 440, (32), portrait, 4 plates.—(2), vi, 468, 1 folding leaf, 9 plates.—(2), vi, 552, (6).   C., B.   550

*** The engraved title is:

The / Works / of / Benjamin Franklin, L. L. D. / Vol. I / Printed, / for Longman, Hurst, Rees & Orme, Paternoster Row, London.

*** "The editor was a Mr. Marshall. His name is not connected with the work; but he performed his part with good judgement, and used much diligence in searching for essays and papers, that had not before been comprised in any collection. Mr. Benjamin Vaughan, who was then in London, rendered him important assistance." *Sparks.*

*** The editor, in his preface, first gave publicity to the charge that William Temple Franklin had been bribed by the English government to suppress his grandfather's writings. This was noticed in the *Edinburgh Review* and in *The American Citizen,* and this latter article was reprinted in *The Argus or London Review in Paris* of March

28, 1807.   To this Temple Franklin wrote a denial, which appeared in the latter periodical for March 31. 1807.   See No. 561.

⁎ Reviewed by Lord Francis Jeffrey in the *Edinburgh Review*, VIII, 327; *Monthly Review*, N. S. LVII, 441, and by James Cheetham in the *American Citizen* for September, 1807.

1806. Works. London: [1811.]

The / Complete / Works / [*550*] / Written by himself. / Second Edition. / In Three Volumes. / Vol. I. / London: / Printed for Longman, Hurst, Rees, Orme, and Brown, / Paternoster-Row; / and J. Johnson & Co. / St. Paul's Church-Yard. / [1811.]

3 Vols. 8vo.

C. 551

⁎ A reissue of the first edition, with the change of printed titles as noted, and lacking the last six pages ("Works lately published") of Vol. III.

1808–9. Works edited by Duane. See 1818.

1811. Essays.

The / Essays, / Humorous, Moral and Literary / of the late / Dr. Benjamin Franklin. / Boston: / Published by John West and Co. / No. 75, Cornhill. / 1811. / E. G. House, Printer.

12mo. pp. 182, (2).

B. 552

⁎ This is a reprint of the second volume of No. 437, with the addition of the "Busy-Body" essays.

1812? Essays.

The / Franklin Family / Primer / Containing / A new and useful Selection / of / Moral Lessons; / adorned with a variety of / Cuts, / Calculated to strike a lasting impression / on the / Tender minds of Children. / By a Friend to Youth. / Improved Edition. / Boston: / Printed by and for Manning & Loring / . . .

Min. pp. 72.

C. 553

⁎ Contains a brief biography of Franklin, and three of his essays.

1817. Correspondence. Paris: 1817.

Correspondance / Inédite et Secrète / du / Docteur B. Franklin, / Ministre Plénipotentiaire des États-Unis d'Amérique / près la Cour de France, / depuis l'année 1753 jusqu'en 1790; / offrant, en trois parties complètes et bien distinctes, / 1° Les Mémoires de sa Vie privée; / 2° Les causes premières de la Révolution d'Amérique; / 3° l'Histoire des diverses Négociations / entre l'Angleterre, la France et les États-Unis. / Publiée, pour la première fois, en France, / Avec des Notes, additions, etc. / Tome Premier. / Paris, / Janet Pere, Libraire-Éditeur, / rue Saint-Jacques, No. 59. / M.DCCC.XVII.

2 Vols. 8vo. pp. vj, 542, portrait.—viij, 480, facsimile.   B. C.   554

⁎⁎⁎ This is a piracy of Vols. v and vi of Duane's edition (No. 568), wretchedly translated and edited by Charles Malo, who was somewhat assisted by MM. Cohen and Breton.   Upon the appearance of the first volume, the publishers of the French edition of the Private Correspondence (No. 559) announced their edition, with the statement that this work was incomplete.   Malo replies in the preface to the second volume, and virtually charges Temple Franklin with being the "assassin" of his grandfather's memory.   Mardelle answers in the preface to his edition (No. 559), and there was also a newspaper controversy in the Paris press, relative to the comparative value of the two editions.

1817.   Private Correspondence.   London: 1817.

The / Private Correspondence / of / Benjamin Franklin, LL. D. / F. R. S. &c. / Minister Plenipotentiary from the United States of America at the Court of France, / and for the Treaty of Peace and Independence with Great Britain, &c., &c. / Comprising / A Series of Letters / on / Miscellaneous, Literary, and Political Subjects: / Written between the years 1753 and 1790; / illustrating the / Memoirs of his Public and Private Life, / and developing / the Secret History / of his / Political Transactions and Negotiations. / Now first Published from the originals, / by his grandson / William Temple Franklin. / London: / Printed for Henry Colburn, / British and Foreign Public Library, Conduit Street Hanover Square. / 1817.

4to. pp. xxiii, (1), 449, facsimile.   C., B.   555

⁎⁎⁎ This volume also forms volume III of Temple Franklin's edition of Franklin's writings (No. 561), but copies were separately sold; and, owing to the delay in the publication of the first volume of that work, this was the first issued.   It is reviewed, by Lord Francis Jeffrey, in the *Edinburgh Review*, XXVIII, 275; *Monthly Review*, N. S. LXXXIII,

18 and 133; *Analectic Magazine*, IX, 553, and *Literary Gazette*, Jan. 25, 1817.

1817. Private Correspondence. London: 1817.

The / Private Correspondence / of / Benjamin Franklin, / L. L. D., F. R. S. &c., / Minister Plenipotentiary from the United States of America / at the Court of France, and for the Treaty of Peace / and Independence with Great Britain, &c. &c. / [*555*] / by his grandson / William Temple Franklin. / In Two Volumes. / Vol. I. / London: Printed for Henry Colburn, / Public Library, Conduit Street, Hanover Square. / 1817.

2 Vols. 8vo. pp. xvi, 456, facsimile.—xii, 392.   556

⁎*⁎ This title and collation are given on the authority of *Sabin*. See Note to No. 562.

1817. Private Correspondence. London: 1817.

The / Private Correspondence / [*556*] / Vol. I. / Second Edition, with Additions.   London: [*556*]   1817.

2 Vols. 8vo. pp. xvi, 493, facsimile.—(4), 452.   c. 557

1817. Private Correspondence. London: 1817.

The / Private Correspondence / [*556*] / Vol. I. / Third Edition, with Additions. / London: [*556*]   1817.

2 Vols. 8vo. pp.   B. 558

1817. Private Correspondence. Paris: 1817.

Correspondance / choisie / de Benjamin Franklin, / traduite de l'Anglais. / Édition publiée par W. T. Franklin. / . . . / A Paris, / Chez Treuttel et Würtz, Libraires, rue de Bourbon, No. 17; / Et à Strasbourg, même Maison de Commerce. / A Londres, / Chez H. Colburne, 50, Conduit Street, New-Bond. / 1817.

8vo. pp. xxxj, 409, (1).   c. 559

⁎*⁎ Translated by M. de la Mardelle, who has added a preface relating to the charges against Temple Franklin made by Charles Malo in No. 554, and severely criticising the latter, both on that account and for the many errors in his two volumes.

⁎*⁎ *Sabin* gives the size as quarto, and *Brunet* says there were two volumes, both of which are errors.   The half title is:

Œuvres / posthume de Benjamin Franklin / Tome Premier / Correspondance choisie.

1817. Private Correspondence.   London: 1833.

Private / Correspondence / [*556*] / and Independence with Great Britain, &c. &c. / Edited by his Grandson, / William Temple Franklin. / In Two Volumes. / Vol. I. / London: / Published for Henry Colburn, / by R. Bentley, New Burlington Street. / 1833.

2 Vols. 8vo. pp. xvi, 456, facsimile.—xi, (1), 392. C., B.   560

1818. Works edited by Temple Franklin.

Memoirs / of the / Life and Writings / of / Benjamin Franklin, LL. D. / F. R. S. &c. / Minister Plenipotentiary / from the United States of America, at the Court of France, / and for the Treaty of Peace and Independence with Great Britain, / &c. &c. / Written by himself to a late period, / and continued to the time of his death, / by his Grandson; / William Temple Franklin. / Now first published from the original MSS. / Comprising the / Private Correspondence and Public Negotiations of Dr. Franklin, / and a selection from his / Political, Philosophical, and Miscellaneous Works. / London: / Printed for Henry Colburn, / British and Foreign Public Library, Conduit Street. / 1818.

3 Vols. 4to.   B., C.   561

Vol. I.   Life. pp. (2), x, 449, (1), lxxxviii, (4), portrait.

Vol. II.   Correspondence. pp. (4), xxiii, (1), 449, facsimile.

Vol. III. Works. pp. viii, xi–xvi, (2), 570, 2, 7 plates.

⁎ This is the first publication of any of the autobiography as written by Franklin, and of the third part in any form. It is followed by a continuation which is of great value. The volumes of this and succeeding editions were sold separately as "Memoirs," "Private Correspondence," and "Posthumous Writings," and so are noticed with more detail in Nos. 555 and 567. It is reviewed in the *Monthly Review*, LXXXVI, 25; *Analectic Magazine*, XI, 449; by A. C. Norton in the *North American Review*, VII, 289; by John Foster in the *Eclectic Review* for 1818; and by F. B. Hoffman in his *Œuvres*, IV, 470.

⁎ Franklin by his will, left the bulk of his books and manuscripts to his grandson, William Temple Franklin, who at once (1790) came to London and began the preparations for, and announced an edition of his grandfather's writings. The times were so unpropitious for an elaborate work, however, that a publisher could not be found, and

Temple Franklin was himself diverted from the venture by a profitable agency in an American land company, and so the enterprise dragged along till 1818, when both quarto and octavo editions were printed. This delay of twenty-eight years occasioned much gossip, which first came into print in the *National Intelligencer*, and finally crystallized in a charge, made in the preface of Marshall's edition of Franklin's writings (No. 550), that Temple Franklin "had found a bidder . . . in some emissary of government, whose object was to withhold the manuscripts from the world." This attack was commented upon in the *Monthly Review*, the *Edinburgh Review*, and the *American Citizen*, whose Anglo-phobic editor made it the basis of a savage attack on both Temple Franklin and the British government. This latter diatribe was reprinted in Paris in *The Argus or London Review* of March 28, 1807. To this Temple Franklin wrote a brief and dignified reply, which was published in the latter paper of March 31, 1807 (and republished in the *London Chronicle*), which should have ended the matter for all time. The slander has, however, proved of feline nature. Thomas Jefferson, always a newsmonger, added fuel to the flame by some inaccurate "recollections," and Charles Malo, in editing his pirated edition of Franklin's correspondence (No. 554), virtually called Temple Franklin the assassin of his grandfather's memory. In this work the editor laughingly notices these attacks, but does not even consider a denial or refutation necessary, which led both Mr. Sparks and Mr. Bigelow to give further currency to the charges in their editions of Franklin's writings, and though both Mr. Stevens and Prof. McMaster have given Temple Franklin fair treatment in this respect, the slander is apparently by no means buried.

1818. Works.

Memoirs / of the / Life and Writings / of / Benjamin Franklin / [+561+] / By his grandson, / William Temple Franklin. / Comprising the / Private Correspondence / And Public Negociations of Dr. Franklin. / And his select / Political, Philosophical and Miscellaneous Works. / Published from the original MSS. / Vol. I. / Life / London: / Printed for Henry Colburn, Conduit Street.   1818.

6 Vols. 8vo.

562

Vols. I–II.   Life.   pp. xii, 542, portrait.—(2), 450.

Vols. III–IV.   Correspondence.   pp. xvi, 493.—viii, 523, 8 plates.   pp. xvi, 456, facsimile.—xii, 392.

Vols. V–VI.   Works.

*** This title and collation is given on the authority of *Sabin*. I have only seen this octavo edition as "second" or "third edition," and I think it was only so issued, the quarto edition being the first.

1818. Works.

Memoirs / [*562*] / Published from the original MSS. / Second Edition. / Vol. I. / Life. / London: / [*562*] 1818.
6 Vols. 8vo.   P. H. S. 563

Vols. I–II.   Life. pp. xii, 542, portrait, 2 plates.—(4), 452.
Vols. III–IV. Correspondence. pp. xxiv, 486, facsimile.—xi, 480, (2).
Vols. V–VI. Works. pp. xvi, 493.—viii, 523, 8 plates.

1818. Works.

Memoirs [*562*] / Third Edition. / Vol. I. / Life. / London: / [*562*] 1818.
6 Vols. 8vo. pp. (?)   564

1818. Works.   Paris: 1817–1819.

Mémoires / sur / la Vie et les Écrits / de Benjamin Frank-lin, / . . . . . / Publiées / sur le manuscrit original rédigé par lui-même / en grande partie, et continué jusqu'a sa / mort, / Par William Temple Franklin, / son petit-fils. / Tome Premier, / Avec un Portrait de B. Franklin. / A Paris, / Chez Treuttel et Würtz, Libraires, rue de Bourbon, No. 17; / Et à Strasbourg, même Maison de Commerce. / A Londres, / Chez H. Colburne . . . / 1818.

3 Vols. 8vo. pp. (2), xiv, 290, portrait.—(2), 435, plate.—xxxj, 459,
(1).   c. 565

*** The third volume is the same as No. 559. The three volumes form a translation, made by M. de la Mardelle, of part of Temple Franklin's edition, but was never carried further. *Sabin* gives a quarto edition, and states the translation to be by Le Veillard, both of which are errors.

1818. Works.   Weimar: 1817–1819.

Dr. Benjamin Franklin's / nachgelassene / Schriften und Correspondenz, / nebst / seinem Leben. / Aus dem Eng-lischen übersetzt. / Erster Band. / Mit Franklin's Portrait. / Weimar, / Im Verlage des Landes-Industrie-Comptoirs. / 1817.
5 Vols. 8vo.   B. 566

Vols. I–II.   Correspondence. pp. xii, (4), 439, (1), portrait.—(2), 396.
Vols. III–IV. Life. pp. (4), 460.—(2), 448.
Vols. V.   Works. pp. viii, 340.
*** The preface is signed "D. H."

1818. Works. Kiel: 1829.

Benjamin Franklin's / Leben und Schriften, / nach der von seinem Enkel, / William Temple Franklin, / veranstalteten / neuen Londoner Original-Ausgabe; / mit Benutzung / des / bei derselben bekannt gemachten / Nachlasses und Früherer Quellen / zeitgemäss bearbeitet von A. Binzer. / Erster Theil. / Kiel, / Universitäts-Buchhandlung. / 1829.

> 4 Vols. 12mo. pp. (6), 303.—246, vi.—249, vi.—(2), 218, vi. B. 567
> *⁎* Only two titles were issued to the four volumes.

1818. Works. London: 1833.

Memoirs / [+ 562 +] / New Edition / London: / Published for Henry Colburn, / by R. Bentley, New Burlington Street. 1833.

> 6 Vols. 8vo. pp. as in No. 562. c. 567
> *⁎* "The so-called new edition of 1833 is the first edition of 1818, with new title pages only." *Sabin.*

1818. Works edited by Duane. Philadelphia: 1808–18.

The / Works / of / Dr. Benjamin Franklin, / in / Philosophy, Politics and Morals: / containing, beside all the Writings published / in former Collections, his / Diplomatic correspondence, / as minister of the United States, at / the court of Versailles; / a variety of literary articles, / and / Epistolary correspondence, / never before published: / with / Memoirs and Anecdotes of his life. / Vol. II. / Philadelphia: Printed and published by William Duane. / 1809.

> 6 Vols. 8vo. (no. pp. 489–498). B., C. 568
> Vol. I. [1818]. Autobiography. pp. (2), xxi, (1), 519, portrait, plate, 2 facsimiles.
> Vol. II. [1809]. Review of Pennsylvania. pp. (6), xxxv, (1), 431.
> Vol. III. [1808]. Scientific. pp. (6), v, (1), 477, 12 plates.
> Vol. IV. [1809]. Political. pp. (10), 407, portrait.
> Vol. V. [1809]. Correspondence. pp. (6), viii, (2), 434.
> Vol. VI. [1817]. Correspondence. pp. (6), xxiii, (1), 564.
> *⁎* The engraved titles are: "The / Works / of / Benjamin Franklin / Vol. II. / Philadelphia. / Printed and published by William Duane / 1809," except Vol. I. which is "Memoirs / of the / Life and Writings / of / Benjamin Franklin / LL.D. F. R. S. / Written by Himself / Philadelphia: / Printed and published by William Duane. / 1818." The

printed title of Vol. I. also differs from the rest of the set, being: "Memoirs / . . . . . / Vol. I. / Philadelphia: / Printed by T. S. Manning. 1818."

₊*₊ This edition was begun in 1808, but owing to the delay of Temple Franklin in printing his edition (with whom Duaue had agreed to an exchange of material), it was not completed till 1818. The editor added many pieces to what had hitherto been printed as Franklin's, derived almost wholly from the books and MSS. which came into his possession by his marriage with the widow of Benjamin Franklin Bache, but the work is so full of blunders and misstatements that its chief value has been to other editors of Franklin. It is reviewed in the *Analectic Magazine*, IX, 553.

1819. Political and Scientific Writings.

The / Posthumous / and / Other Writings / of / Benjamin Franklin, / L L. D. F. R. S., &c. / Minister Plenipotentiary from the United States / of America at the Court of France, and for the Treaty of / Peace and Independence with Great Britain, / &c. &c. / Published from the originals, / by his grandson, / William Temple Franklin. / In Two Volumes. / Vol. I. / London: / Printed for Henry Colburn, Conduit Street. / 1819.

2 Vols. 8vo. pp. xvi, 493.—viii, 523, 8 plates.   569

₊*₊ This title and collation are given on the authority of *Sabin*. See Note to No. 562. They are Vols. v and vi of No. 563.

1819. Political and Scientific Writings.

The / Posthumous / [₊569₊] / Vol. I. / Second Edition. / London: / [₊569₊] / 1819.

2 Vols. 8vo. pp. xvi, 493.—viii, 523, 8 plates.   c. 570

1819. Political and Scientific Writings.

The / Posthumous / [₊569₊] / Vol. I. / Third Edition. / London: / [₊569₊] / 1819.

2 Vols. 8vo. pp. xvi, 493.—viii, 523, 8 plates.   571

1820. Essays.   London: 1820.

Essays and Letters, / by / Dr. Benjamin Franklin. / Part I. / Moral and Philosophical / Vol. I. / [Part II.] Commercial and Political / Vol. II.]   MDCCCXX.

Min. pp. (4), 176.—(2), 164.   A. 572

₊*₊ The engraved title of Vol. I. is: "Dr. B. Franklin's Essays. / Vol. I. / [vignette portrait] / London, Published by John Sharpe, Piccadilly. / 1820," and that of Vol. II: "Essays / by / Dr. Benj. Franklin / Vol. II / London, Published by John Sharpe, Piccadilly / 1820."

1820. Essays.   New York: 1821-2.

Essays and Letters, / by / Dr. B. Franklin. / Part I. / Moral and Philosophical. / Vol. I / [Part II. / Commercial and Political. / Vol. II.]   New-York: / Published by R. & W. A. Bartow & Co., and by / W. A. Bartow & Co., Richmond, (Vir.) / Gray & Bunce, Printers. / 1821.

Min.   pp. 213, (2), portrait.—(2), 216.   B.   573

** Vol. I has no engraved title. That of Vol. II is: Essays / by / Dr. Benjⁿ Franklin / Vol. II. / New York, Published by R. & W. A. Bartow.

1824. Mélanges edited by Renouard.   Paris: 1824.

Mélanges / de Morale / d'Économie et de Politique, / extraits des ouvrages / de Benjamin Franklin, / et précédés d'une Notice sur sa vie, / par A. Ch. Renouard, Avocat. / Tome Premier. / Paris, / Chez Antoine-Augustin Renouard, / Rue de Tournon, No. 6, / 1824.

2 Vols. Min.   pp. vij, (1), 252, portrait.—(4), 186, facsimile. B. 574

1824. Mélanges.   Paris: 1825.

Miscelanca / de Economia, / Politica y Moral, / Extractada de las Obras / de Benjamin Franklin, / y Precedida de una Noticia sobre su Vida. / Traducida del Frances por R. Mangino, naturol de / Méjico, . . . / Tome Primero. / Paris, En la Libreria de Bossange Padre, Calle de Richelieu, No. 60. / 1825.

Min.   pp. (4), ij, 237, portrait.—(4), 230, facsimile.   B.   575

1824. Mélanges.   Paris: 1826.

Mélanges / [*575*] / par A. Ch. Renouard, Avocat. / 2ᵉ edition, revue et augmentée. / Tome premier. / Paris, J. Renouard . . . / 1826.

2 Vols. Min.   pp. as in No. 575.   576

1824. Mélanges.   Volterra: 1834.

Saggi / di / Morale / e / d'Économia Privata estratti dalle Operi / di / Beniamino Franklin / Prima Traduzione Italiana. / V. I. / Volterra. / 1834.

Min.   pp. 190, (1), portrait.—192.   B.   577

1824. Mélanges.   Paris: 1853.

Mélanges / de / Morale, d'Économie / et de Politique. / Extraits des Ouvrages / de Benjamin Franklin / Et précédés d'une Notice sur sa vie par A. Ch. Renouard / Conseiller à la Cour de Cassation / Troisième Édition Revue et augmentée. / Paris / Jule Renouard et Cie, Libraire-Editeur / rue de Tournon, 6. / 1853.

12mo. pp. 376, covers.   B. 578

_**_* The date on the cover is 1854.

1829. Essays.   Paris: 1829.

Écrits Populaires / de Franklin, / choisis et approprié / aux Lecteurs Français / Par le Compagnon de Simon de Mantua. / Paris, Louis Colas, Libraire, rue Dauphine, No. 32. / 1829.

Min. pp. xii, 59, (1).   B. 579

1833. Familiar Letters, edited by Sparks.   Boston: 1833.

A / Collection / of the / Familiar Letters / and / Miscellaneous Papers / of / Benjamin Franklin; / Now for the first time published. / Boston: / Published by Charles Bowen. / 1833.

12mo. pp. xvi, 295, (1).   C. 580

_**_* Though the title states that the contents are "for the first time published," some of the letters had been printed before. The "Miscellaneous Papers" consist of Franklin's MS. annotations from five pamphlets formerly in the Athenæum of Philadelphia; Walpole's Grant, and the "Craven Street Gazette." Reviewed in *American Monthly Review*, IV, 124; *Monthly Review*, CXXXII, 239; and by W. B. O. Peabody in the *North American Review*, XXXVII, 249.

1833. Familiar Letters.   London: 1833.

Familiar Letters / and / Miscellaneous Papers / of / Benjamin Franklin; / now for the first time published. / Edited by Jared Sparks, / . . . / . . . / . . . / with explanatory notes. / London: / Jackson and Walford, / St. Paul's Church-Yard. / 1833.

8vo. pp. xvi, 295, (1).   C. 581

1834. Essays edited by Howard.   London: [1834?]

The / Beauties / of / Franklin, / consisting of / Selections from his Writings. / By Alfred Howard, Esq. / London: / Printed by T. Davidson, / . . .

Min. pp. (2), 186, (2), portrait.   P. H. S.   582

1834. Works edited by Duane.

Memoirs / of / Benjamin Franklin. / Written by Himself, / and continued by his grandson and others / with his Social Epistolary Correspondence, Philosophical, Political, / and Moral Letters and Essays, / and his / Diplomatic Transactions as agent at London and Minister / Plenipotentiary at Versailles. / Augmented Edition / with a / Postliminious Preface. / In Two Volumes. / Vol. I. / Philadelphia: / M'Carty & Davis, No. 171 Market St. / 1834.

2 Vols. 8vo. pp. (2), xxxvii, (1), 624, portrait.—(2), vii, (1), 517, plate.   583

*** The engraved title is: The / Life and Writings / of / Benjamin Franklin / . . . . . / Philadelphia / Published by M'Carthy & Davis.

*** This is a republication of Duane's edition, published in 1818, "augmented equal to the contents of a volume more than was contained in that edition." There is a reissue by the same publishers dated 1840.

1834. Works. New York: 1859.

Memoirs / [*583*] / with a / Postliminious Preface / By William Duane. / In two Volumes. / Vol. I. / New York / Derby & Jackson, 119 Nassau Street / 1859.

2 Vols. 8vo. pp. as in No. 583.   584

*** The British Museum Catalogue gives an edition "N. Y. 1845."

1834. Works. New York: 1861.

Memoirs / [*584*] / Vol. I. / New York: / H. W. Derby, 625 Broadway. / 1861.

2 Vols. 8vo, pp. as in No. 583.   585

1835. Essays. Paris: [1835?]

Instructions / du / Peuple Français; / Livres vendus au prix constant. / Mélanges / de / Morale, d'Économie et de Politique, / Extraits / des ouvrages de Benjamin Franklin. / Paris, / Imprimeur de A. Firmin Didot / Rue Jacob, No. 24.

Min. pp. 39, (1).   B.   586

1835. Essays.

Esprit / de Franklin / ou / Trésor di Sagesse. / Paris. / Louis Janet, / Libraire, / Rue Saint Jacques, No. 59.

Min. pp. viii, 152, portrait, plate.   B. 587

1840. Works edited by Sparks. Boston: 1836–40.

The / Works / of / Benjamin Franklin; / containing / several political and historical tracts / not included in any former edition, / and / many letters official and private / not hitherto published; / with / notes / and / a life of the author / By Jared Sparks. / Volume I. / Boston: / Hilliard Gray, and Company. / 1840.

10 Vols. Rl. 8vo. and 8vo.   B., C. 588

Vol. I.   Life. pp. xxxvii, (4), 612, portrait, plate.
Vol. II.   Essays. pp. ix, (2), 557, portrait.
Vol. III.   Essays. pp. xiv, 577, portrait.
Vol. IV.   Essays. pp. ix, (2), 339, portrait, 2 plates.
Vol. V.   Essays. pp. xiii, (2), 516, facsimile, 2 plates.
Vol. VI.   Scientific. pp. xiii, (2), 578, 11 plates.
Vol. VII.   Correspondence. pp. xxxi, (2), 568, portrait.
Vol. VIII.   Correspondence. pp. xxii, (2), 554.
Vol. IX.   Correspondence. pp. xxi, (2), 550.
Vol. X.   Correspondence. pp. xix, (2), 540, 4 ll.

₊*₊ Mr. Sparks added some six hundred and fifty pieces to what had before been printed in editions of Franklin's writings, with many long and scholarly notes, which in spite of succeeding editions still makes this among the most valuable. Reviewed by F. Bowen in the *North American Review*, LIX, 446; and by H. T. Tuckerman in the same, LXXXIII, 402.

1840. Works. Boston: 1856.

The Works of [+588+] Boston: Whittemore, Niles and Hall. 1856.

10 Vols. 8vo. pp. as in No. 588.   589

1840. Works. London: 1882.

The Works of / [+588+] / London: Benjamin Franklin Stevens / 4 Trafalgar Square, Charing Cross / 1882.

10 Vols. 8vo. pp. as in No. 588.   590

1841. Essays.

This Impression was taken / . . . / At the identical Press, at which / Dr. Franklin worked in London as a journeyman, in the year 1725–6. / [Liverpool : Mitchell, Heaton & Mitchell.   1841.]

4to.   Broadside.   S. D.   590

✱✱ A leaflet, containing Franklin's poem on "Paper" and his "Twelve Rules of Conduct."

1842? Essays.

Dr. Franklin's Moral Table for Perfecting the Human Character.   [n. p., n. d.]

4to.   Broadside.   B.   591

1847. Essays.

Mélanges / d'Économie Politique / . . . / Paris, / Chez Guillaumin et Cie . . . / . . . . . / 1847.

2 Vols.   8vo.   592

✱✱ The half title at p. 621 is "Franklin / La Science / du / Bonhomme Richard, et autre opuscules." It includes Nos. 28, 30, 69, 107, 330, 348, "Economical Project," "Petition of the Left Hand," "Price of Wheat," "Liberty of Commerce," and extracts from letters.

1850. Essays.

Essays; / Humorous, Moral and Literary. / By Dr. Franklin. / London: / Published by J. S. Pratt. / MDCCCL.

Min.   pp. (4), (11)–147.   593

✱✱ See No. 531.

1852. Essays on Commerce, etc., edited by McCulloch.

A / Select Collection / of / Scarce and Valuable / Economic Tracts / from the originals of / Defoe, Elking, Franklin, Turgot . . . / . . . / With a Preface, Notes and Index. / London: / MDCCCLIX.

8vo.   C.   594

✱✱ The half title at page 161 is "Extracts / from the / Works / of / Dr. Franklin / on Population, Commerce, / &c." Edited by J. R. McCulloch for Lord Overstone. Only 150 copies privately printed.

1853. Select Works edited by Sargent.

The / Select Works / of / Benjamin Franklin; / including / His Autobiography, / with Notes and a Memoir / by Epes Sargent. / Boston: / Phillips, Sampson and Company / 1853.

12mo.   pp. (2), xiv, 502, portrait, facsimile.   B.   595

✱✱ The first title is: "The / Select Works / of / Franklin / edited by

/ Epes Sargent. / Boston: / Phillips, Sampson & Co." *Swift* gives re-issues, dated 1856, 1857 and 1858.

1853. Select Works.

The / Select Works / [*595*] / Boston: / J. L. Shorey. / 1866.

12mo. pp. 256, facsimile.   B. 596

1866. Correspondence.

Correspondance / de / Benjamin Franklin / Traduite de l'Anglais et Annotée / par / Édouard Laboulaye / . . . . / Tome Premier / 1757–1775 / Paris / Libraire de L. Hachette et Cie / . . . / 1866 / . . .

2 Vols. 12mo. pp. (4), vii, 462, (2) covers.—(4), iv, 528, covers. 597

⁎ See No. 598.

1867. Essays.

El Libro / del / Hombre de Bien / Opusculos Morales, Económicos y Politicos. / Estractados de / Benjamin Franklin / . . . . . / Barcelona. / Libreria de D. Juan Oliveres, . . . / . . . / 1867.

12mo. pp. 402, (2), covers.   597*

1867. Essays.

Essais / de morale et d'économie politique / de / Benjamin Franklin / Traduits de l'Anglais et annottés / par / Édouard Laboulaye / . . . . . Paris / Libraire de L. Hachette et Cie / . . . / 1867 / . . .

12mo. pp. (4), 348, covers.   598

⁎ This, with Nos. 421 and 497, constitute a four volume edition of Franklin's writings, but each work was also sold separately.

1889. Works edited by Bigelow. New York: 1887–89.

The Complete Works / of / Benjamin Franklin / including / his private as well as his official and scientific correspondence, and / numerous letters and documents now for the first / printed with many others not included in / any former collection / also / the unmutilated and correct version of his autobiography / compiled and edited / by / John Bigelow. / . . . / Vol. I / New York and London / G. P. Putnam's Sons / The Knickerbocker Press / 1887.

10 Vols. 8vo.   B. 600

Vol. I.   [1725–1744]   pp. xxxii, 523, portrait.
Vol. II.   [1744–1757]   pp. xiii, 523, 4 plates.
Vol. III.   [1758–1766]   pp. xiii, 511, 2 plates.
Vol. IV.   [1767–1772]   pp. xvii, 558, portrait, plate.
Vol. V.   [1772–1775]   pp. xv, 564, 1 plate.
Vol. VI.   [1776–1779]   pp. xx, 485.
Vol. VII.   [1780–1782]   pp. xxiv, 497.
Vol. VIII.   [1782–1784]   pp. xix, 522.
Vol. IX.   [1784–1788]   pp. xiv, 484, 3 plates.
Vol. X.   [1788–1790, Supplement] pp. xx, 448.

*** Mr. Bigelow has not only corrected many of Mr. Sparks' errors, but has added some six hundred new pieces to what had hitherto been printed as Franklin's. The chronological arrangement is also a great improvement on the classical one of all prior editions. Reviewed in *New York Times*, June 24 and Dec. 9, 1888; by Edward Eggleston in New York *Commercial Advertiser*, Sept. 14, 1888; and in the *Critic*, Dec. 15, 1888.

The following is the prospectus of the work:

The Complete Works / of / Benjamin Franklin / . . . . . / to be edited by John Bigelow. / This Edition (which will be the most complete ever issued) will be / limited to six hundred sets, / . . . . . / G. P. Putnam's Sons, / New York. / . . . . .   4to. pp. (4).   600*

PART TWO.

PERIODICALS AND SERIALS

CONTAINING

WRITINGS OF FRANKLIN.

_**_* This list only includes such periodicals and serials as contain original publications contributed by Franklin in his life time. It is of necessity imperfect.

1722. The New England Courant. Boston.

⁕ See No. 3.

1729. The Weekly Mercury. Philadelphia. 601

⁕ "The Busy Body" series. See *Sparks,* II, 13.

1729. The Pennsylvania Gazette.

⁕ See No. 11.

1752. Votes and Proceedings of the House of Representatives of the Province of Pennsylvania. Philadelphia.

602

⁕ "You [Franklin] encumbered the Minutes with such a load of scurrilous messages of your own drawing, and such long reports put together from law books, old histories and journals." *William Smith in No. 278.*

⁕ A description of the issues of the "Votes" is given by *Hildeburn.*

1756. The Gentleman's Magazine. 603

⁕ See also *A General Index . . . to the Gentleman's Magazine,* and Vol. LX, 571.

1756. Feb. Military Act of Pennsylvania.
1756. Mar. Dialogue between X, Y and Z.
1757. Sept. Vindication of Pennsylvania. [Signed] "William Franklin."
1764. April. Parable against Persecution.
1764. April. Narrative of Massacre.
1768. Jan. Defense of the Americans. "A. B."
1768. Jan. Cause of American Discontents. "F. † S."
1768. July. Magic Squares.
1768. Oct. Magic Circle.
1768. Nov. Trade of the Northern Colonies. "F. B."
1768. Nov. Trade of the West Indies. "F. B."

1756. Philosophical Transactions of the Royal Society. 604

⁕ See *Index to the Philosophical Transactions of the Royal Society.*

1759. The London Chronicle. 605

⁕ I have only been able to examine an imperfect file of this paper.
1759. May 10. "A New England Man."

1759. Sept. 1. "F." ?
1759. Sept. 11. "F" ?
1759. Dec. 25. "A. Z."
1760.   ?   "A Briton."
1765. May ? "A Traveller."
1766. Feb. 6-8. "A Lover of Britain."
1766.   ?   "Arator."
1767. April 7. "F. B."
1767. July 11. "B. F."
1767. Nov. 24. "B. F."
1768. Jan. 7. "F. S."

1759. Grand Magazine. London. 606

*** "I can only send you . . . some little sketches that have been printed in the *Grand Magazine*, which I should hardly own did I not know that your friendly partiality would make them seem at least tolerable." *Franklin to Kames*, Jan. 3, 1760.

*** I have been unable to examine a file of this magazine. The pieces are inedited.

1759? Monthly Review. London. 607

*** Dr. Franklin . . . recommended him [Dr. Edward Bancroft] to the editors and proprietors of the Monthly Review, in which his standing share was to review all publications relative to America. This information I had from Dr. Franklin himself. I understood this very well, as I thought—to wit, that Bancroft was the ostensible reviewer, but that Franklin was always consulted before the publication." *John Adams' Works, III, 142.*

1767. Pennsylvania Chronicle. 608

*** The following is a copy of a paper in the Stevens-Franklin Collection:

"List of some Papers in Goddard's Pennsylvanian Chronicle,—written by Benj. Franklin.

1767. Feb. 16. Two Letters signed, F. B. & N. N.
  "   " 23. Two Dr. signed *Pacificus* & *Homespun* (or Honestus).
1767. Mar. 9. Two Dr. signed N. N. & F. B.
  "   " 23. Two Dr. signed Homespun & F. B.
  "   June 1. Remarks on the Report published in the last Chronicle, by B. F. Esq.
  "   June 8. Two Papers, signed A Friend to both Countries and *Benevolus.*
1768. Mar. 14. Extract of a Letter from London.
  "   April 25. Letter signed F. † S.
  "   Oct. 12. Queries signed N. M. C. N. P. C. H.

1768. Dec.   5. Piece signed *Day Light*, another signed N. N.
  "   "   12. Piece signed *New England*.
1769. Jan'y 16. Letter to Gov. Shirley—& Remark.
  "   Feb.   6. Letter addressed to Thomas Crowley, signed *Francis Lyon*.
  "   Apr.   3. Extract of a Letter from Paris to a Gentⁿ in London.
  "   June 26. Intelligence from London.
  "   "   9. A little paper signed "Twilight."

1767. The Political Register. London. 608*

** Almon states that Franklin contributed to this, but I can assign nothing to his pen in it except possibly that signed "B. F." in No. XVIII, p. 137.

1772. London Packet. 609

1772. June 3. "A New Englandman."

1773. Public Advertiser. London. 610

1773. "A. P."
       A Well-wisher to the King and all his Dominions.
       A Londoner.
1773. Prussian Edict.
1774. A Friend to the Poor.
  ?   J. J.
  ?   Z. Z.
1777. July 18. Vindication of Congress.

1774? Public Ledger. London. 611

—— —— "A Londoner."

1776. Pennsylvania Evening Post. Philadelphia. 612

** See No. 322.

1776. Affaires de l'Angleterre et de l'Amérique. 613

** See No. 326.

1777? Journal de Paris. 614

—— — A Subscriber.

1785. Memoirs of the Literary and Philosophical Society of Manchester. Vol. II. 615

** Contains Franklin's:
"On the different quantities of Rain which fall at different heights over the same spot of ground." See No. 356.
"Meterological Imaginations and Conjectures."

1786. Transactions of the American Philosophical Society. 616

Causes and Cure of Smoky Chimneys.   II, 1.
Slowly sensible Hygrometer.   II, 51.
Stove for burning Pit-coal.   II, 57.
Maritime Observations.   II, 294.
Formation of the Earth.   III, 1.
New Theory of Light.   III, 5.
Queries and Conjectures.   III, 10.

1787. American Museum.   616*

I.   1.   Consolation for America.
      113.   Notes.
      125.   Parable against Persecution.
      243.   Speech of Polly Baker.
      311.   Establishment of the R. I. Mint.
      452.   Meteorological Imaginations.
II.   17.   Remarks on Paper Money.
       86.   Origin of tobacco.
       87.   Way to make Money Plenty.
      211.   Advice to Emigrants.
      558.   Final Speech in Convention.
V.   109.   Increase of Mankind·
      313.   Gulf Stream.
      233.   Positions on Trade.
      283.   A Prussian Edict.
      353.   Remarks on Smuggling.
      343.   Remarks on Indians.
VI.   295.   Court of the Press.
VII. 101.   On Privateering.
      265.   Petition of the Left Hand.
      314.   Way to Wealth.
      316.   Economical Project.
VIII. 12.   Extracts from Autobiography.
      169.   The Whistle.
      183.   The Ephemeræ.
X.   336.   The Slave Trade.
XI.   67.   Art of Dreaming.

1788. Repository for Select Pieces. London.   617
1788. May. Letter on China.

1789. Federal Gazette.   618
1789. Sept. 12.
1790. Mar. 25. Historicus.

PART THREE.

STATE PAPERS AND TREATIES

IN THE FORMATION OF WHICH

FRANKLIN AIDED.

_**_* The references appended to these titles are only such as relate to the authorship or construction of each paper, and to its correct title. The other references are given in the Reference List.

1785. Treaty with Prussia.   632

₊₊ "The best lesson of humanity which a philosophical king (Frederick II.), acting in concert with a philosophical patriot (Franklin), could possibly give to the princes and statesmen of the earth." *Monthly Review.*

1787. Constitution of the United States.   633

₊₊ See *The Madison Papers*, or *Elliot's Debates*, v; and Yates' *Secret Proceedings of the Federal Convention.*

PART FOUR.

WORKS

CONTAINING

LETTERS OF FRANKLIN.

PART FIVE.

PSEUDONYMS

USED BY

FRANKLIN.

[307]

PART SIX.

WRITINGS

WRONGFULLY OR DOUBTFULLY

ASCRIBED TO

FRANKLIN.

Hooped Petticoats Arraigned and Condemned by the Light of Nature and the Law of God. [Boston: James Franklin. 1719.] 767

₊ In the *Brinley Catalogue* (lot No. 7838), it is suggested that this is by Franklin, and Mr. McMaster goes farther by saying "there is much reason to believe that he was . . . the author." Whether a catalogue maker has a right to make his wares sell for a higher price by ascribing them without proof to a celebrated pen, is a question in ethics for Mr. J. Hammond Trumbull, but such "notes" should certainly not be used in writing the literary biography of the said pen.

The Infallibility of Human Judgment . . . By Mr. Lyons. London: 1724. 768

₊ Mr. Stevens catalogued this in such a way as to make Mr. Swift think that it contained Franklin's "Dissertation on Liberty and Necessity," and it is accordingly so entered in his list. It does not however contain it.

M. T. Cicero's Cato Major. See No. 44.

Letters between Theophilus and Eugenio . . . Philadelphia: 1747. 769

₊ Sabin ascribes this to Franklin "on the authority of an auction catalogue." The compiler has an English edition printed in 1720.

Necessary Truth. See No. 65.

Memorial of the Case of the German Emigrants. London: 1754. 770

₊ *Sabin* gives this in his list of Franklin titles, but does not authenticate it, so in the absence of proof we may safely conclude it is not by him.

A Brief State of the Province of Pennsylvania . . . London: 1755. 771

₊ *Rich* states that according to an MS. note in his copy, William Smith was assisted in this by Franklin. As it is in direct opposition to the latter's opinions, it is hardly necessary to bring forward the personal enmity between the two to disprove it.

Historical View.   See No. 253.

True and Impartial State.   See No. 260.

Interest of Great Britain.   See No. 262.

Continuation of the Account of the Pennsylvania Hospital.   See No. 99.

The Quaker Unmasked.   Philadelphia: 1764.   772

 ⁎ A reply to this charges Franklin with writing it.   Hildeburn states it was written by David James Dove, but I think this is an error.

Cogitata De Cometis.   Communicated by Benjamin Franklin.   London.   1767.   773

 ⁎ This is by John Winthrop, of Harvard College.

Philosophical Essays.   Edinburgh.   1768.   774

 ⁎ Ascribed to Franklin in bookseller's catalogue.   It is erroneous.

Letters to several friends by Arouet de Voltaire.   Translated by Benjamin Franklin.   London: 1770.   775

 ⁎ Entered under Franklin in the Catalogue of the British Museum. It is the Rev. Dr. Franklin.

A Few Reasons in favor of Vendues.   Philadelphia: 1772.   776

 ⁎ Sabin places this in his Franklin list.   I think it is certainly not by him.

Principles of Trade.   See No. 330.

An Appeal to the Justice and Interest of the People of Great Britain . . . London: 1774.   777

 ⁎ Almon claims that Franklin had "a considerable share in the composition."   Arthur Lee unquestionably wrote it.

A True State of the Proceedings in the Parliament of Great Britain.   London: 1775.   778

 ⁎ Reprinted as Franklin's, in the *Prior Documents*, and from there taken by Mr. Sparks for his edition of Franklin.   It was really written by Arthur Lee, from material furnished by Franklin.

Plan offered by the Earl of Chatham, to the House of Lords . . . . . London: 1774.   779

 ⁎ Accredited to Franklin by some of the contemporary politicians and newspapers.   See Sparks' *Works of Franklin*, v, 51.

View of the Title to Indiana.   Philadelphia: 1776.   780

 ⁎ Sabin places this in his Franklin list with a query.   I can see no present reason for ascribing it to him.

Ledger of Doctor Benjamin Franklin. See No. 325.

Matroco. Drame burlesque. Paris: 1777. 781

  *** Accredited to Franklin's pen in *Affairé de l'Angleterre et de l'Amérique*, VII, cxxviij.

Address to the Holders of British Stock in Holland. [n. p. n. d.] 782

  *** Included in MS. list of Frankliniana by Henry Stevens, but why I cannot say.

Two Letters from Dr. Franklin. See No. 346.

Constitution of the Pennsylvania Society for promoting the Abolition of Slavery. Philadelphia: 1788. 783

  *** Ascribed to Franklin by Mr. Swift. Franklin was in France during the preparation of the constitution, and so could hardly draw it.

Avis aux faiseurs de Constitutions. See No. 382.

An Essay on the African Slave Trade. Philadelphia: 1790. 784

  *** *Sabin* improperly ascribes it to Franklin. It is of English origin.

Forged Letters.

  *** The . . . English papers teemed with forged letters, long, tedious, flat and dull, in the name of Dr. Franklin . . . The Doctor declared them all forgeries. John Adams' *Works*, IX, 99.

WORKS

RELATING TO, WRITTEN TO, OR DEDICATED TO

FRANKLIN.

_**_* Arranged alphabetically by author or editor, or by the first word
of title, articles excepted, if the former are unknown.

[*Abbott, Jacob.*]
Franklin, / the Apprentice Boy / New York: / Harper & Brothers, Publisher. [1855.]

12mo. pp. 160, plates.   B. 790

  ** *Sabin* (No. 25610) gives a title: "Franklin the Apprentice. New York. Harper & Brother 1856," which I presume is the same as the above.

Abbott, John Stevens Cabot.
American Pioneers and Patriots / Benjamin Franklin / A Picture of the / Struggles of our Infant Nation, / one hundred years ago / By John S. C. Abbott / . . . / Illustrated / New York: / Dodd, Mead & Company, Publishers. [1876.]

12mo. pp. vii, 5–373, plates.   B. 791

Abbott, J. S. C.
Benjamin Franklin, / Printer's Boy, Statesman, Philosopher, / and Patriot. / By John S. C. Abbott / with numerous illustrations / London: / Ward, Lock & Co., / Warwick House, Salisbury Square, E. C.

12mo. pp. iv, (2), 6–373.   792

The Addition to the Epitaph, without the Copperplate / [Philadelphia: Anthony Armbruster. 1764.]

Folio. Broadside.   P. 793

  ** A burlesque in the form of a prayer, by David James Dove?" Title and note from *Hildeburn.* See No. 997.

An Advertisement, and not a Joke. / A Speech there is which no Man spoke: [Philadelphia: William Bradford.]

4to. Broadside.   P. 794

  ** See McMaster's *Benjamin Franklin,* p. 186.

[*Almon, John.*]
Benjamin Franklin [in Biographical, Literary and Political Anecdotes] London: 1797.

Vol. II, pp. 175–344.   795

[321]

_**_* A sketch of Franklin by a printer who had much intercourse with him in his second visit to England.

An Answer to Mr. Franklin. *See No. 278.*

Annual Dinner / of the / Typothetæ / Of New York / in honor of the birth-day of / Benjamin Franklin / . . . / Tuesday, January 17th, 1884.

8vo. pp. 14, covers.   796

_**_* Many of the speeches relate to Franklin.

[Same] 1885.

8vo. pp. 11, covers.   797

[Same] 1886.

8vo. pp. 15, covers.   798

[Same] 1887.

8vo. pp. 12, covers.   799

[Same] 1888.

8vo. pp. 14, covers.   800

An / Answer / to the / Plot / [Philadelphia: Anthony Armbruster. 1764]

Folio. Broadside.   P. 801

_**_* "Ten Verses not very complimentary to Franklin." Title and note from *Hildeburn.* See Nos. 855 and 937.

Apperçu Hazardé. *See No. 859.*

Aquarone, Bartolomeo.

Vita di Benjamino Franklin. Milano: P. Carrera. 1867.

Min. pp. ⁻6.   802

_**_* Title from *Swift.*

Arman, Bly.

L'Art de faire sa fortune de l'Aquévir, d'Augmenter de la Conserver, par un ancien ouvrier devan millionaire, ou La vie de Benjamin Franklin en exemplis inédit de la science de bonhomme Richard. Paris: 1872.

8vo. pp. 16.   803

The / Author / of / Quaker Unmask'd, / strip'd / Stark Naked, / Or The / Delineated / Presbyterian / Play'd / Hob With. / Philadelphia. / Printed [by Anthony Armbruster] in the Year M,DCC,LXIV.

8vo. pp. 12.   P. H. S. 804

*** Charges Franklin with being the author of *The Quaker Unmasked*, whom it attacks both on that and political grounds.

Bache, *Alexander Dallas.*

Attempt / to fix the date of the observation / of / Doctor Franklin / in relation to the / North East Storms / of the / Atlantic Coast of the United States / By A. D. Bache. / . . . . . / From the Journal of the Franklin Institute / Philadelphia: / Printed by Jesper Harding. / 1833.

8vo. pp. 6.   B. 805

[Bache, *Richard Meade.*]

(Reprinted from Penn Monthly for May, 1882.) / The Lost Papers of Benjamin Franklin. [Philadelphia. 1882.]

8vo. pp. 18.   806

Baker, *P. Carpenter.*

Franklin. / An Address / delivered before / The New York Typographical Society, / on / Franklin's Birthday / January 17, 1865 / By Peter C. Baker. / New York: / Baker & Godwin, Printers / . . . / 1865.

8vo. pp. 28.   B. 807

*** Mr. Baker has also delivered:
European Recollections. An Address . . . on Franklin's Birthday, January 17, 1861 . . . New York. 1861.   808

A Battle! A Battle! A Battle a Squirt; / Where no Man is kill'd, and no Man is hurt! / To the Tune of / Three new blue Beans, in a new blue blown Bladder; / rattle Bladder, rattle Bladder! / To which is added, / The / Quaker's Address, versifi'd; / and / King Wampum, on Harm watch Harm / catch. / . . . . . / [Philadelphia:] Printed [by Andrew Stewart] and sold at the Blue-Nose, near / Brazen-Nose-College, Germantown. [1764.]

Sm. 8vo. pp. 11, (1), plate.   809

*** The plate represents Franklin in his study with a not over-complimentary accompanying stanza. See *Hildeburn*, No. 1959.

Bauer, *J. C. B.*

Franklin and Washington / oder / Sammlung / der / merkwürdigsten bekannten Zuge / aus / dem Leben dieser um Amerika verdienten Männer / Von / Johann Christian Au-

gust Bauer / Prediger zu Güldengossa Leipzig. / Berlin.
1806. / In der Frolich'schen Buchhandlung.

12mo. pp. xiv, 350.

810

[*Beaumarchais, Pierre Auguste Caron de.*]

Le Vœu de toutes les Nations et l'Interet de toutes les
puissance dans l'abbaissement et l'Humiliation de la
Grande Bretagne. [n. p.] 1778.

8vo. pp. (6), 74.

811

₊₊* Dedicated to Franklin.

+ Second Edition, corrigée par l'Auteur. [n. p.] 1778.

8vo. (2), 74.

812

Benjamin Franklin. A Book for all. *See No. 889.*

Benjamin Franklin / "Doer of Good" / A Biography /
. . . / Edinburgh / William P. Nimmo. [186–?]

12mo. pp. 326, portrait.

B. 813

Benjamin Franklin / "Doer of Good" / A Biography /
. . . / Edinburgh / William P. Nimmo. / 1872.

12mo. pp. 322, plates.

B. H. S. 814

₊₊* Also issues with change of date.

Bessière, L.

La Jeunesse de Franklin. Senlis: 1866.

12mo. pp.

815

Bessière, J. F.

Franklin. Comédie historique en cinq actes et en
prose. Par J. F. Bessière. Paris: l'auteur. 1838.

8vo. 6 sheets.

816

Bettziech-Beta, H.

Benjamin Franklin. / Sein Leben, Denken und Werken.
/ Von / Heinr. Bettziech-Beta. / Leipzig: / F. A. Brock-
haus. / 1853.

8vo. pp. (4), 108.

817

"Unterhaltende Belehrungen zur Förderung allgemeiner Bildung.
Band 18."

B. Franklin: / Vir vixit integer, liber obit, / Regnatur
innotatus: / Pri. Gall. Lib. An. M.DCC.XC.

Sm. 4to. Broadside.

N. 818

Biddle, James.

To the / Freeholders and Electors / Of the Province of Pennsylvania. [Philadelphia: William Bradford. 1765.]

Folio. Broadside. 819

₊₊ A savage attack on Franklin and his party. It is signed James Biddle, but William Franklin says the principal officers of the Government employed Biddle to read it aloud to the public. See No. 855.

Bigelow, John.   See No. 424.

Bigelow, John.

Franklin, A Sketch. Boston: Little, Brown, & Co. 1879.

Min. pp. 30. B. 820

Blaine, James G.   See Nos. 900–1.

Bloomfield, O. B. F.   See No. 904.

Boucher, J.

A / View / of the / Causes and Consequences / of the / American Revolution / . . . . . / By Jonathan Boucher, . . . / . . . . . / London: / . . . / M.DCC.XCVII.

8vo. pp. (6), xciv, (2), 596. 821

₊₊ The tenth discourse "on the character of Ahitophel" is clearly, in spite of the author's partial disclaimer, intended to represent Franklin, and the "Appendix" to it is made up of one of the most unfair and untruthful attacks ever made on him.

Boyhood and Manhood.   *See No. 890.*

A / Brief Memoir / of / the Life / of / Dr. Benjamin Franklin, / with an appendix. / Compiled for the use of Young persons. / New York: / Printed and sold by Mahlon Day, / At the New Juvenile Book-store, / No. 372, Pearl Street / 1824.

Min. pp. 90, plate. 822

Brinley, F.

Address / delivered before / The Franklin Debating Society / in / Chauncey Hall, January 17, 1830, / being the Celebration of / their Seventh Anniversary / and / the Birth of Franklin / By Francis Brinley, Jr. / Boston: / Printed for the Society, by Isaac R. Butts. / M.DCCCXXX.

8vo. pp. 16. B. 823

Brougham, J.

French's Standard Drama / No. CLXVI. / Franklin: /
A new and Original / Historical Drama / in / Five Acts. /
By John Brougham, Comedian. / . . . . . / New-York: /
Samuel French / . . . / [1856]

12mo. pp. 27, (1), cover.   P. 824

Brown, H. S.

Lectures to the Men of Liverpool, / by / Hugh Stowell
Brown. / Poor Richard's Almanac / Fourth Edition. /
Price One Penny. / Liverpool: / Gabriel Thomson, . . . /
. . . . . / 1857.

12mo. pp. 142.   825

Burdick, W.

An / Oration / on the / Nature and Effects / of the / Art
of Printing. / Delivered / In Franklin Hall, July 5, 1802,
/ before the / Boston Franklin Association, / By / William
Burdick / . . . . . / Printed by Munroe & Francis, Boston . . . 1802.

8vo. pp. 31.   826

Butler, J. M., editor.

Franklin / before the Privy Council / White-Hall Chapel,
London, 1774, / on behalf of the / Province of Massachusetts, / to advocate the removal of Hutchinson and Oliver.
/ Philadelphia: / Published by John M. Butler, / 242 Chestnut Street. / 1859.

8vo. pp. v, 134, plate.   827

   *** This is a reprint of a chapter from Bancroft, No. 916, and Lord
Chatham's speech. It was prepared by J. M. Butler as an advertisement of the engraving of a picture.

Cadet, Felix.

Histoire de l'Économie politique.   Les précurseurs:
Adam Smith, Franklin, ... Paris: Guillaumin. 1871.

8vo. pp.   828

   *** Title from *Swift*.

Caritat.   See No. 841.

Casette Verte.   *See Nos. 975–6.*

Catalogue of Books.   *See Nos. 968–9.*

Cantwell, Edward.

Benjamin Franklin. Oxford, N. C.: Published by the Franklin Society. 1867.

8vo. pp. 31.   B. A.   829

Cecil, E.

Life of Franklin, Written for Children. By E. Cecil. Boston: Crosby, Nichols and Company. 1859.

Min. pp.   B. A.   830

Celebration / The One Hundred Eighty-Third Anniversary / Birthday of Benjamin Franklin / Tremont House, Chicago, January 17, 1889. / "Strange that Ulysses does a thousand things / so well"—Iliad / [Chicago. 1889.]

8vo. pp. (4), covers.   831

[Chalmers, George.]

Second Thoughts: / or, / Observations / upon / Lord Abingdon's Thoughts / on the / Letter of Edmund Burke, Esq. / To the Sheriffs of Bristol. / By the author of the / Answer to Mr. Burke's Letter / . . . . . / London: / Printed for T. Cadell, . . . / M.DCC.LXXVII.

8vo. pp. (4), 72.   832

_**_* Lord Abingdon had spoken of Franklin as a "great philanthropist and friend of liberty." This stirred Mr. Chalmers into a savage and rather lengthy philippic against Franklin, a fair idea of which may be gathered from the following passage: "Trained in the hardy school of private treachery, stained with the honourable blood of injured friendship, he thought he was qualified to be a public traitor—and he did not err. Unhappy man! His ambitious villainy is stopt for want of space."

+ Second Edition. London: . . . 1777.
8vo. pp. (4), 74.   833

Chaplin, J.

Life of Benjamin Franklin. By Jeremiah Chaplin. Boston. D. Lothrop & Co. 1876.

Min. pp.   834

Chatenet. See No. 853.

City Document.   *See No. 912.*

City Document.   No. 26 | City of Boston. | Franklin Fund | . . . | April 11, 1853.

8vo. pp. 7.   835

⁎ A report by the Committee appointed to examine the accounts and a history of the Franklin fund.

City of Boston | Ceremonies | at the | Inauguration | of the | Statue of Franklin, | September 17, 1856. | Boston: | Geo. C. Rand & Avery, | City Printers, | No. 3, Cornhill. | 1856.

Min. pp. 16.   836

City of Boston | Inaugural of the Statue | of | Benjamin Franklin. | . . . . . | Aug. 23, 1856.

4to. Broadside.   B. 837

⁎ An account of the celebration.

Coombe, T.

A | Sermon | Preached before the Congregations of | Christ Church and St. Peter's | Philadelphia, | On Thursday, July 20, 1775. | . . . . . | By Thomas Coombe, M. A. | . . . . . | Philadelphia: | . . . | M,DCCLXXIV.

8vo. pp. (4), 29.   P. H. S. 838

⁎ Dedicated to Franklin.   There are other editions as follows:

+ Second Edition | Philadelphia: | . . . | M.DCC.LXXV.

8vo. pp. 4, 29.   839

+ Philadelphia | Printed, | Newport, Rhode Island, Reprinted . . . 1775.

8vo. pp. 23.   840

Comme on Devient.   *See No. 847.*

[*Condorcet, Marie Jean Antoine Nicolas de Caritat, Marquis de.*]

Éloge | de | M. Franklin, | Lu à la séance publique de l'Académie | des Sciences, le 13 Nov. 1790 | . . . . . | A Paris, | Chez Pyre, Libraire, rue de la Harpe, No. 51. | Petit, Libraire, au Palais Royal, No. 250. | 1791.

8vo. pp. (2), 42, covers.   S. D. 841

⁎ Also printed in *Œuvres de Condorcet*, III, 372.

Condorcet.

Lofreden | over | den Heer | Benjamin Franklin. | In

eene openbare zitting van de Akade- / mie der Weten-schappen te Parijs, den / XIII. van November, 1790, uit-gesproken, / door den Heer / De Condorcet. / Uit het Fransch vertaald. / . . . . . / Te Rotterdam, / Bij J. Meyer, / 1791.

8vo. pp. (4), 68.   842

Costa, Benjamin Franklin De, editor.

Soldier and Sage / Memorials / of / George Washington / and / Benjamin Franklin / Philadelphia: / McCalla & Stavely. / 1876.

Min. pp. 18, covers.   843

The Counter Medley, being a proper answer to all the Dunces of the Medley and their Abettors. [Philadelphia: 1764.]

Folio. Broadside.   P. 844

  ⁎ A political squib on Franklin and his party.

Courcy, De.   See No. 865.

De Courcy.   See No. 865.

De Groot.   See No. 944.

De Lescaux.   See No. 899.

Demoulin, G.

Bibliothèque / des Écoles et des Familles. / Franklin / par / Mme Gustave Demoulin / Deuxieme Edition / Paris / Librairie Hachette et Cie. / 79, Boulevard Saint-Germain, 79 / 1882 / . . .

Min. pp. 36, covers.   845

Deschanel, E.

Bibliothèque / des Écoles et des Familles. / Benjamin Franklin / Par Émile Deschanel / Paris / Libraire Hach-ette et Cie / 79, Boulevard Saint-Germain, 79 / 1882 / . .

12mo. pp. 191, (1), covers.   B. 846

D' Estaing.   See No. 859.

Douay, E., editor.

Comme on devient un Homme d'après les idées de Ben-jamin Franklin. [Edited by Edmund Douay.] Paris: [1865.]

12mo. pp.   847

Dove, D. J.   See No. 793.

[*Duane, William.*]

Remarks / upon / a Speech / Delivered by / Mrs. E. Cady Stanton! / during the / Summer of 1870. / Philadelphia: / Merrihew & Son, Printers, No. 135 North Third Street. [1870–1?]

8vo. pp. 7.   848

*** Mrs. Stanton, in her speech (see *N. Y. World*, June 4th, 1870), had charged Franklin with having a good time in Europe, while he left his wife at home to take care of his children and property!

[*Duane, William, editor.*]

Letters / to / Benjamin Franklin, / From / his Family and Friends / 1751–1790. / New York: / C. Benjamin Richardson, / 348 Broadway. / 1859.

4to & 8vo. pp. 195.   849

*** 10 copies quarto, 250 copies octavo. Reviewed in *London Athenæum*, July 23, 1859, and in *Historical Magazine*, III, 30. An "Erratum" is given in the *Historical Magazine*, III, 66.

Dubourg, Jacques Barbeu.

Petit Code de la Raison Humane.   Paris: 1774.

8vo. pp.   850

*** Dedicated to Franklin.

+ Passy: Private Press of Franklin.   1782.

8vo. pp.   851

+ Paris: 1789.

o. pp.   852

Du Chatenet.

Benjamin / Franklin / Sa Vie, ses succés / Dans l'art de faire le bien / Par E. Du Chatenet. / Limoges / Eugène Ardant et Cie, éditeurs.

12mo. pp. 180, plate.   P. H. S.   853

Durgin, C.

An / Oration / delivered before / the Franklin Debating Society, at their Anniversary, January 17, 1831, / being the / Birth-Day of Franklin / By Clement Durgin / Published by Request. / Boston: / Published by John H. Eastburn. / 1831.

8vo. pp. 23, covers.   854

Dwight, Theodore F.   See No. 901.

The Election. Humbly Inscribed to the Saturday Nights Club in Lodge Alley. [Philadelphia: 1765.]

Folio. Broadside.   P. 855

∗⁎∗ This and Nos. 801, 819 and 856, all relate to Franklin's attempted re-election to the Pennsylvania Assembly. Many other pieces which relate more or less to the Pennsylvania politics of the time, and therefor to Franklin, will be found in Hildeburn's *Issues of the Pennsylvania Press.*

The Election a Medley, Humbly Inscribed to Squire Lilliput, Professor of Scurrility. / Philadelphia: 1764.

Folio. Broadside.   P. 856

Éloge.   See No. 841.

Elsner, Heinrich.

Befreiungskampf den Nord-Amerkanischen Staaten. Mit den Lebensbeschreibungen der vier berühmtesten Männer derselben, Washington, Franklin, Lafayette und Kosciuszko . . . . . Stuttgart: J. Scheible. 1835.

8vo.   pp. (1), 768, plates.   B. A.   857

Emmons, N.

The Dignity of Man. / A / Discourse / Addressed to the Congregation in / Franklin, / Upon the occasion of their receiving from Dr. Franklin, / The Mark of his Respect in a rich / Donation of Books, / Appropriated to the Use of a Parish-Library / By / Nathaniel Emmons, / Pastor of the Church in Franklin. / Providence. / Printed by Bennett Wheeler, / West-Minster Street. / [1787.]

8vo.   pp. 48.   B.   858

[*Estaing, Comte Charles Hector D'.*]

Apperçu Hazardé / sur l'Exportation / dans les Colonies / Dédié a feu M. Franklin / . . . . . / A Paris, De l'Imprimerie de L. Potier de Lille, / rue Favart, No. 5.   1790.

8vo.   pp. (2), 64.   859

Examination.   *See No. 986.*

Farine, C.

Benjamin / Franklin / Docteur en Droit / . . . . . /

D'après les documents authentiques recueillis dans ses œuvres posthumes et dans ses papiers de famille. / Par Charles Farine, / Avocat à la cour Royale de Paris. / . . . . / . . . / Tours, / R. Pornin et Cie, Imp.-Libraires–Éditeurs. / 1846.

12mo.   pp. (4), 284, portrait.   860

Fauchet, Claude.

Éloge Civique / de / Benjamin Franklin, / Prononcé, le 21 Juillet 1790, / Dans la Rotonde, / Au nom de la Commune de Paris, / Par M. l'Abbé Fauchet. / . . . . . / A Paris, / Chez J. R. Lottin, ... / G. L. Bailly, ... / Vict. Desenne, . . . / J. Cussac, . . . / M.DCC.XC.

8vo.   pp. (2), 50.   861

Fauchet.

Éloge Civique / [*861*] / Par M. l'Abbé Fauchet. / . . . . . / [n. p.] 1790.

8vo.   pp. 32.   862

Fields, James Thomas.

Ode / for the Inauguration of / Franklin's Statue, / . . . Sept. 17, 1856. / Written by James T. Fields. / Set to music by / Nathan Richardson / . . . . . / Printed by Stacy & Richardson, 11 Milk Street / Boston. [1856.]

8vo.   Broadside.   B. 863

First Annual Parade / of the / Boston / Fire Department / . . . . . / for the Inauguration of the / Franklin Statue. / Geo. C. Rand & Avery, Printers, 3 Cornhill, Boston. [1856.]

4to.   pp. (4).   B. 864

Francis, ——?

Franklin / A Passy, / ou / Le Bonhomme Richard / Vaudeville anecdotique en un acte, / par MM. Francis et Decourcy / représenté, pour la première fois à Paris, / sur le théatre du palais royal, le 19 Mai 1832. / Prix: / Fr. 50c. / Paris, / Quoy, Libraire-Editeur, / au Magazin général de pièces de theatre, / boulevard Saint-Martin, No. 18. / 1832.

8vo.   pp. 34, (2).   865

Franklin, J.

Life and Times of Benjamin Franklin, by J. Franklin and J. A. Headington.   4th edition.   St. Louis: J. Burns. 1880.

8vo.   pp.   866

*** Title from *The American Catalogue.*

Franklin, William.

The Answer of his Excellency William Franklin, Esq.; . . . / . . . to the invidious Charges of the Proprietary Party, Con- / tained in a Libel, read by Mr. James Biddle . . . / . . . on Saturday last, and afterwards published and industriously dispersed through the / Province. / [Philadelphia: B. Franklin and D. Hall.   1765.]

Folio.   Broadside.   867

*** See No. 819.

Franklin, W. T.   See No. 561.

Franklin Desiderata.   *See No. 968.*

Franklin before the Privy Council.   *See No. 827.*

Franklin Festival. / The New York Typographical So- ciety / . . . / 149th Anniversary of the birth of / Benja- min Franklin, / . . . / . . . Jan. 17th, 1855. / [Programme of] Literary and Musical Exercises. / . . . . . . / Baker, Godwin & Co., Printers, 1 Spruce Street.   New York.

Folio.   Broadside.   868

Frankliniana, / ou / Recueil d'Anecdotes, bons Mots, / Réflexions, Maximes et Obser- / vations de Benjamin Franklin; / . . . / Par Un Américain / A Paris, / Chez Tiger, Imprimeur-Libraire, rue du Petit-Pont St-Jacques, No. 10. [about 1815.]

Min.   pp. 108, portrait.   869

Franklin Medallion.   *See No. 876.*

Franklin Memorial Window / for the / New University Building.   [Philadelphia: 1871.]

8vo.   pp. (3).   870

*** A report by the Committee, asking for money.

The Franklin Statue. [New York: 1871.]

4to. Broadside.   871

*** A statement that subscriptions for the pedestal for De Groot's statue are payable to Samuel Sinclair.

Franklin Statue! / The Verd Antique Marble Co. / . . . . . [Boston: 1856.]

4to. Broadside.   872

*** A description, in the form of an advertisement of the statue.

Franklin the Apprentice. *See No. 790.*

From the Illustrated Magazine of the Eighth Exhibition / under the direction of the Massachusetts / Charitable Mechanic Association. / The Seventeenth of September, 1856.

4to. pp. (3).   873

*** An account of the Boston statue of Franklin.

Gilpin, H. Dilwood.

The Character of Franklin. / Address delivered before / the Franklin Institute of Pennsylvania, / on the / Evening of the Fourth of December, 1856. / By Henry D. Gilpin. / Philadelphia. / King & Baird, Printers, No. 607 Sanson Street. / 1857.

8vo. pp. 50, covers.   874

Goodrich, S. G.   See No. 905.

Green, S. Abbott.

The / Story of a Famous Book: / An Account / of / Dr. Benjamin Franklin's Autobiography / By / Samuel A. Green, M. D. / Boston: / For Private Distribution. / 1871.

8vo. pp. 14, covers.   875

*** A few copies reprinted from the *Atlantic* for February, 1871.

Green Box. *See No. 973.*

Groot, A. De.   See No. 944.

[*Groux, Daniel E.*]

Franklin Medallion / Struck for the / Inauguration / of the / Statue of Franklin, / Boston, / September 17th, 1856. /

8vo. pp. (4), plate.   s. d.   876

Hale, E. Everett.

Franklin in France. / From Original Documents, / most of which are now published for the / first time. / By / Edward E. Hale / and / Edward E. Hale, Jr. / Part I. / The Alliance. / Boston: / Roberts Brothers. / 1888.

> 2 Vols. 8vo. pp. xvi, (2), 478, 4 plates.—(10), 470, portrait. B. 877
>
> *⁎* Review by F. J. Turner in *The Dial*, VIII, 7; IX, 204; *The Nation*, XLIV, 368; *Athenæum* for 1887, II, 77; and by J. B. McMaster in *The Atlantic*, LX, 318.

Harpel, O. H.

A Franklin Memento. By Oscar H. Harpel. Cincinnati, 1877.

o. pp. 4.   878

Headington, J. A. See No. 866.

Hildebrand, R.

Benjamin Franklin / als Nationalökonom / von / Dr. Richard Hildebrand / (Separatadruck aus B. Hildebrand's Jahrbüchern für National- / ökonom und Statistik Bd. I. S. 577–602 und S. 643–678) / Jena, / Druck und Verlag von Friedrich Manke. / 1868.

8vo. pp. 61.   879

Hill, G. C.

Benjamin Franklin / A Biography / by George Canning Hill / New York: / R. Worthington, 770 Broadway / 1884.

12mo. pp. 333, plate.   880

Holley, Orville Luther.

The Life / of / Benjamin Franklin. / By O. L. Holley. / Boston: / Published by Bazin & Ellsworth, / 13 Washington Street. [1848?]

> 8vo. pp. (2), 468, 20 plates.   881
>
> *⁎* Also re-issues with the following imprints:
>
> + Boston: Sanborn, Carter, Bazin & Co. [n. d.]   882
> + Boston: John Philbrick, 62 Hanover Street. [n. d.]   883
> + Philadelphia: G. G. Evans. 1860.   884
> + New York: G. F. Coolidge & Brother. [n. d.]   885

Horn, W. O. See No. 924.

Hugenholtz, Petrus Hermannus.

Benjamin Franklin / Door / P. H. Hugenholtz, Jr. [Amsterdam: Roeloffzen & Hübner. 1871.]

12mo. pp. 24.   886

Hulbert, Charles.

Biographical Sketches / of / Dr. Benjamin Franklin, / General Washington, and Thomas Paine / with / an Essay / on / Atheism and Infidelity / By C. Hulbert / . . . / London / Published by G. & W. B. Whittaker, for C. Hulbert, . . . / . . . / 1820.

Min. pp. iv, (2), 90, portrait, covers.   P. H. S. 887

Humble Attempt. *See No. 888.*

[Hunt, Isaac.]

A / Humble Attempt / at / Scurrility. / In Imitation of / Those Great Masters of the Art / the Rev. Dr. S[mi]th; the Rev. Dr. Al[iso]n; the Rev. / Mr. Ew[i]n[g]; the Irreverend D. J. D[o]ve; and the Heroic / J[oh]n D[ickinso]n, Esq.; / Being a / Full Answer / to the / Observations / on / Mr. H[ughe]s's / Advertisement. / By Jack Retort, Student in Scurrility. / Quilsylvania: Printed, 1765. [Philadelphia: Anthony Armbruster.]

8vo. pp. 42, (1).   P. 888

_**_*John Hughes offered to give five pounds to the Pennsylvania Hospital if the charges against Franklin could be proved true. This advertisement called out a savage attack on Franklin, to which the above is a reply.

[Hutchins, Samuel.]

Benjamin Franklin: / A Book / for / The Young and the Old. / For All. / Cambridge: / Printed for the Author. / MDCCCLII.

12mo. pp. 36.   889

_**_* Also issues with change of date.

Hutchinson, T. See No. 916.

[Hyde, Mrs. Anna M.]

The / Boyhood and Manhood / of / George Washington

/ and / Benjamin Franklin. / Centennial Edition. / New York: / The World Publishing House, / . . . / 1876.

12mo. pp. 255, viii, 288.   890

  *** Each sketch has a separate title.

Ide, Simeon.   See Nos. 159 and 188.

[*Ide, Simeon.*]

The Young Franklinsonian. / Grandfather's Story: / Written for Children / of / Mechanics and Farmers, / by their Well Wisher. / Hartford, Connecticut: / Wm. L. Mott, . . . / . . . / [1889.]

Min. pp. 128, (7).   891

  *** In 1816 Mr. Ide published an edition of Poor Richard, to which he prefixed a brief life of Franklin. This is reprinted in the above, together with some of Franklin's essays, and an autobiography of Mr. Ide, who still lives.

Interesting Collection of Modern Lives; with Observations on the Characters and Writings of the following Eminent Men, Jeffrey Lord Amherst, ... Dr. Benjamin Franklin . . . . . London: G. Riebau. 1792.

8vo. pp.   892

  *** Title from *Sabin*.

In the Senate of the United States / May 1, 1882, Ordered to be printed. / Mr. Hoar, from the Joint Committee on the Library, submitted the fol- / lowing / Report: /

8vo. pp. 7.   893

  *** "47th Congress, 1st Session. Senate Report No. 504." Advising the purchase of the Stevens Franklin Collection.

Jewett, J. L.

Franklin—His Genius, Life and Character. / An / Oration / delivered before the / N. Y. Typographical Society, / on the occasion of / The Birthday of Franklin, / at the / Printers' Festival, / Held January 17, 1849. / By / John L. Jewett. / . . . / New York: / Harper & Brothers, . . . / M.DCCC.XLIX.

8vo. pp. 37, covers.   s. d. 894

Jonhanneaud, P.   See No. 198.

Jordan, T.

Benjamin Franklin / and Popular Ethics. / A Lecture delivered before the / St. Michaus Young Men's Christian Association, / by the / Rev. Thomas Jordan, A. M. / . . . . . / Dublin: / Hodges, Smith, and Company / Grafton-Street . . . / 1864. /

12mo.   pp. 26.

895

Joseph and Benjamin.   *See No. 936.*

Kell, Karl Julius.

Lebensbeschreibung Benjamin Franklin's, des that-kräftigen Mannes und freisinnigen Volksfreundes.   Eine Volksschrift.   Leipzig: Klinkhardt.   1848.

8vo.   pp.

896

⁎ Title from *Swift*.

Knowles, William J.

Features of Inauguration / of the / Franklin Statue in Boston, / September 17th, 1856. / By W. J. Knowles. / Boston: / Printed for the Author. / 1856.

12mo.   pp. 12.

897

Laboulaye, E.   See No. 246.

Le Roy, Julien David.

Lettre / A M. Franklin, / Sur les Navires des Anciens sur ceux / des Modernes, / . . . / . . . Par M. Le Roy, / . . . . . / A Paris, Chez Nyon . . . / . . . M.DCC.-LXXXVII.

8vo.   pp. (4), 43, plate.

898

Lascaux, Paul de.

Benjamin Franklin, sa vie, ses ouvrages, ses découvertes.   Mirecourt, Humbert.   1864.

Min.

899

⁎ Title from *Sabin*.

Letter / from / The Secretary of State / transmitting / A Communication from Benjamin F. Stevens / . . . / . . . stating that he is authorized to sell . . . / . . . "Henry

Stevens Franklin collection of manuscripts and Books." /
January 20, 1881 / . . . . . [Washington: 1881.]

8vo. pp. 5.   900

 ⁎⁎⁎ "46th Congress, 3d Session. Senate. Ex. Doc. No. 25."

Letter from / The Secretary of State, / transmitting / A
report of Theodore F. Dwight on the papers of Benjamin
Franklin / offered for sale by Mr. Henry Stevens . . . /
 . . . . . / Washington / . . . / 1881.

8vo. pp. 99.   901

 ⁎⁎⁎ "47th Congress, 1st Session. Senate. Mis. Doc. No. 21." Contains a reprint of No. 966.

A / Letter / to / Benjamin Franklin, L L. D. / Fellow of
the Royal Society / In which his Pretensions to the Title
of Natural / Philosopher are Considered. / . . . . . / London: / Printed for J. Bew, No. 47, Paternoster-Row; and
sold by Messrs. / Fletcher, Parker, and Prince, at Oxford.
/ M.DCC.LXXVII.

8vo. pp. 24.   902

 ⁎⁎⁎ It attacks Franklin chiefly because he was self-educated and had
worked at a press. From an allusion in the *Critical Review* the author
was apparently connected with Oxford University.

 ⁎⁎⁎ Savagely reviewed in the *Monthly Review*, LVIII, 126, and the
Critical Review, XLV, 79.

Letters of Governor Hutchinson. *See No. 916.*

Letters to Benjamin Franklin. *See No. 849.*

Levray, A.

Petite Bibliothèque de l'Enfance / Benjamin Franklin /
par / Alph. Levray / Paris / J. Bonheure et Cie, Éditeurs
/ 48, Rue de Lille, 48. / 1878.

8vo. pp. 72, portrait.   903

The Life and Adventures of Obadiah Benjamin Franklin
Bloomfield, M. D., a native of the United States, now on a
tour of Europe. Written by himself. Philadelphia: for
the proprietor. 1818.

12mo. pp. xi, 219.   904

 ⁎⁎⁎ "A squib on Franklin's Memoirs." Title and note from *Swift.*

The Life of Benjamin Franklin. Illustrated by Tales,

Sketches and Anecdotes.   New York: Collins & Hannay. 1832.

Min. pp. 180.   905

₊*₊ This is classed by S. G. Goodrich among the "spurious Parley books, and he adds a note stating that "The name of Parley is not in the title page, . . . but is put upon the back, and they are sold as Parley books, but without authority." As the copyright is in the name of S. G. Goodrich, it is difficult to understand what the above note means. The following, and No. 908, are editions of the same book.

The / Life / of Benjamin Franklin / Illustrated by / Tales, Sketches, and Anecdotes / adapted to the use of Schools. / With engravings / Philadelphia: / Thomas Cowperthwait and Co. / No. 253 Market Street. / 1842.

12mo. pp. 181, plate.   s. d. 906

The Life / of / Benjamin Franklin, L L. D. / Printed and Sold by George Nicholson, Poughnill near Ludlow, / . . . . . [n. d.]

Min. pp. (2), 56, covers.   907

₊*₊ By an error, this title was given among the editions of the autobiography (No. 297). It is, however, a worthless little chap book life.

Life of Benjamin Franklin.   See Nos. 926 and 1002.

Lives of Washington and Franklin.   By Peter Parley. London.   Tegg.   1839.

12mo. pp.   908

₊*₊ Title from *English Catalogue of Books*. See No. 905.

Loughborough.   See No. 889.

Lubimoff, A. N.

[Benjamin Franklin (In Russian). Moscow: Katkoff. typ. of the University.   1881.]

o. pp.   909

₊*₊ Title from *Swift*.

Lyon, J.

Remarks / on the / Leading Proofs / offered in favor of the / Franklinian System / of / Electricity; / with experiments / to shew the Direction of the Electric Effluvia, / visibly passing from what has been termed / negatively Electrified / Bodies. / By the Rev. John Lyon, Dover, Kent.

/ . . . . . / London: / Printed by J. Phillips, . . . / and
sold by J. Dodsley, ... / M,DCC,XCI.

8vo.   pp. 47, (1).   910

McMaster, J. B.

American Men of Letters. / Benjamin Franklin / As a
Man of Letters. / By / John Bach McMaster, / . . . / Boston: / Houghton, Mifflin and Company. / . . . / The Riverside Press, Cambridge. / 1887.

12mo.   (10), 293, (4), portrait.   911

⁕ Prof. McMaster has told so much of this side of Franklin's life,
that had not the introduction to this list been already virtually written,
I should not have added it.   It is reviewed by Lindsay Swift in *The
Nation*, XLVI, 98; by W. Ray in *The Dial*, VIII, 218; and in *The Atlantic*, LX, 318.

[McLeary, Samuel F.]

City Documents.—No. 89, / City of Boston. / A Sketch
/ of the / Origin, Object and Character / of the / Franklin
Fund, / for the benefit of / Young Married Mechanics / of
/ Boston. / Published by order of the Board of Aldermen.
/ 1866.

8vo.   pp. 38, portrait.   912

McNeile, H.

(The Profits of this work, both in England and America,
will be applied / in aid of the London Printers' Pension
Society.) / A Lecture / on the / Life of Dr. Franklin. / By / the Rev. Hugh M'Neile, A. M. / As delivered
by him at the Liverpool Royal Amphitheatre, / on Wednesday evening, 17th Nov. 1841, / with the addition of a
prefatory / note to the reader / by / John B. Murray, Esq.
/ of New York. / Liverpool: / Printed and published by
Mitchell, Heaton and Mitchell, / . . . / London: W. E.
Painter . . . / . . . / 1841.

8vo.   47, plate, facsimile, covers.   913

+ Published by / Henderson Greene, New York. / Carey and Hart,
Philadelphia; . . . / . . . . . / 1841.

8vo.   pp. 42, (2), facsimile.   914

Mason, H.

Poetry / A Poem delivered before / The Franklin Debating Society / in / Chauncey Hall, January 17, 1830 / being the celebration of their Seventh Anniversary / By Henry Mason / . . . . . / Boston: / Printed for the Society, By Isaac R. Butts. / MDCCCXXX.

8vo. pp.   B. 915

[*Maudit, Israel, editor.*]

The / Letters / of / Governor Hutchinson, / and / Lieutenant-Governor Oliver, &c. / Printed at Boston. / And Remarks thereon. / With / the Assembly's Address / and the / Proceedings / of the / Lords Committee of Council. / Together with / The Substance of Mr. Wedderburn's Speech / relative to those Letters. / London: / Printed for J. Wilkie, at Number 71, in / St. Paul's Church-Yard. MDCCLXXIV.

8vo. pp. (4), 126.   916

** Between the covers of this pamphlet is the most dramatic incident in Franklin's life. The letters of Hutchinson and Oliver, obtained by Franklin by means still unknown and transmitted by him to Massachusetts (where they set the country ablaze), were made the excuse for the attempted destruction of Franklin, and Alexander Wedderburn's "philippic" against him for this action is hardly to be equalled for savageness and personality when the place of delivery, occasion, and standing of the two men is considered. From the ethical standpoint, the attack seems in a measure justified, yet what Walpole called the "pert oration" has left no slur on Franklin's character, while its author has sunk into an insignificance from which even Junius' saying that there was "something about him which frightened even treachery," could not save him.

+ The Second Edition / London: / Printed for J. Wilkie, at Number 71 in / St. Paul's Church-Yard. MDCCLXXIV.

8vo. (4), 142.   917

Mayhew, H.

Young Benjamin Franklin; / or, / The Right Road through Life. / A Story to show / how Young Benjamin learnt the principles / which raised him from a printer's boy to the / First Embassador of the American Republic, / A Boy's Book on a Boy's own Subject. / By / Henry Mayhew /

. . . . . / With illustrations by John Gilbert / London: / Griffin, Bohn and Company / . . . / 1861.

12mo. pp. xvi, 534.   918

+ Seventh Thousand / London: / James Blackwood & Co. Lovell's Court . . . [n. d.]

o. pp.   918*

+ New York: Harper Brothers. [n. d.]

Min. pp.   919

Memorial of the Inauguration. *See No. 961.*

Memoirs of Benjamin Franklin. *See No. 998.*

Micheels, J.

Benjamin Franklin, / Een Levensbeeld, / door / J. Micheels, / Leeraar aan het Konin Klyk Athenæum te Gent / Gent, / Boekhandel W. Rogghe (J. Vuylsteke) / Kalanderburg, 13. / 1878.

12mo. pp. vii, 120, covers.   920

Mignet, François Marie Auguste.

Petits Traités / Publiés par / l'Académie de Sciences / Morales et Politiques. / Vie / de Franklin, / a l'Usage de tout le monde. / Par M. Mignet, / de la section d'Histoire Générale et Philosophique. / Premiere Partie. / Paris, / Pagnerre, Libraire / . . . / Paulin et Cie, / . . . / Firmin Didot Frères, Libraires, / . . . / . . . / 1848.

2 Vols. 12mo. pp. 230, covers.—87–230, covers.   921

Mignet, F. M. A.

Benjamin Franklin / Eine Biographie / von / F. A. Mignet / Aus dem Franzosischen von Dr. Ed. Burchardt. / Leipsig / Verlag von Carl B. Lorck. / 1855.

12mo. pp. (4), 143, (9), covers.   922

Mignet, F. M. A.

Een Man uit het Volk; / als Voorbeeld hoe men door eigen vlijt en dengd / tot rijkdom en aanzien kan geraken / voorgesteld in het leven van / Benjamin Franklin, / door / F. M. A. Mignet. / Naar het Fransch / door / Mr. G. Mees Az / Een Volksboek / Te Deventer, Bij / A Ter Gunne. [1857.]

12mo. pp. xii, 175, (2), portrait, covers.   923

Mignet, F. M. A.

Mignet / Vie de Franklin. / Avec Commentaire. / Édition Stéréotype. / Munsters, / Imprimerie et Libraire de Theissing.

Min. pp. 212, cover.   924

Milon, C.

Denkwürdigkeiten / zur Geschichte / Benjamin Franklin's / von / C. Milón / . . . / St. Petersburg, 1793 / bey Johann Zacharias Logan.

12mo. pp. (2), 110.   925

Mirabeau. See No. 949.

Montgomery, H. See No. 435.

[*Moon, William.*]

Life of Benjamin Franklin, / Volume I. / Embossed in / Dr. Moon's Type for the Blind / Published at Moon's Institution for Embossing and Circulating / . . . Books . . . for the Blind . . . / Brighton, Sussex.

2 Vols? Oblong. 8vo.   826

Mornington, Earl of. See No. 995.

New York Typothetæ. / January 17, 1889. / One Hundred and Eighty-third Anniversary of the Birth Day of / Benjamin Franklin. [Menu. Homer Lee Bank Note Co. N. Y.]

12mo. pp. (8).   927

Nixon, W.

Prosody made Easy. / . . . . . / By the Rev. William Nixon, A. B. / Formerly Principal of the Dublin Academy. / . . . . . / Philadelphia: / Printed and sold by William Spotswood, / . . . . . / M.DCC.LXXXVI.

8vo. xvi, (3), 36.   928

  ⁎ Dedicated to Franklin.

Nollet, Jean Antoine.

Lettres / sur / l'Électricité. / . . . . . / Par M. l'Abbé Nollet. / . . . . . / A Paris: H. L. Guérin. / . . . / . . . . . / M.DCC.LIII.

12mo. pp. xi, (1), 264.   929

  ⁎ "Nine letters; six of which are addressed to Benjamin Franklin." Note from *Swift.*

Norton, J. N.

Life / of / Doctor Franklin. / By John N. Norton, A. M. / Rector of Ascension Church, Frankfort, Kentucky; . . . / . . . . . / New York: H. B. Price, 884 Broadway. / 1861.

12mo. pp. 258, (9), portrait.   S. D.   930

﹡*﹡ Reviewed in *Historical Magazine*, v, 95.

+ Claremont, N. H.: S. Ide. 1861.

Min. pp.   931

+ Kentucky: S. F. M. Major & Co. 1861.

Min. pp.   932

Observations / On a late / Epitaph, / In a Letter from a Gentleman in the / Country, / To his Friend in Philadelphia; / . . . / Philadelphia: / Printed by Anthony Armbruster, in Arch-street, / by whom all Manner of Printing-work is / done, both in English and German, with / the greatest Accuracy and Expedition.   [1764.]

8vo. pp. 8.   P. 923

﹡*﹡ See No. 997.

[*Oertel, Phillip Friedrich Wilhelm.*]

Benjamin Franklin. / Lebensbild eines Ehrenmannes in Amerika. / Der Jugend und dem Volke erzählt / von W. O. v. Horn. / New York. / E. Steiger. / 1865.

Min. pp. 77, 4 plates.   924

Oertel, P. F. W.

Benjamin Franklin [+924+] Zweite Auflage. Wiesbaden: Julius Niedner.   1869.

Min. pp. 116.   925

Order of Exercises / at the Inauguration of the Statue / of / Benjamin Franklin, / September, 1856.

4to. Broadside.   B. 926

L'Origine del Fulmine.   Poemetto.   Pisa: 1777.

8vo. pp. 16.   927

﹡*﹡ "Dedicated to Franklin."   Title and note from *Swift*.

Parker, Theodore.

Franklin [in Historic Americans.]   Boston: 1870.

12mo. pp. 312.   928

﹡*﹡ Reviewed by Edmund Quincy in *The Nation*, Feb. 2, 1871.

Parley, Peter. *See No. 905.*

Parton, J.

Life and Times / of / Benjamin Franklin. / By / James Parton, / . . . / . . . / . . . / . . . / Vol. I. / New-York: Mason Brothers, No. 7 Nassau St. / . . . / . . . / London: Trübner & Co. 60 Paternoster Row / 1864.

2 Vols. 8vo. pp. 627, 2 portraits.—707, 2 portraits.   929

** Between the "old school" imaginative biography of Mr. Weems and the "new school" critical biography of Prof. McMaster, this biography may be said to be the half-way post. It is the most elaborate yet written, and as popular taste seems to have altered in regard to the length of biography, it is likely to remain such. It is reviewed in *London Athenæum*, 1864; *North American Review*, July, 1864; *Atlantic*, Sept. 1864; *London Quarterly*, XXIII, 483; *Littell's Living Age*, LXXXIV.

** Reissues as follows:

+ New York: Mason Brothers 1865.   930
** A limited edition of one hundred copies in quarto size.

+ Boston: Ticknor & Fields. 1867.   931

+ Boston: J. R. Osgood & Co. [n. d.]   932

Paul Jones, ou prophéties sur l'Amérique, l'Angleterre . . . . . [etc.] Dedié à S. E. Mgr. l'Ambassadeur Franklin . . . . . De l'ère de l'Independance de l'Amérique l'an V.

8vo. pp. 120.   934

Pictorial life / of / Benjamin Franklin; / embracing / Anecdotes / illustrative of his character. / Embellished with Engravings. / Philadelphia: / Lindsay and Blakiston, / . . . / [1846.]

16mo. pp. 208.   935

** Also issue dated 1847 on title.

[Playfair, William.]

Joseph / and Benjamin / A / Conversation / Translated from a French / Manuscript. / London: / Printed at the Logographic Press/for J. Murray . . . /MDCCLXXXVII.

12mo. pp. (4), xv, (1), 238, portrait.   936

** This is evidently a skit on the intended meeting between Franklin and Joseph II. of Austria. It is decidedly silly.

Plain Dealer.   *See No. 996.*

The / Plot. / By way of a / Burlesk, / To turn F[rankli]n out of the Assembly; between H[ockley]. and P[ugh]; Proprietary Officers, being two / of the Wiser Sort.   [Philadelphia:] Printed [by Anthony Armbruster] in the Year 1764.

Folio. Broadside.   937

₊*₊ See Nos. 780, 801 and 855.

Priestley, Joseph.

Some / Account / of a new / Electrometer / contrived by / Mr. William Henley, / and of several / Electrical Experiments / made by him; / In a Letter from Dr. Priestley, F. R. S. / To Dr. Franklin, F. R. S. / London / W. Bowyer and J. Nichols. / M.DCC.LXXIII.

4to. pp. 8, plate.   938

Printers' Banquet / Celebration / of the / 147th Anniversary / of the birth of / Benj. Franklin / . . . . . / January 17, 1853. / . . . . . / [New York:] George F. Nesbitt & Co. . . .

Folio. Broadside.   939

Preusker, C.

Gutenberg und Franklin. / Eine Festgabe / zum vierten Jubilaum der / Erfindung der Buchdruckerkunst / zugleich / mit Antrag zur Gründung von / Stadt- und Dorf-Bibliotheken. / Allen Buchdruckern, Buchhandlern, Gelehrten, / überhaupt / allen deutschen Männern, / welche an fortschreitender Menschheits-Bildung / regen Antheil nehmen, / gewidmet / von / Carl Preusker, / Konigl. Sachs. Rentamtsmann zu Großenhayn, Ritter des K. S. Civil-Verdienstordens. / Leipzig, 1840 / Verlag von Heinrich Weinedel.

8vo. pp. (2), 64, covers.   940

₊*₊ Reviewed in *Leipziger Tageblatt*, March 17, 1840.

Proceedings / at the / Printers' Banquet, / held by the N. Y. Typographical Society, / on the occasion of / Franklin's birth-day, Jan. 17, 1850, / at / Niblo's, Broadway / New York: / Charles B. Norton / . . . / 1850.

8vo. pp. 64, covers.   941

Proceedings / in / the House of Representatives of the United States, / on / the Presentation / of / the Sword of Washington / and the / Staff of Franklin / February 7, 1843. / Washington: / Gales and Seaton / 1843.

8vo. pp. 15.   B. 942

Proceedings / of the / Franklin Typographical Society, / at the observance / of the / Semi-Centennial of its Institution, / January 17, 1874; / with a brief Historical Sketch. / Boston: / Published by the Society / 1875.

8vo. pp. 60, covers.   943

Reasons on which were founded. *See No. 277.*

Record / of the / Proceedings and Ceremonies pertaining / to the erection of / the Franklin Statue / in Printing-House Square, / Presented by Albert De Groot, / to the Press and Printers of the City of New-York / New-York: / Francis Hart & Co. . . . / 1872.

8vo. pp. 104, plate.   944

Reddingius, Wibrandus Gerardus.

Het leven von B. Franklin, een leerboek voor kinderen. Gronigen, 1807.

8vo. pp.   945

** "*Oettinger* mentions an edition in 1816." Title and note from *Swift.*

Regnier, ——? editor.

Recueil / des / Loix Constitutives / des / Colonies Angloises, / . . . . . / Dédié à M. le Docteur Franklin. / A Philadelphie, [Paris] . . . . . / M.DCC.LXXVIII.

12mo. (10), 370.   946

+ En Swisse, chez les libraires Associés. M.DCC.LXXVIII.

12mo. pp. (12), 370.   947

Remarks. See No. 848.

Rice, R.

Observations / on / The Expectation of Lives / . . . . . / In a letter from / Mr. R. Rice, F. R. S. / to / Benjamin Franklin . . . / London, / Printed by W. Bowyer and J. Nichols. / MDCCLXIX.

4to. pp. 39.   948

Riquetti, Honoré Gabriel, Comte de Mirabeau.

Discours / du Comte de Mirabeau. / Dans la Séance du
11 Juin, / sur la Mort / de Benjamin Francklin. [sic.] /
Imprimé par ordre de l'Assemblée National. [Colophon.]
A Paris, / Chez Baudouin, Imprimeur de l'Assemblée /
Nationale, rue du Foin St. Jacques, No. 31. / 1790.

8vo. pp. 3.   949

  *** "Proces Verbal No. 315." This little leaflet is unknown to all
former bibliographers of Franklin. The "Discours" is reprinted in
Mirabeau's Works, and "Extracts" are printed in Bingham's "Columbian Orator."

Romayne, T.

A / Letter / from / Thomas Romayne, Esq. / to / Benjamin Franklin . . . / Inclosing an account of / some Observations / on / Atmospherical Electricity / . . . . . /
London, / Printed by W. Bowyer and J. Nichols. / M.DCC.-
LXXII.

4to. pp. 10, plate.   950

Roy, Le. See No. 898.

Ruelle, Charles.

La Science Populaire / de / Claudius / Simple discours
sur toutes chose. / Sur la Vie / de Franklin. / A Paris, / Chez
Jules Renouard, Libraire, / Rue de Tournon, No. 6 / 1837.

Min. pp. 4, 214, covers.   B. 951

Rush, B.

An / Oration /| delivered before the / American / Philosophical Society / . . . 27th of February, 1786; / . . . . .
/ By Benjamin Rush, M. D. / Philadelphia: / Printed by
Charles Cist. / MDCCLXXXVI.

4to. pp. (6), 40.   952

  *** Dedicated to Franklin. See Sparks' *Works of Franklin*, x, 255.
+ The Second Edition. / Philadelphia, Printed: / London, Reprinted;
for C. Dilly, . . . / M.DCC.LXXXVI.

8vo. pp. (8), 81.   953

[Sanderson, John.]

Franklin [in Biography of the Signers to the Declaration.] Philadelphia: 1822.

Vol. 11, pp. 1–153.   954

Santon, J.

Denkwürdiges Gespräch zwischen Franklin und Washington. Königsberg: Nicolovius. 1815.

8vo. pp.

955

✱ Title from *Swift*.

Say, J. B.   See No. 133.

Schmaltz, Carl.

Leben Benjamin Franklins.   Leipzig: Schmidt.   1840.

8vo. pp.

956

Schmidt, F.

Benjamin Franklin. / Ein Lebensbild für Jung und Alt. / Von Ferdinand Schmidt. / . . . . . / Berlin / Verlag von Hugo Kaftner.

Min. pp. 136, portrait.

B. 957

The / Scribbler / Being a / Letter / From a Gentleman in Town / To his / Friend in the Country, / Concerning the present State of Public / Affairs; / with a Lapidary Character. / . . . / [Philadelphia:] Printed [by Anthony Armbruster] in the Year MDCC,LXIV.

8vo. pp. 24.

958

✱ See No. 997.

Scudder, H. E.   See No. 430.

Second Thoughts.   See No. 832.

Selter, Johann Christian.

Lebensbeschreibung B. Franklin's.   Berlin, 1797.

12mo. pp.

959

✱ Title from *Oettinger*.

[Shillaber, Benjamin Penhallow.]

A very Brief and very Comprehensive Life / of / Ben. Franklin, Printer, / Done into Quaint Verse, by one of the Typos. / September 17th, 1856.

Folio. Broadside.

960

✱ The verse is "quaint" as the following specimen shows:
"And the Queen frowned not in check,
When this plain republican Mister
Threw his arms about her neck,
And very gallantly kissed her!"

[*Shurtleff, Nathaniel Bradstreet, editor.*]

Memorial / of the / Inauguration of the Statue / of / Franklin. / Prepared and printed / by authority of the City Council, / Boston. / 1857.

8vo. pp. 412.   961

[Smith, John Jay.]

Benjamin Franklin [in the National Portrait Gallery of Distinguished Americans.]   N. Y.   1835.

Vol. II. pp. 1–20.   962

Sketch. *See No. 912.*

Smith, William. See No. 278.

Smith, W.

Eulogium / on / Benjamin Franklin, / . . . . . / Delivered March 1, 1791, in the German Lutheran Church of the / City of Philadelphia, / before the American Philosophical Society and agreeably to / their appointment, / By William Smith, D. D. / . . . . . / Printed by / Benjamin Franklin Bache, / Philadelphia, 1792.

8vo. pp. (2), 40, v, (1).   963

₊*₊ Dr. Smith was aided in the preparation of this address by David Rittenhouse, Thomas Jefferson, Jonathan Williams, and Benjamin Rush. The piece forms a somewhat amusing contrast to the savageness of the Doctor's earlier writings against Franklin.

Smith, W.

Eulogium / on / Benjamin Franklin, LL.D. / President of the American Philosophical Society, &c. &c. / Delivered / March 1, 1791, in Philadelphia, before both Houses of / Congress, and the American Philosophical Society, &c. / By William Smith, D. D. / . . . . / London: / Printed for T. Cadell in the Strand. / MDCCXCII.

8vo. pp. (4), 39.   s. d. 964

Soldier and Sage.   See No. 843.

Stanley, John.

The Life of Benjamin Franklin.   With Selections from his miscellaneous works.   Illustrated by Newton Fielding. London: Simpkin. 1849.

8vo. pp.   965

Stevens, B. F.   See No. 900.

Stevens, H.

Benjamin Franklin's / Life and Writings / A Biblio-
graphical Essay / On the Stevens's Collection of / Books and
Manuscripts / Relating to Doctor Franklin / By Henry
Stevens / . . . . . / London Printed by Messrs. Davy &
Sons . . . / . . . . / cIɔ.Ic.ccc.Lxxxi.

Rl. 8vo. & 8vo.   pp. viii, 40, 5 plates.   966

⁎ Like all Mr. Stevens' lists, this shows great accuracy so far as
the printing of the titles is concerned, and it has been of much use to
the compiler of this list.   Its permanent value, however, is much
marred by the use for which it was intended to serve, and Mr. Stevens'
notes and introduction are written with a greater regard for the "upset
price of £7,000," then for the love of fact.   It was also printed in his
Historical Collections, i, and in No. 875.

Stuber, H.   See No. 437.

Sumner, Charles.

Monograph / from / An Old Note-Book; With a post-
script. / "Eripuit cælo fulmen, sceptrumque tyrannis." /
(Reprinted from the Atlantic Monthly for November, 1863).

8vo.   pp. 17.   967

⁎ This is an investigation of Turgot's famous line on Franklin.
See *Notes and Queries*, iv, 443; v, 17, 144, 549, 571; vi, 88; and *Historical Magazine*, viii, 112.

[*Swift, Lindsay.*]

Franklin Desiderata.   [Boston: 1882.]

Long folio.   pp. 4.   968

⁎ This is a reprint, in galley slips, of the list of Franklin books
published in the Bulletin of the Boston Public Library.   The following is an enlargement of it.

[*Swift, Lindsay.*]

Catalogue / of works relating to / Benjamin Franklin /
in the / Boston Public Library / including / the collection
given by Doctor Samuel Abbott Green, / with the titles
of similar works / not in the library. / Boston / Published
by order of the Trustees / 1883

Rl. 8vo.   pp. 42.   969

⁎ This list is divided into three parts, the first devoted to Frank-

lin's own writings, the second to those about him, and the third to those printed by him, (with an appendix giving a list of the issues of paper currency printed by him), each arranged alphabetically.

Not only have I taken many titles from this work, but also derived the greatest aid in other respects from it, which I wish here to acknowledge. Without it my list would be even more imperfect than it is, and had I been aware of its existence before I began my work, the present list would never have been started.

Thayer, W. M.

The | Printer Boy; | or, | How Benjamin Franklin made his mark. | An Example for Youth. | By | William M. Thayer, | . . . | Boston. | J. E. Tilton and Company | 161 Washington street. | 1861.

12mo. pp. xvi, 261.   970

+ London: | James Hogg & Sons. [n. d.]
12mo. pp. xvi, 264, plates.   971

Thompson, N. A.

Inauguration | of the | Statue of Franklin | Boston, September 17, 1856 | Notice to Marshals. | . . . . . | N. A. Thompson, Chief Marshal. | Boston, September 12th, 1856 | Press of Geo. C. Rand and Avery | . . . [1856.]

4to. Broadside.   B. 972

[*Tickell, Richard.*]

The | Green Box | of | Monsieur de Sartine, | found at | Mademoiselle du The's Lodgings. | From the French of the Hague edition. | Revised and corrected by those of Leipsic and | Amsterdam. | . . . | London: | Sold by A. Becket . . . | . . . | MDCCLXXIX.

8vo. pp. (4), 71.   B. 973

⁎ I am uncertain whether this English edition or the so-called French original first appeared in print. It contains a number of spurious letters of Franklin, and the whole work is a satire on the French alliance.

"A new production of Tickell:—it has appeared and is a most paltry performance. It . . . pretends to be his [Sartine's] correspondence with the Opposition. Nay, they are so pitifully mean as to laugh at Dr. Franklin, who has such thorough reason to sit and laugh at them.

What triumph it must be to him to see a miserable pamphlet all the revenge they can take!" *Walpole.*

+ The Second Edition. / London: / Sold by A. Becket, . . . / . . . / MDCCLXXIX.

8vo. pp. (4), 71.

974

[*Tickell, R.*]

La Cassette Verte / de / Monsieur de Sartine, / Trouvée chez / Mademoiselle du Thé / . . . / (Cinquiéme Edition revue & corrigée sur celles / de Leipsic & d'Amsterdam.) A La Haye: [London] / Chez la Veuves Whiskerfeld, . . . / . . . / M,DCC,LXXIX.

8vo. (4), 76.

975

+ Sixième Edition. . . . / . . . . . / A La Haye: / Chez la Veuve Whiskerfeld, . . . / . . . / M,DCC,LXXIX.

8vo. pp. (4), 76.

976

Toderini, G.

Filosofia Frankliniana / delle punte preservatrici dal fulmine, / particolarmente applicata / Alle Polveriere, alle Navi, e a Santa / Barbara in Mare / Dissertazione / Del P. Giambattista Toderini / Della Compagnie di Gesù, / Letta in Mia Admanza Accademica / degli Icuentici / vel Palazzo / del Sig. Conte Pràzza in forti / L'Anno 1770 / In Modena MDCCLXXI / . . . . .

4to. pp. 65.

P. H. S.   977

Tomkinson, E. M.

The World Workers. / Benjamin Franklin / By E. M. Tomkinson. / Cassell & Company / . . . . . / 1885.

12mo. pp. 128, portrait.

978

To the / Freeholders / and / Electors / Of the City and County of Philadelphia. / [Philadelphia: William Bradford. 1764.]

Folio. pp. 2.

P.   979

*** "An Anti-Franklin election address." Title and note from *Hildeburn.*

To the / Freeholders / And other Electors of Assembly-Men, for / Pennsylvania. / [Philadelphia: Anthony Armbruster. 1765.]

Folio. pp. (2).

P.   980

*** "A Franklin election circular." Title and note from *Hildeburn.*

Triqueti, Henry De.

Benjamin Franklin / Discours adressé aux Apprentis par M. H. De Triqueti. / Secrétaire du Comité de Patronage / dans la séance mensuelle du 4 Mai 1856.

8vo. pp. 12, covers.   B. 981

Tronche, Louis.

La Jeunesse de Franklin, drame en cinq actes, mêlé de chant. Paris: Beck. 1860.

8vo. pp.   982

Venedy, Jacob.

Benjamin Franklin / Ein / Lebensbild / von / J. Venedy. / Freiburg im Breisgau / Friedrich Wagner 'sche Buchhandlung. / 1862.

8vo. pp. (4), 355, covers.   983

La Vœu de toutes les Nations. See No. 811.

Waller, J. B.

Reminiscences / of / Benjamin Franklin / as a Diplomatist. / By J. B. Waller. / Chicago: / Jameson & Morse / Printers. / 1879.

8vo. pp. 39, (4).   984

[*Walsh, Robert.*]

Life of Benjamin Franklin [in Delaplaine's Repository of the Lives and Portraits of Distinguished American Characters.] Philadelphia. 1815.

Part III. pp. 41–124.   985

[*Webster, Noah.*]

An / Examination / into the / leading principles / of the / Federal Constitution. / . . . . . / By a Citizen of America. / . . . . . / Philadelphia: / Printed and sold by Prichard & Hall, . . . / . . . / M.DCC.LXXXVII.

8vo. pp. 55.   986

✱✱* Dedicated to Franklin.

+ [Brooklyn, N. Y.: Privately Printed. 1887.]

8vo. pp. 41.   987

Webster, N.

Dissertations / on the / English Language: / with Notes, / Historical and Critical. / To which is added, / by way

of an Appendix, / An Essay on / A / Reformed Mode of
Spelling, / with / Dr. Franklin's Arguments on that Subject. / By Noah Webster, Jun. Esquire. / . . . . . /
Printed at Boston, for the Author, / by Isaiah Thomas
and Company, / MDCCLXXXIX.

8vo. pp. 410.

988

✱✱ Dedicated to Franklin.

Wedderburn, A.   See No. 916.

Weems, Mason Locke.

The / Life / of / Benjamin Franklin; / with / many choice
Anecdotes / and / Admirable Sayings / of this / great Man
/ never before published by any of his Biographers. / By
Mason L. Weems / Author of the Life of Washington. /
. . . . / The Fifth Edition, Greatly Enlarged / Balti-
more: / Printed by John D. Toy, for the Author. / 1821.

12mo. pp. 264, portrait.

B. 989

✱✱ See Note to No. 477.

+ The Sixth Edition / . . . . . / Philadelphia: / H. C. Carey & G.
Lea. Chestnut Street. / 1822.

12mo. pp. 264, portrait.

B. 990

+ Stereotyped by L. Johnson. / Philadelphia: / Published by Uriah
Hunt . . . / . . . / 1829.

12mo. pp. 239, portrait.

B. 991

+ Philadelphia: / Published by Uriah Hunt . . . / . . . / 1835.

12mo. pp. 239, portrait.

B. 992

+ Philadelphia: / Uriah Hunt & Son, / . . . . . . / 1845.

12mo. pp. 239, portrait.

993

+ Philadelphia / J. B. Lippincott & Co. / 1884.

12mo. pp. 239, plates.

994

✱✱ I have also found mention in catalogues of issues dated 1825,

1839 and 1854.

Weld, H. H.   See No. 413.

[*Wellesly, Richard Colley, Earl of Mornington.*]

Letters of Themistocles. With an Appendix, Containing the Character of Dr. Franklin. London: 1795.

12mo. pp.

995

What is Sauce. *See No. 997.*

[*Williamson, Hugh.*]

The / Plain Dealer: / Numb. II. / Being a / Tickler, / For the liesure Hour's Amusement of the Author of / Cool Thoughts. / Wherein the Force of his several Argu- / ments in Favour / of a Change of Government is stated in a clear / Light and accommodated to the Comprehension of Readers / of every capacity. / By X. Y. Z. Gentleman. / To be continued. / Philadelphia: / Printed [by Andrew Stewart] in Second-street, where Numb. I may be had. 1764.

8vo. pp. 16.   996

⁎⁎⁎ Written in reply to No. 270.

[*Williamson, Hugh.*]

What is Sauce for a Goose is also Sauce for a / Gander. / Being / A small Touch in the Lapidary Way. / Or / Tit for Tat, in your own Way. / An Epitaph / On a certain great Man. / Written by a Departed Spirit and now / Most humbly inscrib'd to all his dutiful Sons and / Children, Who may hereafter chose to dis- / tinguish him by the Name of / A Patriot / . . . . . / Philadelphia, Printed [by A. Armbruster] in Arch-Street.   1764.

8vo. pp. 8.   P. H. S.   997

⁎⁎⁎ In William Smith's preface to John Dickinson's speech (See No. 280), he gave a very eulogistic Epitaph on William Penn. In Franklin's preface to Galloway's speech (No. 280), he burlesqued this and applied it to Richard and Thomas Penn. This in turn gave rise to the above, which is a most savage Epitaph on Franklin. See also Nos. 793 and 923.

Wilmer, ———?

Memoirs / of the late / Dr. Benjamin Franklin: / with a / Review of his Pamphlet, / entitled / "Information to those who would wish to / Remove to America" / . . . / . . . / . . . / London / Printed and sold for the Author, by A. Grant, . . . / . . . also by J. C. Clarke, . . . / C. Stalker, . . . and W. Richard- / son / M DCC XC.

8vo. pp. 94, portrait.   c.   998

⁎⁎⁎ Jonathan Boucher writes of this as "Mr. Wilmer's *Memoirs*," and from other sources I find that the author was a Maryland loyalist. It is an unfriendly life of him, and on that ground is caustically handled in the *Monthly Review*, IV, 83.

Winthrop, R. Charles.

Achimedes and Franklin / A / Lecture, / Introductory / to a Course on the / Application of Science to Art, / Delivered before the / Massachusetts Charitable Mechanic Association. / November 29, 1853 / By Robert C. Winthrop. / Boston: / Press of T. R. Marvin, 42 Congress Street. / 1853.

8vo. pp. 47, covers.   999

Winthrop, R. C.

Oration / at / the Inauguration / of the / Statue of Benjamin Franklin, / at his native City / Sept. 17, 1856. / By / Hon. Robert C. Winthrop. / Boston: / Press of T. R. Marvin, 42 Congress Street. / 1856.

8vo. pp. 28, covers.   s. d. 1000

Winthrop, R. C.

Washington, / Bowdoin, and Franklin, / as portrayed in / occasional addresses: / by / Robert C. Winthrop. / With a few brief pieces on kindred topics, / and with notes and illustrations. / Boston: / Little, Brown, and Company. / 1876.

8vo. pp. 186, plate.   1001

[*Woods, Leonard.*]

The Life / of / Benjamin Franklin, / Including a Sketch of / The Rise and Progress of the War / of Independence / and of / the various Negotiations at Paris for Peace; / with the History of / his Political and other Writings. / London: 1826 / Printed for Hunt and Clarke, Tavestock-Street, Covent-Garden.

12mo. pp. 407, portrait.   1002

٭*٭ This devotes considerable space to the "Parable against Persecution," which led Mr. Duane in No. 583 to criticise the author's remarks. This was in turn replied to in *The Literary and Theological Review* (of March, 1836) by "The Editor of a recent Epitome of Franklin's Memoirs," which is dated "Bangor." This seems to fix the authorship on Mr. Woods, who was then a professor in Bangor, and was editing this very magazine.

SUBJECT INDEX

AND

REFERENCE LIST

TO

FRANKLINIAN LITERATURE.

$*^*_*$ In this section are classed references to all the preceding books, together with brief titles of many works relating to Franklin in a lesser degree. No attempt has been made to include the standard histories and more prominent works of this period.

Biography.

The Autobiography.

Nos. 383–437, 448, 477, 561, 600, 875.

American Museum, VIII, 12.

Cabanis (P. J. G.) Œuvres de. V, 221.

Journal de Paris. No. 83. 1791.

Manuel de l'Amateur d'Autographe. p. 337. Paris. 1836.

Romilly, (S.) Memoirs of. 1, 319, 408.

Vaughan, (W.) Memoirs of. p. 6. London: 1839.

Biographies—Important.

Nos. 383, 409, 423–4, 427, 790, 841, 911, 927, 929–31, 954, 962, 985, 998.

Biographies—Unimportant.

Nos. 133, 188, 198, 249, 802–3, 810, 817, 825, 829, 834, 845–7, 853, 857, 860, 866, 869, 879, 880–87, 889, 892, 894–6, 903, 905–8, 918–26, 930–2, 934–5, 945, 951, 955–7, 960, 965, 970–1, 977, 981, 983, 989–95, 999–1000, 1002.

American Magazine. p. 109. Phila. 1789.

Abbott (J.) Harper's Magazine. IV, 185, 289.

Barbiera (G.) Memoir di.

Brissot de Warville (J. B.) Travels in America. 1, 179.

Briggs (C. F.) Homes of American Statesmen. p. 65.

Brougham (H.) Statesmen of the time of George III. III.

Cabanis (P. J. G.) Œuvres. V, 217.

Campbell (H.) Our Continent. 11, 673.

Cantie (C.) Storia Universale Biographie.

Carson (H. L.) Hist. of the Celebration of the Constitution. 1, 163.

Chadwick (J. W.) Brooklyn Eagle. Jan. 16, 1887.

Charles (V. P. E.) La Dix huitième Siècle. 1, 306.

Crevecœur (H.) Voyages dans la Haute Pennsylvania. 1, 353.

Curtis (G. T.) History of the Constitution. 1.

Duyckinck (E.) National Portrait Gallery. 1, 9.

Dwight (N.) Signers of the Declaration. p. 171.

European Magazine. XXIII, 404.

Everett (A. H.) Critical and Miscellaneous Essays.

Francis (J. W.) The Printer. July, 1859.

Frefanelli (S.) Storici Sugli Stati Unito. Foligno: 1866.

Gentleman's Magazine. LX, 571.

Goodrich (G. A.) Lives of the Signers. p. 261.

Goodrich (S. G.)　Lives of Benefactors.　p. 113.
Hawthorne (N.)　Biographical Stories.
Hildebrand (J. C.)　Hist. Gallery of Portraits.　I.
History of North America.　II, 420.　Leeds: 1820.
Howe (H.)　Memoirs of American Mechanics.　p. 37.
Historical Magazine.　XIV, 59.
Hundred Greatest Men.　VIII, I.　London: 1880.
Hunt (W.)　American Biographical Panorama.　p. 65.
Judson (L. C.)　Sages of the American Revolution.　p. 101.
Lincoln (R. W.)　Lives of the Presidents.
Mackay (C.)　Founders of the American Republic.
McMaster and Stone.　Pa. and the Federal Constitution.
Perry (B. F.)　Biographical Sketches of American Statesmen.　p. 308.
Podcniejnik.　Nos. 4, 5 and 6.　1859.
Political Magazine.　I, 631.　London: 1780.
Polyanthus.　April.　Boston: 1814.
Pursuit of Knowledge under Difficulties.　London: 1830.
Sainte-Beuve (C. A.)　Causeries de Lundi.　VII, 100.
Smith (J. J.)　National Portrait Gallery (Herring-Longacre) II.
Stuber (H.)　Columbian Magazine.　IV-V.　Phila.　1790-1.
Town and Country Magazine.　IX.　London: 1777.
Tuckerman (H. T.)　Biographical Essays.
Watson (J. F.)　Annals of Philadelphia.　p. 519.
Whipple (E. P.)　Harper's Magazine.　LII, 403.

　Biography—Juvenile.
Nos. 790-2, 813-5, 830, 890-1, 916, 982.

Genealogy and Family.

Cole (J.)　Hist. and Antiq. of Ecton, England.　Scarborough.　1825.
Cole (J.)　[Reprint of excerpt from same].　Phila.: 1865.
Everett (E.)　Essays.　III.　485.
Harper's Bazar.　May 22, 1880.
Heraldic Journal.　II, 97.
Historical Magazine.　I, 144.
Massachusetts Hist. Soc. Proceedings.　III, 27, 174; XIX, 310.
New Eng. Hist. and Genealogical Register.　VIII, 374; XI, 17.
Savage's Genealogical Dictionary of New-England.　II, 299.

In Boston.　1706–23.

Buckingham (J. T.)　Specimens of Newspaper Literature.　I, 49.
Everett (E.)　Essays.　II, 1; IV, 108.
Everett (E.)　Mount Vernon Papers.　p. 21.
Goddard (D. A.)　Winsor's Memorial Hist. of Boston.　II, 387.
Shurtleff (N. B.)　Description of Boston.
Towle (G. M.)　Winsor's Memorial Hist. of Boston.　II, 269.

In London. 1724–6.

No. 913.
Printing Times and Lithographer's Journal. June 15, 1886.
Solly (E.) The Bibliographer. Dec. 1882.

In Philadelphia. 1726–57.

Dinwiddie Papers. II, 15, 41.
Pennsylvania Gazette, Feb. 15, 1738.
Pennsylvania Records. I–XII.
Letters and Papers relating to Pennsylvania. Phila. 1855.
Smith (H.) Life of William Smith. I, 341.
Tyerman. Life of Whitefield.
Webster (R.) Hist. of the Presbyterian Church. pp. III, 416.
Westcott and Scharf. History of Philadelphia: I, 218.

Albany Congress.
Adams (J.) Works. x, 62.
Docs. Relating to the Colonial Hist. of N. Y. VI, 853.
Force (P.) American Archives. 4th Series, II, 396.
Hopkins (S.) Representation of the Plan formed at Albany. n. p. 1755.
Hutchinson (T.) History of Massachusetts.
Mass. Historical Soc. Collections. 3d Series, v, 1.
Minot (G. R.) History of Massachusetts. I, 188.
Sedgewick (T.) Life of William Livingston.
Smith (W.) History of New York. II, 183.

In London. 1757–62.

Docs. Relating to the Colonial Hist. of N. Y. VII, 337.
Penn. Mag. of History and Biography. VIII, 408.
Tytler (A. F.) Life of Henry Home, Lord Kames.

In Philadelphia. 1763–4.

Nos. 270–83, 793–4, 801, 804, 819, 844, 855–6, 867, 888, 923, 937, 958, 980–1, 996–7.
Hildeburn (C. R.) Issues of the Pennsylvania Press. II, 1.
Pennsylvania Archives. IV.
Pennsylvania Journal. Nov. 1, 1764.
Pennsylvania Mag. of History and Biography. I, 311; v, 64.
Reed (W. B.) Life of Joseph Reed. I, 36.
Smith (H.) Life of William Smith. I, 587.

In London. 1764–1775.

Barrows (J.) Life of Richard Earl Howe. p. 78.
Bougher's Repository. April, 1883.
Burke (E.) Appeal from the New to the Old Whigs.

Burton (J. H.) Life and Correspondence of David Hume.
Dartmouth. Hist. Mss. Commission Reports, 11, V.
Doc. Relating to the Colonial Hist. of N. Y. VIII, 218.
Lettsom (J. C.) Works of John Fothergill. London: 1780.
Pennsylvania Mag. of Hist. and Biography. XII, 100, 224.
Pitt (W.) Correspondence of. IV, 376, 381.
Priestley (J.) Memoirs of.

Stamp Act.

Nos. 287–97.
Bigelow (J.) Life of Franklin. I, 510.
Historical Magazine. I, 57.
Pennsylvania Mag. of Hist. and Biography. X, 92, 96, 217, 220.
Tucker (J.) Humble Address and Earnest Appeal.

Walpole Grant.

Nos. 311, 317.
Almon (J.) Biographical, literary and political Anecdotes. II.
American Historical Record. III, 204.
Historical Magazine. I, 86; XIII, 18.
Journals of Congress. May 1st, 1782.
N. Y. Documentary History. II, 998, 1001.
Stone (W.) Life of William Johnson.
View of the Title to Indiana. Phila. 1776.
Walpole (H.) Journal of the Reign of George III. I, 204.
Washington (G.) Writings of. (Sparks) II, 357, 483.
[Young (A.)] Observation on Waste Lands. London: 1773.

Hutchinson Letters.

Nos. 827, 915.
Adams (J.) Works of. I, 133, 319, 647. II, 318, 333.
Almon (J.) Biographical, literary and Political Anecdotes. III, 236.
Almon (J.) The Remembrancer. 1779. 327.
Annual Register. XVII, 86.
Bentham (J.) Memoirs of. X, 59.
Burton (J. H.) Life of David Hume. II, 471.
Boston Daily Advertiser. April 3 and 5, 1856.
Craftsman, The. Jan. 1, 1774.
Faithful account of the late affair between J. Temple and W. Whately.
London: 1774.
Gentleman's Magazine. XLIII, 617; XLIV, 89, 285.
Huchinson (T.) Diary and Letters of.
Hutchinson (T.) History of Massachusetts. III, 401.
Keppell (G. T.) Memoirs of Rockingham, II, 302.
Lee (R. H.) Life of Arthur Lee. I, 34, 240, 273.
Letters of eminent Persons to David Hume. p. 210.

Massachusetts Hist. Soc. Proceedings. III, 149; XVI, 43.
Monthly Magazine. Nov. 1802.
Morning Post. Jan. 16, 1774.
N. E. Hist. and Genealogical Register. I, 307.
Pitt (W.) Correspondence of. IV, 323.
Public Advertiser. Aug. 26; Sept. 4; Nov. 10, 25; Dec. 11, 30, 1774.
Reed (W. B.) Life of Joseph Reed. I, 61.
Smith (Goldwin). Study of History. 213.
Walpole (H.) Letters of. VI, 69.
Walpole (H.) Journal of the reign of George III. II, 167, 637.
Wells (W. V.) Life of Samuel Adams. II, 72.
Winthrop (R. C.) Speeches of. I, 1.
Winthrop (R. C.) Address before the Maine Hist. Soc. p. 37.

In Philadelphia. *1775–6.*

Adams (J.) Works of. II, 448–501, 511, 516; VII, 281; IX, 373.
Almon (J.) The Remembrancer. VIII, 250.
Carroll (C.) Journal of, in Canada, 1776.
Conn. Historical Soc. Collections. II.
Draper (L. C.) Auto. Collections of the Signers. p. 50.
Force (P.) American Archives. 4th series, VI, 450, 587.
Ford (W. C.) The Nation. March 28, 1889.
Galloway (J.) Examination of, before the House of Commons.
[Galloway (J.)] Reply to the Observations of Sir W. Howe.
Hutchinson (T.) Diary and Letters of. II, 237.
Jefferson (T.) Works of. I, 31.
Journal of the Continental Congress. I; II.
Minutes of the Provincial Council of Pa. X.
New Jersey Colonial Records. X.
Pennsylvania Evening Post. April, 1775.
Pennsylvania Gazette. Dec. 13, 1775.
Phillips (H.) Hist. Sketch of Paper Currency. II, 25, 28, 31.
Secret Journals of the Continental Congress. I.
Virginia Gazette. Dec. 13, 1775.

In France. *1776–1785.*

Nos. 328, 854, 984.
Adams (J.) Works of.
Address and Recommendations to the States by Congress. 1783.
Anecdotes Historique. Paris: 1784.
Bachaumont (L. P. de.) Mémoires sécrete.
Bettelheim. Beaumarchais, eine Biographie.
Bigelow (J.) The Century. XXXV, 741.
Bigelow (J.) Hours at Home.
Bolles (A. S.) Financial History of the U. S. 1774–89.

Chotteau (L.) Guerre de l'Independence.
Chotteau (L.) Le Français en Amérique.
Circourt. Histoire de l'Alliance de la France et l'Amerique.
Correspondence Sécrète sur Louis XVI et Marie Antoinette.
Diplomatic Correspondence. 1783–89.
[Delaunay's] Histoire d'un Pou Français. 1779.
Grimm-Diderot. Mémoires Historiques.
Flassan (G. R. de.) Diplomatique Français.
Force (P.) American Archives. 5th series, III, 894, 926.
Historical Magazine. VIII, 176.
Historical Society of Pa. Collections. I, 135.
Jay (W.) Life of John Jay.
Jefferson (T.) Works of. III, 213.
Jones (J. P.) Life of. N. Y. 1830.
Laurens (J.) Army Correspondence of. p. 21, 30.
Lee (R. H.) Life of Arthur Lee.
Littell's Living Age. VIII, 230; XXXIX, 170.
Loménie (L. de) Beaumarchais et son temps.
Lyman (T.) Diplomacy of the U. S.
Mass. Historical Society Collections. 5th series, IV, 321.
Papers in the Case of Silas Deane.
Pennsylvania Mag. of Hist. and Biography. II, 358; XI, 1; XII, 378.
Portrait du Comte de Vergennes. [Paris:] 1788.
Secret Journals of Congress.
Sedgwick (T.) Life of William Livingston. p. 413.
Sherburne (J. H.) Life of John Paul Jones.
Sparks (J.) Diplomatic Correspondence of the American Revolution.
Spark (J.) Life of Gouverneur Morris. I, 188.
Sumner (C.) Works of. VIII.
Trescott (W. H.) Diplomacy of the Revolution.
Watson (E.) Men and Times of the Revolution.
Wells (W. V.) Life of Samuel Adams. III.
Wharton (F.) International Law Digest.
Virginia State Papers. I, 346.

Negotiations with England.

Almon (J.) The Remembrancer. 1779, 327.
Bezassier (J. D.) Couplets sur la Paix. Noyon: 1783.
[Brizard (G.)] Fragment de Xénophon. Paris: 1783.
Fitzmaurice (E.) Life of William, Earl Shelburne.
Gentleman's Magazine. LV, 561.
Jay (J.) Peace Negotiations of 1782–3.
Mass. Historical Society Proceedings. N. S., III, 89, 349.

In Philadelphia. 1785–90.

Cutler (W. P. & J. P.) Life of Manasseh Cutler. I, 269.
Historical Magazine. x, 213.
Westcott and Sharf. History of Philadelphia.

Federal Convention.

Curtis (G. T.) History of the Constitution. I.
Elliot (J.) Debates. v.
Independent Gazette. (Boston). Dec. 18, 1787.
Plan of the New Constitution. London. 1787.
McMaster & Stone. Pennsylvania and the Federal Constitution.
Martin (L.) Genuine Information. Phila. 1788.
Yates (R.) Secret Proceedings of the Federal Convention.

Death.

Nos. 818, 841–2, 861–2, 949, 963–4.
American Museum. VII, 41, 43; VIII, 211, 213, [12.
American Historical Record. III, 312.
Debates in Congress. (Annals.) II, 1534, 1732, 1770, 1791, 1798, 1883, 1968.
Historical Magazine. I, 83; II, 207, 302, 333.
Jefferson (T.) Works of. III, 139, 218.
Magazine of American History. III, 312.
New York Magazine, I, 239. 1791.
Smith (H.) Life of William Smith. II, 324.

Ana.

No. 869.
Adams (J.) Works of.
American Museum. IX, 116, 176.
Annual Register. XXII, 201; XXXV, 241.
Beer's Almanac for 1799. Hartford.
Fisher (G.) Life of Benjamin Silliman. I, 12, 73.
Hunt (F.) American Anecdotes.
Hutchinson (T.) Diary and Letters of. II, 195.
Jefferson (T.) Works of.
Moore (F.) Diary of the Revolution. I, 389; II, 83.

Artist.

Nos. 64, 284–6.
Adams (J.) Works of. III, 59.
Force (P.) American Archives. 5th series, I, 943.
Gentleman's Magazine. LIII, 269.
Mass. Historical Society Collections. XI, 148, 301, 475.
Morellet (A.) Memoires inédit. I, 300.

Phillips (H.) Historical Sketch of Paper Money. II, 31.
Preble (G. H.) Our Flag. pp. 148, 475.

Educator.

Nos. 40, 75, 83.
American Journal of Education. XXVII, 401; XXVIII, 809.
Smith (H.) Life of William Smith. I, 24-5, 339.

Editor.

Nos. 3, 11, 36, 326, and "Printer."

Humorist.

Nos. 12-9, 24, 31-5, 37-9, 50-7, 73-4, 76, 89-90, 92, 102, 104, 106-252, 314, 330-1, 344-5, 364-6, 381, and "Ana."
Historical Magazine. IV, 16.
Monthly Anthology. VII, 174.

Inventor.

No. 41-2, and "Artist"
American Historical Record. I, 26.
American Medical and Phil. Register. I, 446.
Cutler (W. P. & J. P.) Life of Manasseh Cutler. I, 269.
Ferguson (J.) Select Mechanical Exercises. London: 1778.
Gentleman's Magazine. XLVII, 110; LI, 412.
Laurens (H.) Correspondence of. p. 62.
Magazine of American History. V, 380.
Minutes of the Provincial Council of Pa. X, 283-4, 322.
Phillips (H.) Historical Sketch of Paper Currency. II, 67.
Sargent (W.) Loyalist Verses of Stansbury and Odell. p. 5.

Literateur.

Nos. 875, 911, 966, 968-9.
Allibone (S. A.) Dictionary of Authors. I.
Blackwood's Magazine. XVII, 49.
Duyckinck (E. A. & G. L.) Cyclopædia of American Literature. I.
Richardson (C. F.) American Literature. I.
Tyler (M. C.) History of American Literature.

Moralist.

Nos. 28-30, 37-39, 52-5, 57-60, 69-72, 107-252, 257-60, 329-30, 341, 891.

Orator.

No. 326.
Elliot (J.) Debates on the Constitution. V.
Independent Gazette (Boston) Dec. 18, 1787.

Jefferson (T.) Works of. I, 31.
Madison (J.) Papers of.
Yates (R.) Secret Proceedings of the Federal Convention.

Philanthropist.

Nos. 75, 83, 99, 103, 256, 378, 830, 835, 858, 912.
Cobbett (W.) Porcupine's Works. IV, 363; VII, 82; VIII, 189–92.
Green (S. A.) Inaugural Address as Mayor of Boston. 1882.
Historical Magazine. III, 284.
Boston Evening Traveller. Feb. 8, 1858.
New York Evening Post. Dec. 5, 1887.
Livermore (G. L.) Historical Research on Negroes.
New York Hist. Soc. Publication Fund. I, 255.
Wood (G.) Address on the Pennsylvania Hospital.

Philologist.

Nos. 320, 988.
Ellis (A. J.) On Early English Pronunciation. IV. London: 1875.

Poet.

Nos. 1–2, 12.
Bigelow (J.) Life of Franklin. III, 449.
McVickar (J.) Life of Samuel Bard.
Morellet (A.) Mémoires inédit. I, 296.
Smith (H.) Life of William Smith. I, 341.

Politician.

Nos. 10, 28–30, 61–7, 85–8, 101, 118, 122, 125, 135, 253–5, 262–97, 303–5,
308–9, 311, 314–7, 322, 326–8, 345, 348–53, 367–71, 379, 382, 619–633,
793–4, 801, 804, 819, 844, 855–6, 867, 888, 923, 937, 980–1, 996–7.

Post Master.

Nos. 323–5.
American Weekly Mercury. Nov. 1740.
Annual Register. XVIII, 133.
New Jersey Colonial Records. IX, 262.
New Jersey Hist. Soc. Proceedings. IX.

Printer.

No. 43, 826, 913–4, 941, 968–9.
American Historical Record. II, 165.
American Medical and Phil. Register. I, 446.
Ford (P. L.) Magazine of American History. XV, 452.
Gentleman's Magazine. LX, 571.
Hildeburn (C. R.) Issues of the Press of Pa. 1685–1784.

Hudson (F.) Journalism in the U. S.
Magazine of American History. I, 681.
Mass. Historical Soc. Proceedings. II, 38.
Pennsylvania Mag. of History and Biography. x, 229.
Printing Times and Lithographer's Journal. Nov. 15, 1877.
Solly (E.) The Bibliographer. III, 3.
Thomas (G.) History of Printing.
Valentine (D.) Manual of the Corporation of N. Y. 1857.

Scientist.

Nos. 40–2, 256, 298, 307, 318–9, 354–63, 372–7, 604, 615–6, 805, 910, 978.
American Historical Record. I, 25.
Cutler (W. P. & J. P.) Life of Manasseh Cutler. II, 234.
Draper (J. W.) Harper's Magazine. LX, 265.
Draper (J. W.) Kansas Review. IV, 156.
Gammett (W.) Heroes of Science. p. 33.
Jefferson (T.) Works of. III, 212.
Littell's Living Age. IX, 226.
Nature (La). March 31, 1888.
Weld (C. H.) History of the Royal Society.

Electricity.

Nos. 77–82, 93–97, 307, 318, 929.
Adams (J.) Works of. II, 9, 51; III, 221, 278.
Allen (W. H.) Methodist Quarterly. VI, 100.
Beccaria (G.) Dell' Elettricismo Artificiale.
Bigelow (J.) N. Y. Observer. June 19, 1879.
Gentleman's Magazine. XXII, 227.
Hoadly & Wilson. Observation on Electrical Experiments. London:
   1756.
Hoadly & Wilson. Observations . . . 2d Edition. London: 1759.
Henley (W.) Account of New Experiments in Electricity. London:
   1774.
Henley (W.) Experiments Concerning Rods. London: 1774.
Henley (W.) Experiments and Observations in Electricity. London:
   1774.
Henley (W.) Experiments and Observations in Electricity. London:
   1776.
Kinnersley (E.) A Course of Experiments in Electricity. Phila. 1764.
London Magazine. xx, 336; XXIII, 431.
Moore (F.) Diary of the American Revolution. I, 504, 929, 938, 978.
New Jersey Colonial Records. VIII, 7.
Priestley (J.) A Familiar Introduction to Electricity. London: 1768.
Priestley (J.) History and Present State of Electricity. London: 1767.
Priestley (J.) Additions to History of Electricity. London: 1770.

Prince (T.) Improvement of the Doctrine of Earthquakes. Boston: 1755.
Roberts (G.) Catechism on Electricity.
Smith (H.) Life of William Smith. I, 341.
Whewell's History of Inductive Sciences.
Winthrop (J.) Lectures on Earthquakes. Boston: 1755.
Wilson (B.) Observations on Lightning. London: 1773.
Wilson (B.) Further Observations on Lightning. London: 1774.

Theologian.

Nos. 5-8, 21-3, 25-7, 91, 257-60, 312-3.
Adams (J.) Works of. III, 186, 220.
Bigelow (J.) New York Observer. June 19, 1879.
Historical Magazine. II, 361.
Littell's Living Age. LXIV, 757.
Peabody (W. O. S.) Christian Examiner. XII, 273.
Penn. Mag. of History and Biography. III, 230; IX, 405.
Perry (W. S.) Papers relating to the Church in Pa. p. 421.

Attacks on.

Nos. 277-9, 821, 827, 832-3, 848, 902, 916-7, 973-6, 996-7.
Cobbett (W.) Porcupine's Writings.
Boston Watchman. ? 1879.
Jefferson (T.) Works of. VIII, 108; IX, 138.
Madison (J.) Writings of. I, 78.
McMaster & Stone. Pa. and the Federal Convention. pp. 159, 696.
N. Y. Hist. Soc. Fund Publication. 1878. pp. I, 483.
Smith (H.) Life of William Smith. I, 344.
Stanton (E. C.) N. Y. World, June 4, 1870.

Birthday Celebrations.

Nos. 796-9, 807-8, 823, 831, 854, 868, 874, 894, 915, 927, 939, 941, 943.
Francis (J. W.) The Printer. July, 1859.
Evening Mirror, Jan. 18, 1849.
Evening Mirror, Jan. 18, 1851.
Evening Mirror, Jan. 17, 1852.

Burlesque of.

No. 904.
Hopkinson (F.) Writings of. II, 69.

Dedications to.

Nos. 811-12, 838-43, 850-2, 859, 926, 928, 934, 946-7, 952-3, 986-8.
Mass. Hist. Soc. Proceedings.
Moore (F.) Diary of the American Revolution.

Sparks (J.) Writings of Franklin. VIII, 289.

In Fiction.

Nos. 816, 824, 865, 936, 989–94.
Créquy, Souvenir de la Marquise de. Paris.
[Delaunay]. Histoire d'un Pou Francaise. Paris: 1779.
Hunt (F.) American Anecdotes.
Seriey (A.) Mort de Robespierre. Paris. 1801.
Thackeray (W. M.) The Virginians.
Tupper (M. F.) Washington. London: 1865.

Franklin Fund.

Nos. 835, 912.
Green (S. A.) Inaugural Address as Mayor of Boston. 1882.
New York Evening Post. Dec. 5, 1887.

Franklin (Town) Library.

No. 858.
Boston Evening Traveller, Feb. 8, 1858.
Historical Magazine. III, 284.
New York Evening Post. Dec. 5, 1887.

Franklin's (Private) Library.

Cutler (W. P. & J. P.) Life of Manasseh Cutler. I, 269.
Historical Magazine. X, 123.
Pa. Mag. of History and Biography. VIII, 430.

Medals of.

No. 876.
American Journal of Numismatics. Jan. 1873.
Coin and Stamp Collector's Journal. III, No. 4.
Gentleman's Magazine. XXIII, 538, 587.
Loubat (J.) Medallic History of the U. S. I, 93, 96.
Mass. Hist. Soc. Proceedings. XI, 301.

Poor Richard (Imitators).

Poor Richard Revived . . . Albany: 1799, 1800, 1801, 1802, 1803, 1804, 1805, 1806, 1807, 1808.
Franklin's Legacy or . . . Almanac. Troy: 1802.
Poor Richard's Almanac . . . Boston: 1802, 1803, 1804, 1805, 1806, 1807, 1808.
Franklin Almanac . . . Pittsburg: 1819.
Franklin Almanac . . . Phila.: 1822, 1823, 1824, 1825, 1826, 1827, 1828, 1829, 1830, 1831, 1832.
Poor Richard's New Farmer's Almanac . . . Concord: 1833, 1834, 1835, 1836, 1837, 1838, 1839.

Franklin Almanac . . . New York: 1841, 1842, 1843, 1844, 1845, 1846, 1847.
Franklin Almanac . . . Boston: 1842, 1843.
Franklin Almanac. Rochester. 1843.
Old Franklin Almanac . . . Phila.: 1860, 1861, 1862, 1863, 1864, 1865, 1866, 1867, 1868, 1869, 1870, 1871, 1872.
Franklin Almanac . . . Cincinnati: 1868.
Almanac Franklin . . . Paris. 1869.

Portraits.

Boston Public Library Report No. 20. p. 86.
Catalogue of Hist. Portraits & Relics. (Washington Centennial) N. Y.: 1889.
Hale (E. E.) Franklin in France, I, i, 150.
Historical Magazine. III, 252, 286.
Magazine of American History. V, 380.
Mass. Hist. Soc. Proceedings. X, 412; XI, 150; XII, 51; XIV, 160; XV, 10; XX, 264, 359.
Moore (F.) Diary of the American Revolution. II, 283.
Notes and Queries. VII, 409; VIII, 208; XIII, 12, 122.
Pa. Acad. of Fine Arts. Loan Exhibition of Portraits. 1887.
Winsor (J.) Narrative and Critical History. VII, 37.
Winsor (J.) Memorial History of Boston. II, 291.

Relics.

No. 942.
Mass. Hist. Soc. Proceedings. II, 665; IV, 6; VII, 361; XII, 215.
American Antiquarian. III, 220.
Watson (E.) Men and Times of the Revolution. p. 120.
Watson (J. F.) Annals of Philadelphia. p. 519.

Statues and Busts.

Nos. 836, 839, 863-4, 871-3, 897, 925, 944, 962, 972.
Mass. Hist. Soc. Proceedings. III, 111, 115, 177, 364, 393; XII, 81.
Watson (E.) Men and Times of the Revolution. p. 121.

CHECK LIST

AND

CHRONOLOGICAL INDEX.

_**_* The following is a list of the first part of Franklin's writings and of the Frankliniana, arranged chronologically under the date of printing. Only the first or first two words (articles excepted), are given of Franklin's writings and anonymous works, and the authors' names of the remainder. Works without date are arranged alphabetically at the end, under the same system; but where the date could be positively ascertained they are also entered under that year, with a [to show that it is without date. The references are by title numbers, and roman type is used for Franklin's own writings, and italic for works relating to him. See also the special index at page 109.

GENERAL INDEX.

The list of pseudonyms at page 307 is not indexed.

Whitefield, G., 47.
Wilcke, J. C., 43.
Williams, J., 381.
Williamson, H., lvii, 393.
Willing, T., 123.
Willoughby, B., lvii, 333.
Wilmer, —, lxi, 181, 393.
Wilmot, J. E., 303.
Wilson, —, lvii.
Winsor, J., lxv.

Winthrop, J., lvii, 315; R. C., 395.
Wollaston, W., xv, 3-5
Wood, B., 51.
Woods, L., 395.
Worthilake, 1.
Yale College, lxvii.
Yates, R., 295.
York, J , 165.
X. Y. Z., 393.